JOHN FOSTER DULLES:
1888—1959

• • • • • • •

John Foster Dulles:

1888–1959

· · · · · · · ·

BY JOHN ROBINSON BEAL

Foreword by Thomas E. Dewey

HARPER & BROTHERS   PUBLISHERS   NEW YORK

JOHN FOSTER DULLES: 1888-1959

Copyright © 1951, 1957, 1959 by John Robinson Beal
Life pictures: © 1948, 1955, 1956 by Time, Inc.

Printed in the United States of America

All rights in this book are reserved.
No part of the book may be used or reproduced
in any manner whatsoever without written permission except in the case of brief quotations
embodied in critical articles and reviews. For
information address Harper & Brothers
49 East 33rd Street, New York 16, N. Y.

The first edition of this book was published in 1957
under the title of JOHN FOSTER DULLES: A BIOGRAPHY.

Library of Congress catalog card number: 59-15273

To Betty

Table of Contents

Acknowledgments xi

Foreword by Thomas E. Dewey xiii

1. A New Secretary Takes Over 1
2. He Wrote a Book 16
3. American Roots 22
4. Salt-water Sailor 33
5. A Taste of Diplomacy 44
6. Law and Marriage 54
7. The Lesson of Versailles 61
8. Luck and Adventure in Law 70
9. The Quest for a Just and Durable Peace 86
10. Bipartisanship 95
11. Four Months a Senator 106
12. Pilot Operation: Peace with Japan 115
13. The Call from Ike 129
14. Administrative Troubles 138
15. Life in an Airplane 153
16. The Unpopular Man 164
17. Korea: The End of a War 177
18. Berlin: A Diplomatic Gambit Opens 185
19. Indochina: A Different "Brink" 204
20. Formosa: Deterrence Confirmed 219

Contents

21. The Problem of Subversion   229
22. Nasser and the Dam   246
23. Nasser and the Canal   262
24. The Alliance Splits over Egypt   272
25. Unity in Western Europe   289
26. "Liberation"   309
27. Piecemeal Negotiation   322
28. Three Crises   331
29. The Peacemaker   341
     Index   351

Illustrations

The following are grouped in a separate section after page 46

John Foster Dulles with his sister
John Foster, age 12, with Margaret, Allen, Eleanor Lansing, and
 Nataline Dulles
John Foster Dulles at 7
Dulles as a Princeton University student
Major John Foster Dulles
Dulles wedding party, June 26, 1912
Dulles conferring with Secretary Hull, 1944
Adviser Dulles conferring with Secretary Marshall during Paris con-
 ference
Senator Dulles on campaign, 1949
Three leaders of the Anglo-American alliance
Dulles chats with a Marine in Korea
Allen Dulles confers with his brother
Dulles at work aboard a plane
Dulles with a "devil dancer" in Ceylon
President and Mrs. Eisenhower arrive at the Dulles home
The Secretary's official State Department portrait
Secretary Dulles with his family
The Secretary and Mrs. Dulles play backgammon
Dulles at the wheel of his cruising yawl
Main Duck Island
The Dulles cabin on Duck Island
John Foster Dulles with Winston Churchill and President Eisenhower
 at Walter Reed Hospital
The funeral at Arlington National Cemetery

Acknowledgments

This book was written on the basis of information collected during a period of continuous professional coverage of the foreign policy of the United States, and the people involved in it, before and after John Foster Dulles took office. It benefits from personal interviews with him which provided additional facts about his career and insight into his official actions, for which I was grateful. But the reader must understand that in no sense was he responsible for its contents. Not only did his participation end with the interviews, but the narrative details of various incidents of diplomatic negotiation, including those involving him, came from other sources in the normal course of news coverage.

I am equally grateful to Mrs. Janet Dulles, his wife, to his sister, Eleanor, and to his brother, Allen, for family reminiscences. Members of the Secretary's personal staff were of great assistance, including Roderic L. O'Connor, Mrs. Burnita O'Day, and Miss Phyllis Bernau; and so, too, were numerous officers of the Department of State to whom it is not possible to give individual acknowledgment.

For information about his pre-official career I am indebted to Thomas E. Dewey, Arthur H. Dean, and the late Walter Van Kirk, among others. My thanks go also to Time, Inc., for indulging this

Acknowledgments

extracurricular project, for which, of course, it likewise bears no responsibility, and to *Life* magazine for its courtesy in making pictures available from its files.

JOHN ROBINSON BEAL

Foreword

This book tells the story of one man who was never deceived about the nature of the Soviet menace. Even during the honeymoon of Soviet-American partnership in World War II, as we talked of foreign affairs and thought together on speeches, he saw clearly the shape of things to come.

Foreign affairs had been either his vocation or his avocation during his entire life. His primary dedication was to peace, a peace based on the concept that life is fluid and, if civilization is to survive, there must be means of achieving change without war. When he became Secretary of State in January, 1953, this dedication to peaceful solutions faced the ultimate test.

The death struggle was already on in Korea and, though localized, was a strain on both sides and threatening to spread.

Iran was tottering into the hands of the Soviets with the implication of ultimate Soviet conquest of the whole Middle East and its two-thirds of the known oil resources of the world.

Austria and Germany were both occupied by Russian troops and were harshly divided by the lines Stalin devised and won during the war. Western defense unity in Europe was still a goal to be achieved because Free Germany was not yet a member.

Trieste was a tinder box. The French defense against Communist aggression in Indochina was going badly. Full-scale Communist revolution was in progress in such widely separated places as

Malaya and Kenya. Our own hemisphere had been successfully penetrated: Guatemala was Communist ruled.

The new Secretary of State was confronted with crises already in existence in a dozen spots around the world. Many sparks which had been fanned were already bursting into flames when he took office. Any one of them had the potential of exploding into a world war.

Since we live in a day of Foreign Ministers' Conferences, the meetings to deal with these fires could not be attended by subordinates, else the other nations would also send subordinates. What we needed was at least four Secretaries of State, each with full authority. Since there could be only one, Foster Dulles had to be everywhere.

No ordinary mortal would have been able to do it. Every problem was different. Each one had to be analyzed against a detailed knowledge of the total background of the area, its history and the objectives of the aggressor. It was necessary to think through the approach to each chess game with the Russians, where the stakes involved the lives of millions of human beings or the risk of total war—or both. Yet such was the pressure that there was little time for new study.

It was a blessing that we had a Secretary of State who had already thought his way through most of these crises before he took office. He had behind him nearly fifty years of training, writing and thinking, including the eight preceding years of intense participation in foreign affairs. He knew the nations, their aspirations and their problems. He understood the Soviet techniques because he had dealt with them face to face at conferences from London to Tokyo to Moscow.

It is regrettable that so much of this recent history and so many of the decisions still, of necessity, involve top-secret information. To open the files would betray sources of information and motivations for action which would imperil the security of our country. Thus, the full story of many of the events of the past four years cannot be fully recorded for many years.

The work of the Secretary of State and the Department, more than any other function of government except Intelligence, may be compared in structure to an iceberg. What shows on the surface can only be a small fraction of the total.

Taking over the direction of foreign policy in our country in the year 1953 involved other problems. For a century and a half we as a nation were enabled to preserve our splendid isolation largely by reason of the strength of the British Empire. The cumulative blows of World War I and World War II were almost fatal to the Empire and cost Britain immeasurably in treasure and lives.

Our own industrial growth has conspired with the march of events to make us a single unit of economic and atomic power so great that the leadership of the Free World is ours whether we want it or not. Most of us would prefer not to have the burden and we have little training or experience for this fateful role. We must learn in a few years what it took the British one hundred years to learn. We must learn it or lose the struggle for survival.

Compared with every other national problem, survival comes first. If this book helps to demonstrate the infinite complexities of foreign affairs in today's world, it will serve a great purpose.

The harsh struggle for survival against a malevolent, expansionist dictatorship will face us for many years. Basically this struggle is in the hands of our career foreign service and the Central Intelligence Agency. Each contributed much to the progress recorded in this volume.

Foreword

Entering the foreign service has not in the past been a part of the thinking of our people. Things are too comfortable at home. It is not attractive to go and live and labor all over the world, often amid squalor and physical discomfort. Underpaid as it is, and usually subjected to abuse, the miracle is that our foreign service includes so many thousands of devoted and highly competent people. My own observation has been that the wives of our foreign service officers often work as hard as their husbands but without pay and with few thanks. I hope this book may serve to stimulate interest in these great services and inspire more of our ablest young men to enter them as a career. The survival of the Republic depends on them.

THOMAS E. DEWEY

JOHN FOSTER DULLES:
1888—1959

. . . .

1

· · · · · · · ·

A New Secretary Takes Over

JOHN FOSTER DULLES was sworn in as Secretary of State in a
White House ceremony at 5:30 P.M. on the day following
President Eisenhower's inauguration in 1953. It was the fulfillment
of a lifetime ambition.

The tradition is that any American boy can think of his goal
as the Presidency; Dulles set his heart on achieving a subordinate
but no less honorable role, in which he might work for world
peace. Undecided as a young man whether to become a Presbyterian
minister, like his father, or to go in for law and diplomacy, like
his grandfather, Dulles finally chose the latter. He became one of
the world's most successful and highly paid attorneys; with a
constant single-mindedness he kept his diplomatic objective in
sight, and when his means permitted he devoted his energy to
influencing American public opinion toward his concept of the
path of enduring peace with justice. In this process he carved a
place for himself in the nation's foreign policy councils where what

he said demanded attention. By the time that execution of foreign policy was turned over to the Republicans after twenty years of Democratic administration, his appointment to the Cabinet post came almost as a matter of course.

On the morning after taking the oath of office Dulles showed up for work at nine o'clock, having been asked by his staff not to come in any earlier because they wanted everything to be ready in the large, rose-carpeted room on the State Department's fifth floor which had just been vacated by Dean Acheson. The official limousine, which picked him up at the hotel at which he was temporarily staying, took him to the underground garage from which a private elevator carried him up to the Secretary's suite. He was wearing a dark-blue suit which had a faint dark-green pencil stripe, an Oxford-gray overcoat, and a black Homburg hat. Though his clothes came from one of the best tailors in New York, he wore them like a man who had other things on his mind. His tie was just a shade off center and there were wrinkles in his sleeves at the elbows.

Many times had Dulles been in the room which was to be his office for the next six years. In appearance he looked as he always did, a tall man with his shoulders a trifle hunched, with gray, thinning hair parted on the side of a head which ran straight down at the back to form a thick neck; his blue eyes were sober behind bifocals rimmed with white gold frames. His mouth turned down solemnly at the corners. The net effect was that of an austere, wary, rather unapproachable individual.

The outer offices of the suite were messy with the evidences of moving; telephones were standing on the floor while workmen were installing connections on the new desks that were being moved in.

But in his private office everything was in order.

He had elected to leave the room pretty much as it was. The desk remained with its back to one of the several windows overlooking the street; across from it was a huge grandfather clock in glass and mahogany case. The near side of the room, into which visitors entered from the reception room, was taken up by an arrangement of leather-upholstered sofa and chairs around a low leather-covered coffee table; the far side contained a long conference table surrounded by chairs. Near the latter, on the far wall, was a big portrait of Cordell Hull, flanked by two flags on floor standards, one the Stars and Stripes and one the blue emblem carrying the seal of the department. The only change he had wanted was the hanging of three new portraits. One pictured a distinguished man with white sideburns: his grandfather, John Watson Foster, who had served as Secretary of State from June 29, 1892, through February 23, 1893, in the Cabinet of President Benjamin Harrison. Another was of his uncle, Robert Lansing ("Uncle Bert"), who had been Woodrow Wilson's Secretary of State at the Versailles Peace Conference; the third was of Secretary Robert Bacon, who had served in the Theodore Roosevelt and Taft administrations.

Though he was familiar with the room of old, Dulles felt an exaltation about entering it this time as his own. Twice before he had anticipated the experience, once quite vividly. It symbolized a professional pinnacle toward which he had worked for years. It did not awe him to reach it at last, for in a sense he was only changing desks to continue the type of work in which he had long been engaged; but his exaltation was mingled with a keyed-up feeling of challenge because despite his proficiency in the art of diplomatic navigation and confidence in his ability to run this ship in accordance with the accepted rules of seamanship, it was a much more complicated piece of machinery than any he had handled. There were many more controls on the bridge than he was accustomed to manipulating. And, being a wary man, he was nervous about a few of the crew.

Momentarily these thoughts went through his mind as he sat down at the desk from which he was to operate. On one of the small tables within easy reach of his swivel chair he placed some of his personal reference books, including three he was never without: the Federalist papers, Stalin's *Problems of Leninism,* and the Bible. On another table, immediately behind his chair, were three telephones: one connected with the State Department switchboard, one a private line with an unlisted number, and one, a white instrument, connected directly with the White House switchboard.

One of the first calls that came in over the white phone was from President Eisenhower, who said that for the last two mornings he had found on his desk a top-secret one-page summary of the previous twenty-four hours' most important world developments, compiled by the State Department from the cables of all the intelligence agencies. Ike said he did not feel he wanted that particular service and asked that it be stopped. Such is the momentum of an operating bureaucracy that it took an aide two days to trace the origin of this daily summary in the State Department's secretariat and discontinue the service. The new President felt he would get all the information he needed from his Secretary of State.

On the desk side of the telephone table was a built-in intercommunication system, with a row of switches providing direct access to the desks of key officers in the department. Dulles, who had not been accustomed to use of a "squawk box" in his previous jobs, preferred to use the regular telephone extensions on the departmental switchboard. But he discovered that whenever he leaned back in his chair he inadvertently depressed anywhere from two to half a dozen keys on the intercom, and since they were the type that continued buzzing in the connected office until there was an answer and the Secretary picked up his own transmitter, the effect was to bring assorted assistant secretaries to his office on the double to see what was wanted. After this happened a couple of times he had the intercom disconnected.

Carl W. McCardle, who had been appointed Assistant Secretary of State for Public Affairs, dropped in to discuss an idea Dulles had that one of Dean Acheson's difficulties had been strained relations with the Pentagon. Anxious to get his own relations off on the right foot, he asked McCardle to see if the Joint Chiefs of Staff could come to luncheon. McCardle phoned General Omar Bradley, then chairman, who said, "This is the first time we've had a chance to do business with anyone above assistant secretary. I don't know what engagements the chiefs have, but we'll be there without fail."

Dulles' first official appointment was at 9:22 that morning, with a member of the secretariat with whom he wanted to discuss arrangements for an airplane to take him to Europe on January 30, on the first of a series of trips that made him the most traveled Secretary of State in history. At 9:30 he called in the only four officials of the new regime who had then been appointed and two holdover officials, for the first conference. The new men were Undersecretary Don Lourie, Assistant Secretaries Thruston Morton and Carl W. McCardle, and Legal Adviser Herman Phleger; the holdovers were

Undersecretary David K. E. Bruce and Career Minister H. Freeman ("Doc") Matthews, who was serving as deputy undersecretary.

At ten o'clock he had his first outside visitor, Ralph Cake, Republican national committeeman from Oregon, who had come to offer congratulations. Shortly before eleven he went down in his private elevator to the basement garage and drove in his official limousine, a black 1949 Cadillac bearing U.S. license 120 s, to the Capitol for a session with the House Foreign Affairs Committee. He was invited to stay for luncheon, but because of his date with the Joint Chiefs of Staff, he excused himself after a few bites with his Congressional hosts and returned to the department to lunch again with Generals Omar Bradley, J. Lawton Collins, Hoyt Vandenberg, and Admiral William M. Fechteler.

At 2:15 Assistant Secretary of Defense Frank C. Nash, Assistant Secretary of State John Allison, and Doc Matthews arrived at his office for a study of President Eisenhower's impending "State of the Union" speech from the foreign policy angle. At 2:45 another set of officials, including Assistant Secretary Henry A. Byroade, who was in charge of the Near East, came in to discuss the situation in Egypt, where the Naguib-Nasser government was seeking to oust British troops from the Suez Canal zone. At 3:15 the group was enlarged by the arrival of Paul Nitze, head of the policy planning staff, and Assistant Secretary Harold F. Linder, and the discussion turned to Iran, where Britain was involved in a dispute with Premier Mohammed Mossadegh over the nationalization of oil.

At four o'clock the new Secretary made his first business call on President Eisenhower at the White House. By 5:15 he was back in his office to receive an old friend and fellow Princetonian, Senator

Alexander Smith of New Jersey, who had brought along Governor Alfred E. Driscoll. At 5:30 Dulles acceded to the request of news photographers for a picture in his office, posing with his secretary, Mrs. Burnita O'Day, and his personal assistant, Roderic L. O'Connor. At 5:45 Doc Matthews was back with some official business; at 5:50 Undersecretary Bruce had several questions to bring up. At 6:15 Dulles held an hour's conference with Assistant Secretary McCardle and at 7:15 he saw Douglas MacArthur II, the department's counselor.

Toward the end of the first day the department's news division issued the first press release of the Dulles regime, No. 40 of 1953. It was a statement the Secretary had drafted in pencil on a lined yellow scratch pad aboard the airplane which carried him from New York to Washington to take over his new duties, and was addressed "to my associates in the Department of State and the Foreign Service." It said, in part:

"We are united by the heavy responsibilities that press upon us. We are front-line defenders of the vital interests of the United States which are being attacked by a political warfare which is as hostile in its purpose and as dangerous in its capabilities as any open war. President Eisenhower recently stated, 'This nation stands in greater peril than at any time in our history.'

"The peril is of a kind which places a special responsibility on each and every member of the Department of State and the Foreign Service. It requires of us competence, discipline and positive loyalty to the policies that our President and the Congress may prescribe.

"Less than that is not tolerable at this time.

"Lest any misunderstand, let me add that loyalty does not, of

7

course, call for any one to practice intellectual dishonesty or to distort his reporting to please superiors. Our foreign policies will prevail only if they are based on honest evaluations of the facts. . . .

"It will be necessary, from time to time, to adjust our Department and Foreign Service so that we shall be best able to discharge our responsibilities and reach our chosen goals. This will be done with all of the consideration which the situation seems to permit. But the national welfare must be given priority over individual concerns.

"I know, and our fellow citizens know, that those who comprise the Department of State and Foreign Service are, as a whole, a group of loyal Americans dedicated to the preservation of American ideals."

It was a statement designed to set an opening tone of firmness and direction in the conduct of foreign policy and at the same time to make clear that operating employees were expected to exercise intelligent participation in it, not obsequiousness. But because of the distorted overtones Senator Joseph McCarthy had given the word "loyalty" in his attacks on the State Department and other government agencies, it was misinterpreted, as many subsequent Dulles statements were. What was "positive" loyalty? Did he mean the McCarthy brand of loyalty? In the atmosphere of the day and the job uncertainty inherent in administrative turnover the statement had an unsettling, rather than reassuring, effect on departmental morale. The effects of this, however, can be examined later.

Thus went the first day in office. Because of the new Secretary's familiarity with departmental routine from past experience, it was accomplished with a minimum of awkwardness and with quick attention to the department's substantive affairs. On James F. Byrnes' first day in the office, as successor to Secretary Edward

Stettinius, he found a neat pile of official cables on his desk, all addressed laconically to "Byrnes." Byrnes notified his secretary he did not want to be disturbed, and shut the door. Two and one-half hours later, when pent-up departmental business led one of the higher placed officials to decide the Secretary must be interrupted regardless, Byrnes had written out, in longhand, the answers to forty-seven of the cables. He was unaware that all messages, incoming and outgoing, are addressed personally to the Secretary as a means of ensuring central distribution to the proper officers.

Dulles had, in fact, been making transition to his new responsibility by operating unofficially, prior to assumption of authority, from Suite 3126, where with a small staff he had made such preliminary moves as selecting a committee of distinguished retired Foreign Service officers to advise him on the assignment of career ambassadors. His first official week included such events as attending his first Cabinet meeting, lunching with the President, conferring with ranking career officers George Kennan and Charles E. Bohlen, paying a courtesy call on ailing ex-Secretary Hull, and interviewing Walter S. Robertson, an investment banker and Eisenhower Democrat from Richmond, Virginia, whom Representative Walter Judd of Minnesota had recommended for consideration as Assistant Secretary for Far Eastern Affairs. Robertson later got that appointment from President Eisenhower. Anticipating his first trip, Dulles also had an Air Force medical officer administer a flu shot, and signed his own passport, Diplomatic Passport No. 2, and that of Mrs. Dulles, No. 1.

Like most of the new Cabinet members, Dulles was already a well-known public figure, but one who, having become a powerful policy-making official, required much closer examination. There was no lack of information about his views, for those who took the trouble to look them up. He had made hundreds of speeches on foreign policy, acted as adviser to Democratic Secretaries of State at numerous postwar conferences with the Russians, brilliantly negotiated a treaty of peace with Japan for President Truman, and in 1950 had written a book, *War or Peace,* as a guide to his thinking; much of it became foreign policy. Yet there was naturally a new curiosity about him among those who had paid scant attention to his work and a desire for fuller information on the part of others who wondered what kind of impact he would have on foreign policy practices established over 20 years.

Columnist Stewart Alsop, calling on him in New York shortly after his appointment, found "a solemn looking man with a long, early American face, a penchant for green-tinted suits, and a habit, when deep in thought, of making small clicking noises with his tongue." He thought Dulles looked and talked "much like the traditional American country lawyer—shrewd (and perhaps downright wily when need be), cautious (he often hesitates a full minute before answering a question), highly intelligent, and extremely practical."

Fred Collins, Washington correspondent for the Providence *Journal,* writing after Dulles took office, said that "physical evidence suggests that Mr. Dulles possesses a unique ability to taste ideas, as others with specially cultivated palates taste tea, or wine. Between utterances, his mouth works constantly in the tasting process." Collins' assessment was that Dulles had "a Class A mind which can draw on rich reserves of experience and creative political imagination, and whose adventures are disciplined by a vigorously professed but by no means impractical morality." He also made a comparison with the previous Secretary: "Like Dean Acheson, he is an intellectual, but he is not cursed with his predecessor's impatience with lesser minds. A summary distinction is often made: Acheson had arrogance in office; Dulles has vanity."

Before the new man had been in office a week the public got its own look at Dulles by means of a nation-wide telecast. The spot from which he chose to speak was his own office, with maps to refer to. The informality of the talk, seemingly extemporaneous, the chatty way in which he discussed world problems, and the idiomatic American slurs of diction were in rather startling contrast with the polished, loftily expressed Yale and Harvard Law School accents of Dean Acheson. In his first sentence Dulles referred to himself as "sekketary of State." When he came to locating the trouble spots, he mentioned a place he called "Krea." This habit persisted. In 1954 he attended an Inter-American Republics conference in a Venezuelan city he called "Crackus."

He told his TV audience, "Of course it's obvious that after six days I haven't got the answers to all the problems. It would be ridiculous if I pretended that I did have, but I do think it's worthwhile to tell you what our position in the world is and the spirit with which we approach the solution of these problems."

Dulles applied this chatty tone to foreign policy substance with even more startling results. "President Eisenhower has often used the phrase 'enlightened self-interest,'" he said. "That is going to be the guide as we go on to make our foreign policy. Now in our own interest, our enlightened self-interest, we have to pay close attention to what is going on in the rest of the world. And the reason for that is that we have enemies who are plotting our destruction. These enemies are the Russian Communists and their allies in other countries." The candor of this simply stated basic foreign policy premise of the Eisenhower administration was certainly refreshing, but could it be that the new Secretary was totally insensitive to the time-honored circumlocutions of diplomacy? "Now you may ask," he went on, "how do we know that they are really trying to destroy us? Well, the answer to that one is that their leaders teach it openly and have been teaching it for many years, and everything that they do fits into that teaching."

All the way through, the manner in which Dulles told the American people what they faced was simple, direct, and clearly understandable.

"And in Western Europe," he said, "we find that there is in existence there one of our major foreign policies, the foreign policy that is called by the word NATO; NATO standing for North American Treaty Organization. The purpose there was to tie the Western European countries together with association from the United States and Canada so as to create there a community which would be strong enough to deter any attack on Western Europe by the Red armies. . . . The trouble has been that in the past these Western European countries have used their military strength with which to fight each other and to bleed each other, particularly France and Germany. . . . The present hope is that Germany and France will join in a single European defense community and then we would have a situation where they could not fight each other and where their combined strength with that of their other allies would make it unlikely that the Red armies would attempt to invade Western Europe. That's a good idea and it has had in this country bipartisan support.

"Unfortunately the plan now seems to be somewhat stalled. . . . The United States has made a big investment in Western Europe on the theory that there could be unity there. Of the forty billion dollars which we have sent abroad since the end of the Second World War, almost thirty billions have gone into Western Europe. If however there were no chance, and that I just refuse to believe, but if it appeared there were no chance of getting effective unity, and if in particular France, Germany, and England should go their separate ways, then certainly it would be necessary to give a little rethinking to America's own foreign policy in relation to Western Europe."

This speech was an attempt by Dulles, at the very outset of his term, to give a comprehensive picture of the Eisenhower administration's thinking about foreign policy.

A speech by any Secretary of State presumably takes into account its probable "home consumption" aspects, but normally greater care is taken to convey an American message to foreign governments and the domestic impact is a secondary consideration. In this case Dulles reversed the emphasis.

His theory was that foreign policy, no matter how wise and sound, could not succeed in a democratic republic unless the mass of people understood it and supported it. He had tested the theory in negotiating the Japanese peace treaty and learned that, while it was more troublesome to stir up controversy along the way by being frank about what he was planning to do, the result was to talk out differences and arrive at compromises that provided a firmer base of support when time came for final action. He believed his first job was to restore the American public's confidence in the State Department.

At the same time, Dulles was too experienced at the game not to know that every ambassador in Washington, and every Foreign Office abroad, would currycomb the speech for clues to new American attitudes. Consequently it carried plenty of news for foreigners, too, though that angle was somewhat obscured by the chatty type of talk directed at Americans, and doubly concealed by the fact that he seemed to be speaking extemporaneously. It happens that Dulles had a splendid memory. It was not infallible, but it enabled him to recite with great precision every thought in a speech he had written. Sometimes, even when he appeared to be reading from manuscript, he was speaking from memory and putting the pages aside almost mechanically. His first telecast was not half as casual as it appeared.

Reaction to it varied; comment was generally approving in the United States and uneasy abroad, particularly in France, where it created shocked resentment. A curious reaction was that of Washington's diplomatic correspondents and commentators. Being employed to report on America's impact abroad, they tend to gauge American moves by foreign reaction and to subordinate or overlook the test of American self-interest. Since this was in the first flush of enthusiasm over the new Republican regime, their interpretive dispatches reflected an uncharacteristic restraint. But implicit in most interpretive dispatches was the thought that Dulles made a mistake in speaking off the cuff and that he should not have used TV. One dispatch reported an "air of incredulity" among diplomats over the Dulles statement that President Eisenhower might find a way to make the Korean War enemies want peace. Editorially most American papers approved the speech. The *New York Times* picked out the warning to Europe as its "most trenchant passage" and commented: "It is to be hoped that Europe will heed it—and put new steam behind the unification program."

It was precisely this passage, of course, which raised French hackles. For eight months French cabinets had been sitting on the

EDC treaty and ignoring private American urgings to push for action. The Truman administration had avoided prodding the French officially since it might be regarded as unwarranted interference in internal affairs and cause resentment. Dulles was rude by contrast, and those who felt constrained to be charitable about his first performance did it with a tacit air of indulgence for an understandable mistake by a man who did not yet understand all the angles.

Yet it should not have surprised them. In a chapter in his 1950 book, *War or Peace*, Dulles discussed the need for Western European unity and the reluctance of the United States to apply pressure on Europe's laggards. "There may have been justification in trying a hands-off policy for a time," he wrote, "in the hope that unity would come about of itself. However, it now seems clear that Western European unity will not have any early reality unless strong pressure is exerted by us."

In the same *New York Times* dispatch from Paris giving French reaction to the Secretary's speech, and quoting the local newspapers as calling it "brutal" and "a veiled threat to Europe," was news that the cabinet had that day taken the EDC treaty from its pigeonhole and submitted it to Parliament. In the end EDC was defeated, but Dulles was determined not to let it go by default. Out of the pressure that finally brought a showdown came a substitute, Western European Union, which was adopted.

The Secretary's first diplomatic gambit showed an ability to load a seemingly casual speech with a carefully placed electric charge designed to shock a moribund EDC into revived activity. Correspondent Collins, examining his operating methods, later commented: "Dulles does not always, by any means, move in a straight line toward his goals."

2

. . . .

He Wrote a Book

SECRETARY OF STATE Cordell Hull once described foreign policy as "the task of focusing the attention of the American people on problems beyond our shores." John Foster Dulles took office with a mind sharply focused and a record of having been thinking, writing, and speaking continuously, consistently, and imaginatively about the problems faced by the United States in international relations since 1907, when, as a Princeton junior, nineteen years old, he accompanied his grandfather to a world peace conference at The Hague. When he was thirty he was one of five close advisers to Woodrow Wilson at the Versailles Peace Conference of 1919. The picture he got there of Wilson's idealism in conflict with a vengeful statesmanship at work in Europe left him absorbed, lifelong, with the great problem of how the world might achieve a just and durable peace. Between the World Wars he had thought out, organized, and assembled his ideas.

On the eve of Hitler's attack on Poland he published his con-

16

clusions in a book titled *War, Peace and Change*. In its foreword
he said it represented twenty years of thinking on the subject, since
the Versailles conference. It never drew as much attention as did
his 1950 volume, *War or Peace*, but may in the long run prove of
greater value.

War, Peace and Change was a profoundly philosophical book
which examined the causes of war and the means which had been
employed in history's attempts to avoid war. It reached the conclusion that the successful method must be a mechanism providing
for peaceful change. Change, he argued, was inevitable, and the
reason wars occurred was that "satisfied," dominant nations sought
artificially to preserve the status quo and prevent change, repress-
ing the forces working for change until they exploded in armed
conflict. Some casual readers—and it is impossible to absorb the
book's message casually—interpreted it as an apologia for Hitler
and Mussolini, which it was not. The book was highly concentrated,
written with a terseness verging almost on outline. While it made
judgments and reached conclusions which may be open to argument now, as they were in 1939, there was no idea in it that can
be said to have been proved wrong by events which have taken
place in the eighteen years intervening.

Analyzing the behavior of nations as they are recorded in history,
Dulles concluded that peoples tend to personify their countries
in their international relations, thinking in such concepts as the
Nation-Hero and the Nation-Villain. Because of this, he reasoned,
the sixty or seventy nations of the day were, in their relations with
each other, in much the same position politically as communities of
sixty or seventy individuals before group authority was set up.
Although nations are made up of individuals who are overwhelm-

ingly peace-loving and law-abiding, the ferment of change continues to create situations in which the Nation-Villain impinges
on the pride and sensibilities of the Nation-Hero, leading to war.

Many others have seen the need for a system of international
law and order, and many had devoted themselves to striving for it.
Dulles decided that previous attempts had been falsely based on the
theory of preserving the status quo. If change could be allowed
for peacefully, it might make a difference. Searching for a mechanism, he found a satisfactory germ-idea in Article 19 of the
Covenant of the League of Nations, although the League's impotence by the time he wrote left its application in the realm of
theory. Article 19 provided: "The Assembly may, from time to
time, advise the reconsideration by members of the League of
treaties which have become inapplicable and the consideration of
international conditions whose continuance might endanger the
peace of the world."

In subsequent thinking on this subject Dulles differed from
those who sought suddenly to burst the bonds of national sovereignty. International order, he felt, would have to come at its own
pace, a pace capable of being supported by mass opinion. At the
same time, he recognized that perceptive leadership was necessary.
In a speech at Ohio Wesleyan University in 1942 he outlined
what he thought might be a conservative first step. It was based
on the proposition that scientific developments have made the
world interdependent economically—a proposition well enough
accepted not to require recapitulation here of the logical and
statistical evidence.

"What science can do," said Dulles, "politics must match." The
problem, he contended, was to get started in the right direction.

He rejected isolationism of the Fortress-America thinking. "It is by no means certain," he remarked, "that the rest of the world would tolerate our isolation." He rejected world government. Interdependence, while often existing on a world scale, fell short of being universal. Besides, there was not sufficient world-wide awareness to lead people to accept world government in place of their national governments, and the complications were too great for any governing group honestly to accept, or practically to discharge, a world-wide trustee responsibility. He rejected union of the democracies: "Indeed, the unordered interdependence which leads to war actually is found largely between the democratic and nondemocratic countries. . . . The so-called 'democratic' nations are, generally speaking, the richer and more satisfied. The nondemocratic nations are, usually, the poorer nations. Thus a federation of the so-called democracies would, to others, appear as a banding together of the well-to-do to maintain the status quo. A natural reaction would be a banding together of the dissatisfied peoples in a counteralliance." The League of Nations he considered inadequate because it was "dependent for power upon its constituent members who were the very nations whose separate and self-willed and self-seeking acts were bringing about disorder."

But if a League-type Assembly and Council could be used as a world legislature and appointing authority, and the World Court as a judiciary, he suggested that an initial step might be taken toward supranational executive authority by creation of an Executive Organ which would: (1) operate a Monetary and Banking Corporation as a clearinghouse for world trade; (2) charter commercial companies subject to its own taxation and regulation, and immune from national controls of the same type; and (3) negotiate tariff and trade quotas with individual nations which, for the chartered firms, eventually would replace national quotas.

Establishment of functional agencies not subject to any national sovereign would begin "that dilution of sovereignty which all enlightened thinkers agree to be indispensable," Dulles contended, and at the same time avoid "the mistake of assuming, at the beginning, tasks so vast, so difficult, and so unexplored that failure is likely."

In speeches such as this he enlarged, refined, and added to the basic theory he outlined in *War, Peace and Change*. The 1950 book, *War or Peace*, was a topical application of his theory in the light of experiences as a foreign policy adviser and in anticipation of being charged with responsibility for conducting foreign policy. Before he became Secretary he carried forward the elaboration and refinement of its principles, and in a 1952 article in *Life* magazine he set forth, in advance, quite clearly, the policies of "Liberation" and "Deterrence" and others which became so highly controversial after he took office.

He proclaimed his philosophy in advance, and was destined to be a man of controversy. He had been thinking about war and peace consistently for more than thirty years, and his convictions were profound. Critics who concluded he was a foot-in-mouth diplomat, who talked before he knew what he was doing, misled themselves. He knew what he was doing; what he was doing did not fit the pattern to which they were accustomed. His theories might not work, but he was spurred by the conviction that previous theories for attaining world peace not only had not worked but would not work. Thus he was determined to try his own. He had done it once before, in negotiating peace with Japan. Discarding and overcoming demands for vengeful peace, he wrote a treaty of reconciliation.

If there are three sentences that sum up what made John Foster Dulles tick as he took up the job of Secretary of State, they are the three opening sentences of *War or Peace:*

"War is probable—unless by positive and well-directed efforts we fend it off.

"War is not inevitable, and I do not think it is imminent. Something can be done about it."

And when he wrote those words he was completely aware that the threat of nuclear war, arising out of scientific advance in the period between his two books, made the need for a just and durable peace infinitely more desperate than ever before.

3

· · · · · · · ·

American Roots

JOHN FOSTER DULLES was born on February 25, 1888, in Washington. His father, the Rev. Allen Macy Dulles, D.D., was pastor of the First Presbyterian Church of Watertown, New York, but Mrs. Dulles, who had been Edith Foster, returned to the parental home for the arrival of her first-born. It was four years before her father, John Watson Foster, an Indiana lawyer who had served as minister to Mexico and St. Petersburg, became Secretary of State under President Benjamin Harrison.

Dulles could trace his ancestry back forty generations from the Watertown pastor to Charlemagne (b. 2 Apr. 742, as the family genealogy notes meticulously). Mrs. Dulles has a French poodle which goes by the name Pepi but whose real name is Pepin Le Bref, after Charlemagne's father, Pepin the Short. A French diplomat, who knew about the poodle, exclaimed with the delight of discovery when he learned about the Dulles ancestry: "Ah! Now it is clear why Secretary Dulles is so keen on the unity of Western

Europe! He wants to restore the Holy Roman Empire. But of course!"

The Dulles name (believed to have been Douglas originally) first showed up in a Scot named William Dulles who is recorded as having been an officer at the Battle of the Boyne in 1690. The first of the clan to reach the United States was Joseph, who arrived at Charleston, South Carolina, about 1776, shortly afterward found himself helping to defend the city against an attack by Sir Henry Clinton, and lived to become a well-to-do merchant who moved to Philadelphia in 1792 and lived until 1818. His grandson, Allen Macy Dulles, married Edith Foster and became the pastor at Watertown.

The missionary grandfather of John Foster Dulles died the year after he was born, but his diplomatic grandfather lived until he was grown up. It was only natural, therefore, that when it came to a grandfather's yarn spinning, the boy should hear more about his mother's side of the family. John Watson Foster had lots to tell: about the pioneer days of his father, who had come from England as a lad of fifteen; about his own Civil War experiences, which included action at the capture of Fort Donelson, the Battle of Shiloh, and command of a cavalry brigade under General Burnside in Tennessee; entering service as a major, he was mustered out a brigadier general. By the time his Dulles namesake was born, John Watson Foster was an established family patriarch, a man of position, great dignity, and imposing sideburns, who doted on his first grandchild, wrote two books for him and his generation, and, later on, virtually led him by the hand into his legal and diplomatic careers.

The Foster strain came from England, where it was spelled

Forster. The genealogy goes back to George Forster, a tenant farmer of Gilesfield, Durham, who married a tradesman's daughter named Jane Watson late in the eighteenth century. They had three sons: Matthew, James, and William.

In 1815 the family joined the tide of emigration to America which followed the ending of the Napoleonic Wars. For two years they farmed in upstate New York. In 1817 Matthew started off on foot to find a new home for the family and walked all the way to St. Louis, Missouri, then a city of about four thousand population. Because he foresaw that slavery was likely to be permitted under the Missouri constitution Matthew rejected St. Louis as a place to settle, and remembering the richly timbered land he had passed through in southern Indiana he retraced his steps to a spot in the White River valley about twenty miles east of the old military post of Vincennes. There he got a government patent for eighty acres, and returned to New York, still on foot, to lead the family back.

Detailed information about the homely American beginnings of the Foster clan were preserved because when Matthew's eldest son left for the Indiana State College at Bloomington he was still wearing suits homemade from cloth spun and woven on the farm. All the children remembered vividly the conditions under which they had grown up and the stories their father told them of the trek westward. The third son, John Watson Foster, eventually recorded them in a privately printed life of his father to honor an injunction when Matthew lay dying: "Don't let the little ones forget."

This account tells how the original farm produced corn and pork which soon exceeded local demand. The only outlet for it was downriver, and in 1820 Matthew made a trip to New Orleans as a hired hand on a flatboat to sell some of the surplus. Eleven years later an Illinois lad named Abe Lincoln made a similar trip. Matthew's profits were not sufficient to permit boat passage back, so he walked the twelve hundred miles back, covering as much as fifty miles some days, traversing Indian territory with his money, in Spanish doubloons, buckled around his waist. He made two such trips before he could afford the steamboat back to Indiana.

On the first journey he had noted that there was a scarcity of hoops for the barrels and hogsheads used in the sugar and molasses production of the plantations along the lower Mississippi, with consequent high prices for them. Organizing a co-operative undertaking with his neighbors, he accumulated a stock of hickory hoop-poles sufficient to load a flatboat, and sold them downriver at a handsome profit. Later, operating on his own, he shipped venison, corn, pork, and other local products, opened a store in Petersburgh to sell the wares he brought back, and branched out with two gristmills.

John Watson Foster felt very close to this frontier life, for he could remember the log cabin in which a long rifle was placed over the door. Even though he went on to become a lawyer, a soldier, a diplomat, and a Cabinet member, he was able to pass along to his namesake a vivid sense of the pioneer American spirit in which he had been brought up. In June 1955, when Secretary Dulles received an honorary degree from the University of Indiana, he spoke feelingly about those bits of family history.

"My grandfather, whose name I bear, exerted a great influence over my life," he said, "and he had ideals and purposes which I have tried to make my own. He was a deeply patriotic American. He belonged to the period which saw this country rapidly developing from a small Atlantic coast group into a nation that spread across the continent. He fought to preserve the Union; and then on diplomatic missions and as Secretary of State he helped to spread the influence of this nation throughout the world both in Europe and in Asia."

Since Dulles' adult experiences and thinking had led him to believe in evolutionary supranationalism as a cure for war, it is noteworthy that in this speech he dwelt on the virtues of patriotism. He saw no conflict between love of country and a willingness to subordinate nationalism for world peace.

"In some quarters," he said, "there has developed a tendency to scorn patriotism. Indeed, there are a few who find patriotism unfashionable and who go so far as to assume that institutions and ideas are better if only they bear a foreign label. Also there is a theory that this mood is necessary if we are to develop international institutions and maintain international peace.

"It seems to me that love of country is one of the great and indispensable virtues. No community is weaker because the members of the families which made it up are bound together by distinctive ties of love, respect, and admiration. So I am convinced that the family of nations will not be the poorer or the more fragile because the peoples who form the different nations have a special affection and pride for their own people and for the nation they form. I recall that Saint Paul took great pride, which he did not attempt to conceal, in the achievements of his own people.

"True patriotism, which vitalizes liberty and freedom for ourselves, can never be a purely selfish force. Our people have always been endowed with a sense of mission in the world. They have believed that it was their duty to help men everywhere to get the opportunity to be and to do what God designed."

The affinity between a grandfather and grandson can often rival that between father and son, and it shows through on both sides in this case. In his diplomatic memoirs Grandfather Foster provided a glimpse of his own feeling in recounting his experiences as adviser to the Imperial Chinese government in negotiations with Japan on the Treaty of Shimonoseki, which ceded Formosa to Japan. Viceroy Li Hung-chang invited Foster to remain in China as a government adviser.

"I resolved to decline," the grandfather recalls, "but when I presented to the Viceroy various reasons . . . he gave me to understand that I should receive such compensation as would overcome these objections.

"I then, in an assumed serious tone, told him there was one insuperable obstacle in the way which he must recognize, as he was a follower of the great philosopher Confucius, who taught that children should be trained to respect and venerate their parents and ancestors. I had made an engagement with and a promise to my seven year old grandson that I would come home in time to go a-fishing with him that summer, and that it would destroy all his esteem and confidence in me if I failed in my promise!

"The next season, as good luck would have it, as the seven year old grandson and I were trolling along one of the islands of the St. Lawrence River, I 'struck' a fine fish, which proved a good-sized muskallonge, reaching from the boy's shoulder to the ground. I sent the Viceroy a photograph of the boy with the fish on a gaff-hook hanging from his shoulder."

Fishing in the St. Lawrence and in Lake Ontario in the vicinity of his Watertown home was an important part of the boy's early life. The grandfather had a summer home at Henderson Harbor, overlooking the lake. Grandfather, father, and son often went out in a rowboat or catboat and fished all day long. On such excursions the boy heard his grandfather tell about his experiences in Russia and Mexico and China. Sometimes there were distinguished visitors at the home—Vice-President Charles W. Fairbanks, for one, or Chinese diplomats—and young Foster found himself greatly impressed.

At home the boy had a strict religious upbringing. On Sundays the children were all required to attend Sunday school as well as the three Sunday worship services then in vogue. Monday evenings they attended the young people's service, Wednesday night the weekly prayer meeting. Whenever a Communion service was nearing they were also required to attend the preparatory service on the preceding Friday night.

One of Sunday's regular tasks was to learn some poetry, a chapter of the Bible, from either Psalms or the New Testament, and one or two verses of a hymn. At one time young Dulles could recite all of John's Gospel. "I'm glad I had to do it," Dulles said in later life. "If I hadn't learned the Bible thoroughly I would have lacked a great source of comfort and strength."

Sundays also were distinguished by a big family dinner—chicken and ice cream. The grownups got the white meat and the children the dark, with the result that Dulles always liked the dark meat better. The high point for him was making the ice cream in an old-fashioned freezer, and getting to lick the dasher.

Sunday afternoons the family reading was restricted to religious publications: the *Herald & Presbyter*, missionary stories, or serious literature like *Pilgrim's Progress* and *Paradise Lost*. It was only in later years that standards were relaxed to the point of permitting more secular publications like the *Outlook* and *Independent*. Summers the family lived at a lake shore cottage, walked the three miles to a village church and back along the bluffs overlooking the lake, often singing hymns as they walked. Among the favorites were "Work, for the Night Is Coming" and "Onward, Christian Soldiers." "It was a very rigorous upbringing," Dulles once recalled, "but it was not distasteful."

Dulles went through grammar school and high school in Watertown. He took part in the boys' gangs, organized according to the streets they lived on, which engaged in snowball battles in winter or played one old cat in the spring after school hours. Despite his upbringing, John Foster was not above playing hooky to go fishing.

"They had democracy and discipline in those days," he recalled. "They believed in corporal punishment. I had my hands caned and my ears cuffed for throwing spitballs in school. I don't believe there is any equivalent of that type of public school education today. They preached a good old Americanism. Our heroes were Paul Revere and John Paul Jones. We read the Henty books and the Boys of '76. There was a strong spirit of Americanism and pride in country."

The Rev. Dr. Dulles was a "liberal" minister. He was almost thrown out of the church for contending that the Christian religion did not depend on belief in the Virgin Birth, and he was one of the early preachers who presided at marriages of divorced persons. Later his son took the modernist side in a widely publicized fundamentalist controversy involving this point at the Presbyterian

General Assembly of 1924, in which the preaching licenses of such noted New York Presbyterian divines as Dr. Harry Emerson Fosdick and Henry P. Van Dusen, head of Union Theological Seminary, were challenged.

Under Father Dulles' upbringing the children never felt a conflict between the things they believed and the way they lived. There was no sense of inferiority as minister's children. They had the usual family problems but they adjusted to them. They were spared the more extreme poverty in which ministers' families generally lived. It was true their circumstances were modest, but the Rev. Dr. Dulles made a salary of $3,000, which in those days represented considerable buying power. He also had a private income which enabled the family to travel in Europe during the summers, in an era when steamship passage could be had for as little as $50. They stayed at modest *pensions* and did their sightseeing by bicycle. In this way they visited Germany, France, and Switzerland as youngsters.

Watertown remained "home" to Foster Dulles because he was ready for Princeton by the time the family moved to Auburn, a nearby town, where his father preached and also occupied the chair of apologetics at the Auburn Theological Seminary. At Auburn his sisters and brother Allen entered into the life of the town and became acquainted with youths their own age, of whom Foster, on his visits home during school vacations, was only casually aware. One of these was a girl named Janet Avery, who sometimes attended dancing parties with Allen.

At Princeton Dulles found study very easy and had lots of leisure, which he spent playing whist, later bridge, and poker. In his freshman year he was on the 10-board chess team, but quit because he found it too absorbing. He took part in debate but did not try out for the varsity.

Once a professor who sought to find out whether his course was too hard asked Dulles how much time he spent studying for it. Dulles exaggerated a bit and told him, "One hour a week." It embarrassed the professor. Foster had a knack for exams, being endowed with the ability to cram the course book into his head in a night's intensive study and remember it well enough to pass the next day.

By the time he went to Princeton a curious combination of shyness, intellectual self-confidence, conventional modesty, and unconventional tendency toward iconoclasm had been mixed together in the ego of John Foster Dulles. Some of it showed through the first long theme he submitted for English, which he turned in September 24, 1904. The subject was "My Preparation for English."

"It is hard," wrote the sixteen-year-old freshman, "to write five hundred words on one's preperation in English when one has not spent five hundred minutes preparing it. But that is the task which is before me.

"When I say that I have never spent any length of time in preparing what is called English, I may give a false impression. It is true that I have never taken an English course at school. Altho I have, at one time or another, entered classes, I have as often, voluntarily or otherwise, dropped out.

"As a result of this my knowledge of grammatical rules and parsing is slight. Indeed, it consists chiefly in what I have learned from Latin & Greek, but then, Latin & Greek grammer is the foundation of all others.

"My knowledge of English Literature is somewhat larger, but

that is not saying much for it. Whatever of the masterpieces of literature that I have read, I have read not as a task. In this way they are much more enjoyable than when read and dissected piece meal, as is some times done, and a clearer idea of the whole book is obtained.

"I have read, thus, many of Scott's novels and Dickens, espescialy Pickwick Papers. I have memorized—and forgotten—several short poems of Longfellow, Tennyson & Whittier, but am not so thoroughly acquainted with those books which are required for anterance into most Universities as those who have studied and dissected them with an eye, more directly, toward the examination. The same is true in some degree with Shakespeare, altho I have spent some time in studying his plays.

"As to compositions and essays I have written very few, as the present writing will testify. In fact I am surprised that I was ever allowed to enter the college, as far as English preparation is concerned."

The manuscript of this composition, preserved by his mother and given eventually to his wife, shows that Foster's teacher, apparently giving up the idea of blue-penciling corrections about halfway through, wrote at the top: "Where did you study English? Rewrite."

His Princeton major was philosophy. He was expecting to enter the ministry. Despite the coupled apology and defiance of his freshman English theme, his grades were uniformly good. His senior thesis was on "The Theory of Judgment" and it was good enough to rate an A, contribute to making him Phi Beta Kappa and valedictorian of his class, and earn him the $600 Chancellor Green Mental Science fellowship that gave him a year to study philosophy at the Sorbonne in Paris.

4

· · · · · · · ·

Salt-water Sailor

IN 1901 a Pan-American exposition was held at Buffalo. Dulles, then thirteen years old, had been promised he would be taken to see it, but he came down with typhoid fever just before the scheduled trip. He had a severe bout with typhoid, and underwent the rigorous treatment common in that day—ducking in ice water whenever his temperature went above 102 degrees, with nothing to eat for three weeks but boiled milk.

Missing the exposition was a bitter disappointment. One day, standing on the porch of the family's summer cottage, he saw the speck of a white sail out on the blue of the lake. The little craft came in toward shore and the boy became aware that the grownups were watching him closely, apparently to see his reaction. Suddenly he realized that this boat was intended for him. He had seldom felt as excited about anything. It was his grandfather's gift, a recompense for having had to miss the Buffalo exposition.

Even at that age the boy was a good sailor. Will Stevens, a

33

Watertown resident who acted as guide for fishing trips on which his father and grandfather took him along, had taught him how to handle the 12-foot St. Lawrence skiffs used in the area. Sometimes he and his grandfather, in one boat, would compete with his father and brother Allen in another in a race to get to the fishing spots first.

Fishing, however, was his first outdoor sport. His earliest recorded literary effort related to fishing. It was a block-letter composition (preserved by his mother) with the usual reverse S's and N's of a boy just learning to write at six years, in the form of a letter home. It said:

"Dear Papa, I am at Henderson. Yesterday I were aut fishing and I cot six fishis and Uncle Bert and Aunt and one of my fishis was a big one and it tok three pepol to pull it in 6uly 26th Foster."

Ownership of his own boat enlarged his interest in outdoor life. The boat, a cat, never had a name except "No. 5" derived from the fact that the number happened to be painted on it. It instilled a love of sailing that stayed with him all through life, turned him into a daring but not reckless salt-water yachtsman, and led him later on to buy a cruising yawl on which he and members of his family made exciting cruises down the St. Lawrence and along the Nova Scotia coast to Maine and Long Island. Although he disposed of the yawl when wartime conditions restricted its use, he kept a sailing skiff at his Duck Island retreat in Lake Ontario.

Out of the sailing-fishing excursions of his boyhood came the first awakening of interest in international affairs. While they angled from the boat, or after they had cooked their fish for luncheon at some spot on the shore, Grandpa reminisced with Papa and Uncle Bert (Robert Lansing) about his experiences in Mexico, at the court of the Czar in St. Petersburg, and among the exotic peoples of China and Japan. The conversation fired the youngsters with interest—and not Foster only, for Allen was sufficiently moved to write an essay on British policy in South Africa, taking the Boer side, which so delighted the grandfather that he had it privately printed, complete with boyish misspellings, for family circulation.

No. 5 was too small a boat for use much beyond twenty or thirty miles from home, but that kind of range was enough to make the eastern end of Lake Ontario thoroughly familiar to its owner and to instill fundamentals of sailing which had application in life as well as in sport. He learned that serious sailing called for careful advance planning, taking into account weather probabilities, and he quickly learned to read from the weather signs whether the clouds threatened a real blow or just a passing squall. He discovered he could not be sloppy in taking care of a boat, for it entailed penalty in moments of crisis. He learned self-reliance. One day, out sailing with one of his sisters, a squall hit and the mainsheet tackle broke. His grandmother, watching through binoculars from the porch of their summer home, moaned, "They'll drown, they'll drown!" but Foster fixed the tackle, installed a new sheet, and came in safely. He learned, incidentally, to become a very good swimmer; while in high school he swam some two and one-half miles across Henderson Harbor on more than one occasion.

Sailing taught not only patience, since there was no use fretting during periods of calm, but courage and steadiness when management of the craft called for the calmest kind of taut-nerved operation. One of his sisters recalls an exciting forty-mile sail from Kingston before a brisk wind which kept him alert every moment, handling the tiller so as to take advantage of the breeze and at the same time prevent quartering seas from causing the boat to yaw and throw the boom across in a jibe with force enough to snap it off.

Sailing developed in him an affinity for an outdoor life and probably contributed to his rugged constitution. Possessed of a splendid memory and a strategist's brain, later he became an expert at such intellectual pastimes as bridge and chess, but he abandoned them when they absorbed him to the point of wasting time. He never abandoned swimming, sailing, fishing, hunting, wood chopping, and such kindred physical activities. His father taught him to enjoy long walks and took him on mountain-climbing expeditions in Switzerland. Such outdoor sports undoubtedly explain his ability, well along in his sixties, to stand the pace of a peripatetic life as Secretary of State.

Eventually No. 5 was replaced by a larger catboat, the *Duck,* a centerboarder which though without a cabin was large enough for longer excursions. It was a 10-day cruise aboard the *Duck,* some years after Dulles was a successful lawyer, that led to his acquisition of Main Duck Island, on the Ontario side of the lake about forty miles by air from Watertown.

Foster and Allen and their wives set out to cruise the eastern end of Lake Ontario. It was ambitious for an open boat, but the *Duck* was big enough to carry provisions and, when tied up in a sheltered cove at night, for two to sleep on each side of the centerboard housing. They sailed up through the Bay of Quinte and into the open reaches of the lake. One of their stops was Duck Island, which they had visited before on briefer overnight cruises.

Foster and Janet had had their eye on the island as a particularly favorite spot and that year, 1929, it had been offered for sale by the owner, a Canadian named Cole, known locally as "Old King." He had a house there—a hideous frame structure, the only habitation on the island except for a lighthouse manned by a solitary warden and radio operator and some fishermen's shacks. They arranged to buy it, but it turned out there was no pen or paper at hand to seal the contract, so they shook hands on it. But the deal failed to go through because the owner's son convinced his father it would ruin the lucrative smuggling business he was doing under prohibition. Duck was strategically situated for supplying Rochester and other U.S. cities.

After repeal in 1933 the son offered it to the Dulleses again, at a price considerably below what his father had asked, but by then the depression was on and the Dulleses felt they had enough real estate on their hands with homes in Cold Spring Harbor, Long Island, and Manhattan. In 1941, however, they did buy it, from Cole's widow, and disdaining the ugly house with its "conveniences" which never worked, had a log cabin built by Indians: a rough but comfortable no-conveniences structure containing one great big room, a kitchen, a dressing room, and a washroom, and located on a more suitable part of the island. In 1956 they tore down the old house, which was rotting to pieces.

Ever afterward, the Dulleses used the cabin as their very private retreat, isolated from all but the most emergency communication via radio to the lighthouse keeper. None but they stayed there overnight, and few but their most intimate friends even visited the island while they were there. Occasionally young sailors of another generation have tied up in its lee on summer cruises, as the Dulleses did before they owned it. On one such occasion the visiting mariners were in trouble and Dulles helped them repair the craft and gave them advice on local sailing conditions.

Here the couple fished, hunted, watched birds, tapped the trees for maple syrup, cooked for each other, washed the dishes, and scoured the copper cooking utensils. They did not even have a battery radio to keep up with news of the outside world. Here it was, too, that the Secretary did his heavy thinking. After each major shift in world affairs, as, for example, after the "summit" conference at Geneva, he liked to spend a few days in this rugged outdoor milieu, his active mind at work analyzing the effects of the changed international power factors as he fished or sailed. At night, by the light of a kerosene lamp, he crystallized his judgment of the best course for the United States to follow by writing down his ideas on a yellow scratch pad.

It was aboard the *Menemsha,* successor to the *Duck,* that Dulles displayed his ability to do really rugged open-water sailing. The *Menemsha* was a 40-foot gaff-rigged auxiliary cruising yawl with a combination keel and centerboard, designed and built by George Lawley in 1916. From 1933 through 1941 Dulles logged nearly twenty thousand cruising miles in her, sailing the Great Lakes at first and later the Gulf of St. Lawrence and the Nova Scotia coast. Colored maps on which have been entered the history of these cruises, complete with log notations showing where storms were encountered, whales sighted, and mishaps occurred, were kept in Dulles' hideaway office at the State Department and he reflected a sailor's pride when he talked about them.

A cruise through three of the Great Lakes in 1933, marked by trouble with the engine, bilge pumps, and rigging, was interrupted ignominiously when the boat grounded on a soft mudbank in the Detroit River, fouled the anchor line, and had to be got off by kedging. Later Dulles had a new engine installed and fitted the boat with a new suit of sails, and in 1934 started out on a St. Lawrence-Atlantic cruise with Mrs. Dulles, his daughter Lillias, his son Avery, and Robert F. Hart, Jr., a seasoned yachtsman of Chaumont, New York, whose experience has included sailing in blue ribbon Bermuda races. Threading the Thousand Islands, the party went through the canal system to Montreal without mishap but with one exciting experience when they missed the entrance to one of the locks. They found themselves in fast-moving water headed for the rapids. Coming about, they tried to go back upstream but the engine was barely strong enough to hold its own against the powerful current. So they bore off again and went roaring down through the fast water.

At Murray Bay, Quebec, Mrs. Dulles and Lillias left the party, and Dulles' older son John, his brother Allen, and Ferdinand Eberstadt, New York investment banker, joined the ship. As they sailed along the north shore of the St. Lawrence the air and water became progressively colder but it never prevented the daily swim. They stopped in at Seven Islands, on the Quebec shore north of the western tip of Anticosti Island, and sighted a whale off Anticosti en route to the Gaspé Peninsula. There Allen Dulles and Eberstadt left to return to New York.

Dulles, his two sons, and Hart continued on to Prince Edward Island. It was challenging sailing because of the new hazards to navigation which Dulles was encountering: strong currents, extreme weather, heavy and often continuous fog. Going into the harbor of Charlottetown, P.E.I., the *Menemsha* parted a running backstay and a main shroud, but the crew brought her around into the wind fast enough to save the rest of the rig. Repairs could not be made locally, so the Dulleses returned to New York while Hart got new rigging made in Boston and returned with his brother to sail the boat to Halifax with the help of a local fisherman as hand, and on down the east coast to Gloucester, Boston, and Newport, Rhode Island. Here the Dulles family rejoined the boat for the final leg to their home at Cold Spring Harbor, Long Island, and en route they saw the start of the last of the races for the America's Cup, which that year was held between *Rainbow* and *Endeavor I*. Hart took the boat back to Chaumont, New York, by way of the Erie Barge Canal.

In 1935 the *Menemsha* cruised the Great Lakes again, with Dulles, his two sons, Hart, and a home-town crew member, Art Eldridge. On this cruise Dulles sprained his back badly hauling the anchor and had to be lowered into the water by boatswain's chair for swimming, since it was painful to climb the ladder. The *Menemsha's* log carried one entry noting that the air temperature was 37 degrees and the Lake Superior water 46 degrees. Although the sailors wore their heaviest clothing, including winter underwear, they stripped to the buff each day to go swimming.

On this trip the *Menemsha* suffered the greatest casualty of her cruising career while Dulles owned her. Bob Hart recalls: "We were coming into a harbor at night under power on an absolutely flat sea. Mr. Dulles was at the wheel, Avery was sitting beside him in the cockpit with the charts, doing the piloting, and John and I were below. I was getting supper started with a big bowl of soup on the stove.

"We were probably moving along at about 5 knots when suddenly there was a crash which sounded like an explosion and we stopped dead in our tracks. Of course everything on the boat that was loose and some things that weren't went flying forward, including the bucket of soup. We hit so hard that we couldn't believe that she wouldn't sink within minutes. However, on investigation we found that there were no holes through her and she wasn't making any water.

"The two gas tanks had been torn loose from their fastenings and the gas lines were broken, with gasoline pouring into the bilge. The engine was shut off immediately to prevent fire, but we were, of course, without power. Mr. Dulles, who had been straddling the wheel, was badly bruised, and Avery was momentarily knocked out by being thrown forward against the afterbulkhead of the cabin. John got his head cut when he collided with a gimbaled lamp in the cabin, and I wound up in the forepeak covered with soup.

"We kept a watch all that night to make sure she was not making water, and jury-rigged one of the gas tanks so that we could get under way next day. When dawn came we discovered we had run head-on into a tremendous boulder. The boat had fortunately hit on the forward end of her lead keel, which was about 14 feet long and weighed 8 or 9 tons. The keel was knocked out of shape, and all of the keel bolts were badly bent, which necessitated a very major job before the next season. It was caused, of course, by an error in piloting."

The Dulleses chose to try another St. Lawrence-Atlantic cruise in 1938, stopping among other places at the mouth of the Moisie River, just northeast of Seven Islands and close to the Labrador border. They arrived just in time to see a native wedding ceremony and tried their luck at salmon fishing but without results, being too late in the season. They were stormbound there for one day. "It was one of the few times Mr. Dulles was ever willing to postpone a departure because of weather," Hart says. They cruised leisurely along the Gaspé, Prince Edward Island, the Gut of Canso, and explored the Bras d'Or Lakes on Cape Breton Island. Since they planned to leave the boat in Halifax for the winter, they spent considerable time on the Nova Scotia coast and the Bay of Fundy. It was a trip that required very careful navigation and piloting, for despite the well-marked coast, fog was common. "We went in and out of harbor after harbor in absolutely dense fog," Hart recalls. "In some cases we couldn't see the shore at all, either on our way in or our way out. You have to know what you're doing to keep out of trouble."

The last of the long *Menemsha* cruises was to Lake Superior in 1940. Hart says: "We had some wonderful heavy weather sailing on both Lake Huron and Lake Superior, with one of the hardest sails we ever had on our return coming down Lake Huron. Many, many times throughout these cruises we would be the only boat out because of weather conditions." As a means of entertainment, Dulles promoted bets on such things as the time of landfalls, speed of the boat, best hour's run. Dulles won most of the bets, but not much money, for he insisted on limiting them to a nickel each.

In 1941, having acquired Duck Island, Dulles disposed of the *Menemsha,* knowing that wartime conditions would prevent the kind of cruising he had learned to enjoy. But the qualities of character which sailing brought out in him carried over into not only law but diplomacy. One of his law partners noted that his technique as an attorney displayed the same boldness that caused him to take his boat out on days when others stayed ashore, taking calculated chances for the excitement of the sail but without venturing into recklessness.

Salt-water Sailor

In 1956, called on to speak at a yacht club dinner at Sodus Point, New York, Dulles compared sailing to diplomatic technique. "Sometimes you need a lot of tacking to reach your objective," he said. "When you set out to get somewhere, you have to find out how to reach your goal in spite of winds that might blow against you, and this often calls for a lot of tacking." And the conduct of foreign affairs, he added, calls for the sailor's qualities of patience, endurance, and eternal vigilance.

5

. . . .

A Taste of Diplomacy

GRANDFATHER John W. Foster records in his *Memoirs** that when The Hague peace conference of 1907 was convoked, he attended as a delegate for the Imperial government of China. "I sailed from New York on May 31, 1907," he writes, "accompanied by my wife and my grandson, John Foster Dulles, a student of Princeton University, aged nineteen, who, on our arrival at The Hague, was made a secretary of the Chinese delegation, and because of his knowledge of the French language was enabled to render useful service to the delegation." Dulles had special permission from the university authorities to leave school early and take his exams in the fall when he got back.

General Foster's recorded judgment of this conference was that "in some respects"—today it seems a hardly adequate qualifying phrase—it was "the most important event in the history of the

* John Watson Foster, *Diplomatic Memoirs*, 2 vols., Houghton Mifflin, 1909.

44

human race." He based it on the fact that for the first time "the political representatives of all the nations of the earth had met together" in peacetime, to promote peace and prevent war or mitigate its horrors.

It was the second such conference held at The Hague. The first, in 1899, was attended by only twenty-six nations. The second drew representation from forty-four; two who were invited, Costa Rica and Honduras, did not attend, and two others, Abyssinia and Liberia, were not considered important enough to get bids. Both conclaves were on invitation of Czar Nicholas II of Russia, but the inspiration of the second was really President Theodore Roosevelt. For the sake of good foreign relations and protocol, Teddy indulged the hints from St. Petersburg that, having called the first, Nicholas wanted to send out the invitations for the second.

The first conference was called to consider limitation of armaments, but German objection to this topic caused abandonment of the idea. The conference did, however, adopt three conventions: one for the pacific settlement of international disputes; one regulating the laws and customs of war by land; and one adapting to maritime warfare the principles of the Geneva convention of 1864.

The second conference, which sat from June 15 to October 18, 1907, likewise encountered big-power opposition to discussion of arms limitation. But it enlarged on the beginning previously made in focusing moral opinion on the need for controlling the inclination of nations to go to war to achieve national objectives. It reiterated the principle that nations should seek to settle international disputes by peaceful means; it urged prohibition of forcible collection of debts (i.e., by warfare) by one nation from another; it adopted rules for warning prior to the commencement of hostilities;

it drafted regulations governing land and naval warfare; it proposed establishment of an international prize court; and it urged the signatory nations to set up a permanent international court of justice, a proposal which led, after an intervening World War and years of wrangling over methods of selecting the judges, to creation of the tribunal now seated at The Hague. In all, the second Hague conference drew up thirteen treaties, offering them separately to the participating nations in the hope that the opportunity to pick and choose would gain a wider base of acceptance than if each nation had to take all or nothing.

It was a limited attempt to curb warmaking and was looked on by Europe's statesmen with considerable cynicism. General Foster took note in his *Memoirs* of this cynicism, but he himself refused to shrug off the value of the effort. Writing in 1909, he said: "It was worth more than dollars or pounds, shillings, and pence that the representatives of all the nations of the earth have gathered in one great assembly with the avowed purpose of promoting peace; that they came together upon a perfect equality, the smallest and weakest nation on the same footing as the most populous and powerful; that they remained in session for four months, discussing great questions of world-wide importance in a friendly spirit and without a harsh word or a warlike threat. . . . It is a record of which every lover of mankind may be proud. It is visionary to expect that wars among nations will cease, but let us hope that there is the dawn of a new day when right, not wrong, justice, not force, will rule in the affairs of governments . . . when the patriot will delight, not in the triumphs of formidable navies and vast armies, but in the achievements of peace, industry, and commerce in the friendly competition of the nations."

Feb. 8th 1893 - Foster began to cough with the whooping
cough, which he caught at kindergarten. He coughed for about
a month, but only whooped a few times & had it quite lightly.

Taken Dec. 1891
Age 3 yrs. 10
Margaret. Age 2 yrs. 8 months

John Foster, age twelve, when he was in the Watertown Cadets, with Margaret (now Mrs. Deane Edwards), Allen, Eleanor Lansing, and Nataline (now Mrs. James S. Seymour).

Grandfather John W. Foster turned down an offer to advise the Chinese Imperial Government because he preferred to go fishing with this seven-year old lad.

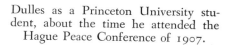

Dulles as a Princeton University student, about the time he attended the Hague Peace Conference of 1907.

Major John Foster Dulles at the time he served with the War Shipping Board during the First World War.

Dulles wedding party, June 26, 1912. Groom was suffering after-effects of malaria, and nurse accompanied the couple on first three days of their honeymoon.

On crutches because of bad nerve in his foot, Dulles confers with Secretary Hull on "bipartisanship" pact covering 1944 campaign.

Adviser Dulles confers with Secretary Marshall during Paris conference.

Senator by appointment, Dulles was defeated for election in 1949 by Herbert H. Lehman.

Three leaders of the Anglo-American alliance.

Dulles chats with Marine in Korea. Ambassador Henry Cabot Lodge is in background.

Pipe-smoking Allen Dulles, director of CIA, confers with brother Foster.

Secretary Phyllis Bernau and confidential assistant William Macomber (back to camera) travel with Secretary for work aboard plane.

Dulles poses with "devil dancer" who entertained his party during visit to Ceylon.

President and Mrs. Eisenhower arrive at Dulles home to attend Secretary's birthday party.

The Secretary's official State Department portrait.

Mrs. Dulles, daughter Lillias, Presbyterian layman John Foster Dulles, and son Avery, a Jesuit priest.

Two-year-old Janet Hinshaw kibitzes as Grandpa and Grandma Dulles play backgammon.

Skipper of the *Menemsha:* Dulles at wheel of the cruising yawl in which he logged
some 20,000 miles of adventurous fresh- and salt-water sailing.

Main Duck Island in Lake Ontario, in aerial shot from family album. The island, acquired by Dulles in 1941, is larger than the Principality of Monaco.

The Dulles cabin on Duck Island, built by Indians.

Dulles gestures from his wheel chair as he talks with Winston Churchill and President Eisenhower. The two statesmen paid him a surprise visit on May 5, 1959, and the three chatted in his suite at Walter Reed Hospital under a portrait of the former Prime Minister by the President.

Wide World

Dr. Russell P. Barnes of New York, secretary of the World Council of Churches, presents the American flag from the casket of John Foster Dulles to Mrs. Dulles after interment services May 27, 1959, in Arlington National Cemetery. Others, from left, are: John Dulles, son; Mrs. Robert Hinshaw, daughter; Father Avery Dulles, son; President

A Taste of Diplomacy

Dulles' part in all this was to help the Chinese delegation with protocol and translations. French was the language of diplomacy and the Chinese delegation for whom he worked spoke English but not French. The tall, thin, leggy young man had spent several summers in France with his father, covering more of the country by bicycle than most tourists ever see, and for one year before entering college had lived with a French-speaking family in Lausanne, Switzerland. He had a much better than college-taught command of the language, and his ability to read a document in French and translate the sense of it into English for a member of the delegation was much more satisfactory than the more laborious ordinary translation routine, which was also more time-consuming. As a result of this knack he was made one of the general conference secretaries as well, and as such saw a lot of other delegation members in addition to his own.

His first job, however, related to protocol. There was a great to-do at the outset, as General Foster records, over the precedence of calls by each diplomat on the others. Some delegation heads were ministers, some were ambassadors; some who represented big countries thought their national prestige required individually higher ranking diplomats from smaller countries to call on them, rather than the other way around. It was an age when such things were considered far more important than they are now. The time once was when duels were fought over fancied slights of protocol; Harold Nicolson, the British diplomat and historian, writes of an incident as late as 1768 when a French ambassador, attending a court ball in London, observed the Russian ambassador sitting in a front seat next to the Austrian ambassador. Climbing over the back benches, the Frenchman shoved himself physically between them, with the result that a duel was fought to maintain national prestige and the Russian ambassador was severely wounded. Growing realization of the seriousness of the world's business had eroded such extreme practices, but at The Hague in 1907 it did seem for a while that the conference would never get under way because of jealousies over the precedence of calls.

Statesmanship finally rose to the occasion. The solution hit on was reminiscent of an incident of protocol which occurred in 1659, when the French ambassador to Holland, de Thou, met the Spanish ambassador, Don Esteban de Gamarra, on a street too narrow for their carriages to pass. After three hours of argument, they decided to tear down a fence so that they could pass each other without either one having to accept loss of face by backing up. Similarly, the gentlemen who gathered to discuss peace in 1907 decided that if everyone called on everyone else at the same hour protocol would be satisfied. In practice this merely meant the delivery of calling cards all around. Accordingly, one afternoon young Dulles put on a Prince Albert and high silk hat and set out in a horse-drawn carriage bearing neat bundles of cards for each of the other delegations, and thus did the honors for the Chinese.

Relatively humble as his job was, it was an exciting thing for the Princeton junior to rub elbows with the most noted statesmen of the day and see the clash of national interests they represented. The first Hague conference had come to nothing in 1899 because of Prussia's refusal to talk disarmament. The Germans were only a shade more tractable at the second. While some delegations argued for conventions that would protect neutrals and civilians from the horrors of warfare, the Germans contended that the best way to eliminate the threat of war was to make it harsher and more terrible, and therefore more to be avoided. Dulles was greatly fascinated by the German delegate, an imposing man with a dueling scar on his cheek, and acquired from him a prejudice against Prussian militarism that lasted ever afterward.

The experience of contact with the foremost international names of the day and acquaintance with their business deepened a conflict that was going on in the young man's mind. Both his parents wanted him to become a minister and carry on a deep-rooted family tradition. While he accepted this as a possibility, he had been drawn also by the example of his grandfather toward law and diplomacy ever since the days he heard the old man spin yarns about them during their fishing excursions. The taste of diplomatic life was exciting. Nevertheless, he returned to his senior year at Princeton still undecided.

The paper Dulles turned in for his senior thesis, nineteen pages of double-spaced typing, is still in his wife's possession. It showed the growth of discipline and conformity since his Freshman English composition, but still carried overtones of independence and a somewhat belligerent modesty of the type used to conceal shyness.

"In general the plan I have followed is this," he wrote in laying out the limits of his philosophy essay. "I have first given briefly that theory of the judgment which is held and developed by Bradley and Bosanquet. I have then made what seem to me a few possible criticisms of that theory and suggested another definition of the judgment which I have briefly worked out, with references to Sigwart, Hobhouse and Baldwin, chiefly in the line of the singular affirmative and negative judgments.

"I have ventured to express my personal opinions somewhat, not because I believe they have any value, nor even in the belief that they will continue to be my opinions for any length of time, but simply because I do hold certain views on the subject and to express them has made the writing of the essay more interesting to me."

His whole thesis was a bit too abstruse for reproduction here, but it might be noted that he disputed a Bradley-Bosanquet theory that in judgment only one idea is necessary. "Now this," said Dulles, "seems to involve the fallacy that because but one idea is expressed there is but one idea in the judgment. . . . When I cry 'fire' in a house, my total judgment is 'there is a fire here which is dangerous.' But I am pressed for time. I know that if I simply express a part of my judgement, the rest of it will be awakened by constant association and habit in the minds of my hearers, and so I cry 'Fire' and that word, awakened in the mind of the auditor, drags after it by association the idea of danger, thus completing in the hearer's mind the total judgement which I had in my own mind but all of which I did not express."

This thesis, as we noted, won him a $600 scholarship at the Sorbonne. Thus in the summer of 1908 the Dulles family was back in Paris again, ensconced in a corner apartment in the Boulevard Raspail with a small balcony out over the street. Foster occupied one of the rooms normally used for servants, up under the mansard roof. The family talked French, discussed family plans, and it was a time of maturing for the children.

There was another family from Auburn, New York, in Paris that summer—the Averys. But Foster scarcely noticed Janet, and Janet's explanation is understandable: "He owned a Prince Albert and went to parties at the Embassy; I still wore hair ribbons."

Since his scholarship was in philosophy, Foster studied philosophy under the noted Professor Henri Bergson. The opportunity to absorb the best of French culture under some of its greatest intellects at this time of his life gave Dulles an appreciation of the French heritage which stayed with him through life and enabled him to maintain a tolerance of and patience with France in her days of political impotence beyond that of many of his colleagues. Had the events of 1954 and 1955 forced him to the "agonizing reappraisal" of U.S. policy toward France of which he warned, the appraisal would have been agonizing to him personally as well as officially.

The pull of his grandfather's career was strong upon him. He did not remember any clear-cut decision for the law and against the ministry as an incident during this period, but the bent of his mind shows in the fact that he elected to take courses in international law at the same time. Mrs. Dulles kept a notebook in which he took down, in French, his teacher's lectures on international fishing rights.

As a Sorbonne student he affected the bowler hat and umbrella then in vogue, and took part in the riots which occurred when the student body split on the issue of canonizing Joan of Arc. One group of partisans wore white ribbons in their lapels, the other blue. When one of the professors blossomed out with a blue ribbon there were riots which caused authorities to shut down the school for several days. Foster stuffed the inside of his bowler with newspapers to cushion the blows of the gendarmes' truncheons and got doused along with the rest when the police unlimbered fire hoses.

By the end of the year his interest in a legal career had won out over the ministry. He picked George Washington University as a law school, primarily because it meant he could live with his grandparents. But with the idea that mastery of Spanish would be an asset to a lawyer practicing in the Western Hemisphere, he decided first to spend some time in Spain. During the summer, before returning home, he went to Madrid and lived for six weeks in the home of a middle-class Spanish family who spoke no English. "It was one of the hardest six weeks I ever spent in my life," he said later. It served to give him a speaking and reading knowledge of Spanish, not as complete as his mastery of French but he improved upon it later when his legal work took him to Latin-American countries. On boyhood trips to Germany with his father, who studied at Heidelberg, he had learned a smattering of German, and his French and Spanish gave him enough of a base to understand some Italian —just enough, in the case of German and Italian, to enable him to get the drift of the news out of the papers when, as a traveling international lawyer and as Secretary of State, he visited those countries.

William Howard Taft was President when Foster returned to Washington, and the Taft boys were his contemporaries. As General Foster's grandson he was invited to parties they attended, and sometimes he squired Martha Bowers, who later married Bob Taft. It was the only really gay social period of Foster's life, and he lived it intensely. He telescoped three years of law into two; after attending classes all day he frequently went home for a nap, then rose at midnight to go dancing. "I don't see how I got through it," he confessed in later years.

But he had a knack for exams, as he had shown at Princeton. He had discovered that if he read the books the night before, their contents would be fresh in his mind in the morning. He acquired the practice of spending the night before a law exam—say on torts —by going through tort case indices and memorizing the important decisions and citations. On arriving in the examination room, before looking at his questions, he would write down the essentials of the cases he had studied, as well as the citations. Then, turning to the examination paper, he attacked the questions and sprinkled the answers with legally erudite references of this nature: "As Judge Smith said in overruling Brown v. Jones (135 U.S. 387) . . ." The effect was that of a man who had prepared himself with a law clerk's help. It greatly impressed his professors.

As a result, he made the highest marks ever made at the school— but in spite of having taken all the required courses he was refused a degree. The scholastic organization to which G.W.U. belonged required three years of study for a degree. It was not until some twenty-five years later, after he had become a leader of the bar, that the university authorities decided he was entitled to be listed on their records as a bachelor of laws.

6

• • • • • • • •

Law and Marriage

A<small>FTER</small> George Washington University, Dulles returned home
to Auburn to qualify for the New York State bar. With
characteristic concentration he shut himself in his room for sixteen
to eighteen hours at a time, cramming himself with lawbook knowledge. With equally characteristic deconcentration, occasionally
he broke it off sharply to go canoeing. The family gradually became
aware that he had a companion on these canoe trips. It was a case,
not uncommon in boy-girl history, of sudden awakening to the
realization that the girl who had been wearing pigtails and hair
ribbons a couple of years before had blossomed into a beautiful
young woman. Though Foster had known Janet Avery since the
family moved to Auburn, he "started fresh" that summer as her
suitor.

The bar exams were held at Rochester. Foster had a dinner date
with Janet for that night, back at Auburn, and during the examination he realized that he would not be able to catch a train

that would get him back in time if he stayed to complete the questions. He thought he had answered enough to pass, so he skipped the last few and caught the train. His family took a dim view of this early employment of the calculated risk principle, but it paid off: not only did he pass the bar exam, he won the girl.

But when he started out to look for a job, the man who was to make a fabulously successful career for himself in law found it extraordinarily hard to get a toehold in the profession. For six weeks he made the rounds of the big New York attorneys without result. In those days—and to some extent still—Harvard was *the* law school to come from, Columbia next best. Harvard-bred lawyers told him disdainfully they considered his college, Princeton, "a country club." Most of them reacted to mention of the George Washington law school by saying, "Never heard of it." One told him, "You don't look very promising to me." It made no difference that he had achieved the highest marks on record at G.W.U. Not only was the school itself a handicap, he did not have a degree.

Thoroughly discouraged, Dulles returned to see his grandfather in Washington. The old man had once been associated, as a fledgling lawyer prior to the Civil War, in the Cincinnati law firm of Algernon S. Sullivan. Sullivan had long since moved to New York and founded Sullivan & Cromwell. General Foster gave his grandson a letter to the surviving partner, William Nelson Cromwell, recalling the old association with Sullivan and mentioning the grandson's excellent grades in law school. "Isn't the memory of an old association enough to give this young man a chance?" he inquired.

Cromwell was in semiretirement by 1911 and it was not his

practice to interview applicants for his law firm. But he made an exception for Dulles. Being a sentimental man, he told his partners, "We must give this young man a chance."

Dulles got $50 a month as a starting law clerk. He was lucky to get anything at all. Until a few years previously the big New York attorneys took on clerks without pay, on the theory they were sufficiently compensated by learning about the practice of law from professionals. Even at that time a few firms kept up the old practice, but Sullivan & Cromwell had joined the more enlightened in deciding that the beginning laborer in the law's vineyard was worthy of $600 a year hire.

It was a fortunate connection. William Nelson Cromwell had been a unique personality in the New York bar, and his firm took a broad and enlightened view of its mission. Cromwell was not personally sensational after the fashion of the flamboyant courtroom orators associated with the era's most notorious criminal cases; but privately he was quite spectacular on a much more important scale. He conceived it his business to know all about the affairs of his clients, their competitive status, the conditions of the industry, and the national economy in general. His most active years coincided with great expansion in the corporate form of business organization, and he used a creative imagination to devise new legal forms designed to support, organize, and finance the nation's burgeoning corporate economy. Too poor to go to college, he died leaving $19,000,000.

Cromwell's most bravura performance was his leadership, in this century's first decade, of the fight to get the United States to build the Panama Canal, winning acceptance of the present route instead of one through Nicaragua. He was counsel for the Panama

Railroad Company, which had built a line across the isthmus, and for the New Panama Canal Company, successor to a bankrupt firm which had been organized by de Lesseps, builder of the Suez Canal.

The normal job for a starting law clerk is to write memoranda on the law for older and more experienced lawyers or to do general work under their direction. Dulles did not do much work of this type. Sullivan & Cromwell had been doing extensive legal business since the 1880's in Latin America, having represented English, French, and German investors in railroads, public utilities, and other ventures. Young Dulles, with his good command of Spanish, was sent to the region on the firm's legal business.

On one of these trips, to British Guiana, Dulles came down with malaria and nearly died. He was dosed with terrific amounts of quinine—50 to 80 grains a day. Quinine is a drug that affects the optic nerve, and the result was that afterward he had to wear glasses and had a noticeable tic in his left eye all through life.

His job on this trip was to prevent, if possible, the imposition of a tariff on U.S. flour in British territories and colonies of the Caribbean region. His client was the New York Produce Exchange. By arguing that tariffs would prevent the United States from buying Caribbean cocoa and coffee, he headed off the tariff in the self-governing territories, but the British crown colonies insisted on an early form of Empire preference by giving Canadian wheat an advantage over American.

At the end of a year Sullivan & Cromwell raised him to $100 a month, and he and Janet Avery were married, June 26, 1912, at Auburn.

Most articles about Dulles have made a special point of the fact that the couple "took a nurse along on the honeymoon," on the reasonable theory that it probably never happened to anyone else. One writer saw evidence of supreme diplomatic talent in Foster's ability to get a bride's consent to a threesome at such a time. Actually Dulles was finishing off a prescribed course of treatment for his malaria, and it involved a three-day delay in the couple's plans, which they spent at her family's summer home at Owasco Lake, after which they did depart, alone, on a real honeymoon in the Catskills.

Foster and Janet Dulles did not waste their money. They used the Madison Avenue street car, which cost a nickel, instead of the Fifth Avenue bus, which cost a dime. Foster ate 10-cent breakfasts at the Automat. But they had a comfortable apartment which cost them $80 a month, and they employed a maid at $25 a month. Obviously, they were not dependent entirely on Foster's salary. Grandfather Foster had encouraged him to get married, and he had made it possible by enabling the young man to draw on an intended legacy. "I'm going to leave each of my grandchildren $20,000, and you might as well have your share now," he explained.

Nevertheless, Janet kept meticulous household accounts. The ledger for 1912 showed such entries as "oranges (3) 10 cents . . . Hester's carfare .20 . . . mistake in adding bill at Dieckmann's .02 . . . porterhouse steak .35 . . . library fine .09." No penny was unaccounted for: "Pd. Foster what I borrowed July 27, .15 . . . to blind man .02 . . . credit for returning bottles .30 . . . dinner (Cafe Abbazzia) with tip .80." The accounts also hinted at occasional splurges: "marcel wave .50; hair net .25; taxi to opera 1.90." It recorded expansion of the family: "12 nipples .60 . . . peanuts (5) balloon (10) for John .15 . . . Lillias' shoes 1.25."

In two or three years, however, Dulles' income as a lawyer made it unnecessary for him to draw further on this reserve source. There was still about $12,000 left as his share when General Foster's will was probated. The grandfather got his reward when Foster and Janet presented him with his first great-grandchild, a boy they named John Watson Foster Dulles, who grew up to become a mining engineer in Mexico. One of the family's vivid recollections is the sight of the venerable, dignified old man, one summer at Henderson Harbor, delightedly piling up stones on the beach for his little namesake to throw into the water.

Because of the cushion which General Foster's money provided, Janet was able from the start to go along on Foster's trips, leaving the babies for others to care for temporarily, and thus becoming a part of his career. One trip she was forced to forgo because it was deemed too dangerous for a woman. That was when Dulles was sent to Panama on a dual mission: he had business to do for his firm and a special agent's commission from the State Department.

The latter was confidential. It was early in 1917, and President Wilson anticipated American entrance into the war, which was to come on April 7. He wanted Secretary Lansing to make sure that the Republic of Panama, bordering the vital canal, was in harmony with American policy and would, in fact, synchronize a declaration of war. In addition, it was known that German spies were operating in Central America, and Wilson wanted arrangements made to round them up when the time came. Dulles was picked because Sullivan & Cromwell was counsel for the Panama government. Another task he was given by Wilson was to overcome a three-cornered feud involving U.S. Minister William Jennings Price, General Goethals, who was in charge of the canal, and General

Edwards, the military commander. None was on speaking terms with the others.

Dulles persuaded the three officials to co-operate on the basis of handling their day-to-day problems. In telling about it later he deprecated his own part in it. "When someone comes with the authority of the President, and carries a warning message, most people are decent enough to abide by it," he said.

The spy hunt was satisfactorily accomplished, too. German agents were rounded up in due time and sent to sit out the war in internment on the island of Tobago. Dulles pursued the roundup into Costa Rica and Nicaragua, on horseback. Because of the danger involved, President Juan Tinoco of Costa Rica insisted on presenting Dulles with a 38-caliber Smith & Wesson revolver. Dulles never had to use it in self-defense, except against a wildcat he encountered in the jungle. Years later the revolver figured in an incident which occurred when he was Secretary. The Russians, who sought to promote the "spirit of Geneva" by sending various delegations to the United States, complained that the McCarran Act's requirement of fingerprinting was "degrading." Dulles was asked his opinion of it at a press conference. He said he did not consider the act degrading; that in fact he submitted to fingerprinting once a year himself. And why did he have to be fingerprinted? To renew his annual permit to keep a revolver. Inquiry disclosed that the revolver was the one which President Tinoco had given him. He took it along when he went to Duck Island, for target practice.

7

....

The Lesson of Versailles

WHEN the United States entered the First World War, Dulles was barred from regular military service because of his poor eyesight. There was, however, great need in Washington for lawyers to handle the legal controls over the economy which war always necessitates. Dulles got an Army commission as a captain (he was promoted to major before it was over) and was assigned to the War Trade Board, of which Vance C. McCormick was chairman, as assistant to McCormick.

The War Trade Board was created to control the nation's foreign commerce during the war, and a War Industries Board, headed by Bernard M. Baruch, exercised similar mobilization powers over domestic production. As McCormick's assistant Dulles had many dealings with Baruch on behalf of his agency, beginning an acquaintance and friendship that lasted to the end.

Dulles helped draft many of the executive orders and proclamations under which the War Trade Board did business, one of them being President Wilson's order of March 20, 1918, seizing 87 Dutch ships which were then in United States ports, representing 354,478 tons of badly needed shipping capacity. This particular draft was one on which Wilson did no more than pencil in a few minor changes before signing. Dulles kept the original copy with Wilson's emendations.

America's merchant marine was small, and Britain's was of course tied up in meeting her own wartime needs. The War Trade Board negotiated with various nations to acquire steamships from them. Satisfactory arrangements were worked out with four big maritime countries: Norway, Sweden, Denmark, and Japan. Holland had 450,000 tons of shipping here when war broke out, but negotiations dragged out interminably. The United States was not willing to ship food supply to a neutral such as Holland unless assured she would make every effort to increase her own production and hold consumption to the minimum; and it also wanted to make sure that Holland did not transship to Germany or release production of her own as a result of receiving food from the United States.

A tentative agreement was reached early in January, but when its consummation continued to be blocked because of strong German pressure on Holland, the War Trade Board decided the only way to proceed was to seize the ships, with adequate compensation to the owners. There was considerable outcry over the order, which some held to be unconstitutional, but it was not formally challenged.

In this job Dulles acquired a comprehensive appreciation of the industrial mobilization required to conduct a war, and something of the military side of it since he had to transact a great deal of business with the War and Navy Departments. After the Armistice, when President Wilson decided personally to head the American delegation to the peace conference, Vance McCormick's knowledge of world trade figures was regarded as necessary and Dulles went with him to Paris.

The ten nations who gathered at Versailles to write a peace with Germany farmed out parts of their work to various commissions. Baruch was named head of the American delegation on the Commission on Reparations. Having been impressed by Dulles' legal ability as he had seen it in action in Washington, he asked for Dulles to serve as the delegation's counsel.

With our recent experience of having paid out some $50,000,-000,000 in various forms of aid to foreign countries since the Second World War, some of it to support our defeated enemies, it takes a bit of mental adjustment to reconstruct the frame of mind in which the victorious Allies of the First World War approached the task of getting reparations for war damage out of Germany.

The Allies were, of course, all in unbelievably bad financial condition, with much property destroyed, and under the yoke of heavy wartime taxes. Some of their leaders had made promises to give the voters relief, promises based on false or exaggerated ideas of what Germany had capacity to pay. David Lloyd George, prime minister of Great Britain, had been re-elected in a campaign promising to collect from Germany the costs of the war to Britain "shilling for shilling, and ton for ton." In France the Chamber of Deputies refused to pass tax bills, and one of the slogans placarded on the walls of the city when the conference delegates convened was "Que L'Allemagne paye d'abord" (Let Germany pay first). Baruch, who later wrote a book about the economic clauses of the treaty, says in its introduction:

"Try as men might, and I submit they did try, the spirit of vengeance or selfish advantage could not be entirely eradicated from the minds of the framers of the treaty. On them the pressure of public opinion in their respective countries was being constantly exerted. In the reparations clauses, the conference was not writing a mere contract of dollars and cents; it was dealing with blood-raw passions still pulsing through people's veins."

When the various nations submitted their ideas in the meetings of the commissions, the Americans discovered they were the only ones with a definite reparations scheme, based on President Wilson's famous "Fourteen Points" speech of January, 1918, as elaborated in subsequent speeches.

The Americans filed a statement, written by Dulles, which involved two main principles: (1) that Germany make good the damages resulting directly from acts clearly in violation of international law, such as her violation of Belgian neutrality, which had been guaranteed by a treaty among Great Britain, Russia, France, Austria, and Prussia; and (2) that Germany make good her pre-Armistice agreement to compensate for all damages to civilian populations and their property, this being construed by the American delegation to mean direct physical damage to property of nonmilitary character and direct physical injury to civilians.

The other delegations merely filed general statements to the effect that, since Germany started the war by a wrongful act, she was responsible for all the resulting damage, direct and indirect. Baruch's counterpart as head of the British delegation, Prime Minister W. M. Hughes of Australia, even went so far as to argue that every Australian who had mortgaged his house to buy war bonds was as rightfully entitled to reparations as a Frenchman whose home had been burned by the Germans.

The Lesson of Versailles

The American delegation's position was that the Allies had in effect entered into a contract with Germany by insisting on an understanding as to the basic terms of peace before consenting to an armistice.

It fell to Dulles, as counsel, to argue the American position before the commission. While various nations took part in the debate, the basic clash pitted Dulles against Hughes.

"It was a matter of considerable chagrin to the American members of this commission when it developed, on analysis of the various memoranda on the principles of reparation, that the memorandum of the United States appeared to be the least drastic in its terms," said Dulles in addressing the commission, February 13, 1919. He said America joined the others in condemning Germany's instigation of the war as an international crime, and reminded the conference that the United States also had a war debt, comparable in magnitude to that of any other nation.

Why, then, was the United States less severe than the other Allies? "Because," said Dulles, "we are not here to consider as a novel proposal what reparation the enemy should in justice pay; we have not before us a blank page on which we are free to write what we will. We have before us a page, it is true; but one which is already filled with writing, and at the bottom are the signatures of Mr. Wilson, of Mr. Orlando, of Mr. Clemenceau, and of Mr. Lloyd George. It is the agreed basis of peace with Germany." He argued that it was the commission's job to pass on to the "construction and application" of the agreed terms.

When Prime Minister Hughes got the floor next day he took strong exception to the American contention.

"The American memorandum admits that Belgium's whole war

costs are a direct consequence of Germany's violation of Belgium's right of neutrality," said Hughes. "That is indisputable; but we cannot stop there . . . Belgium's neutrality was the result of an agreement between certain nations. It was guaranteed by all the signatory powers to the Treaty of London. Great Britain and France were bound by their treaty obligations to defend Belgium's neutrality; and consequently Germany's violation of that neutrality involved, as a direct and necessary consequence, the whole war costs, not only of Belgium, but of Great Britain and France as well. . . .

"But more is involved than even this . . . When Germany violated the treaty, Great Britain and France were *bound* to defend it; the United States and Italy were *entitled* to defend it. Germany was the criminal, Belgium the victim. Great Britain and France may be compared to the policeman whose sworn task is to prevent a breach of the law; the United States and Italy and other nations may be compared to civilians whose right it is—and also whose duty in case of need—to come to the rescue.

"Germany's violation of her international pledge was an act which the whole world had a right to resist; and it follows beyond the possibility of dispute that the whole war costs of the Associated Powers, being a direct consequence of that violation, can also be claimed, and that—even on the narrow basis of the American memorandum—reparation for all those war costs is clearly due from Germany."

Dulles did not think much of the Hughes argument. On February 19 he made a reply. It was a double-barreled answer, contending with the juridical question and at the same time demolishing Hughes's logic.

Juridically he made two points: (1) That the negotiations among
the Allies prior to agreeing to talk armistice with Germany, together
with their acceptance of Wilson's points, contained every element
necessary to constitute a binding contract. (2) That in looking for
"causal relationship" between the violation of Belgian neutrality
and war costs, Belgium's obviously were directly related and it
could be argued that Britain, since she based her declaration of war
on that violation, also was entitled to war costs. But not France;
France did not go to war because Germany violated Belgium; France
got into war because Germany declared war on her and invaded Belgium quite incidentally in the process. On his part, however, Dulles
denied that Britain had a right equal to Belgium's or above that of
any other ally on the ground that when Britain in 1839 assumed
obligations with respect to Belgium she did so under what she then
regarded as adequate consideration—Belgium's agreement not to
demand different frontiers.

Then Dulles turned to the logic of Hughes's argument. "Mr.
Hughes stated that Great Britain and France may be compared to
the policeman whose sworn task is to prevent a breach of the law.
Precisely—but does the policeman receive his hire from the wrongdoer whom he arrests? No; in making the arrest the policeman has
performed his duty—nobly, gallantly, at great sacrifice, if you will;
but still his duty. And the reparation made by the wrongdoer is
made to the victim—not to the guardian of the law.

"If the argument which I make is sound, it leads to the conclusion that Great Britain, and Great Britain alone, shares the special
position of Belgium. This is a conclusion so extraordinary that the
Honorable Mr. Hughes, with that common sense and bigness of

heart for which he is noted, was compelled to repudiate it.

"What form did his repudiation take? Did he say: My conclusion is unsound; therefore I must have reached it by unsound processes of thought? No; he said: My conclusion is absurd; therefore I will multiply it by ten and the absurdity will disappear. After adopting reasoning which if sound led to the establishment of a special privilege for Great Britain in respect of war costs, he illogically, but with a generosity which we can but admire, invited us all to come and share it.

"Gentlemen, if we hold to the domain of reason, we cannot adopt such methods. To demand the gigantic total of war costs would be to jeopardize securing that specific reparation as to which Germany must clearly recognize her liability, and the satisfaction of which will tax her resources to the limit."

Dulles was then just four days short of his thirty-first birthday.

As often happens in the case of friendly antagonisms, Hughes and Dulles acquired a personal admiration for each other and shared a common annoyance over some of the other statesmen with whom they had to deal at Versailles. One day Hughes sent over to Dulles the following note, handwritten on a piece of scratch paper, complaining facetiously about a boresome speech by the Belgian representative: "There is one thing for which I shall *never* forgive the Germans. They were in Belgium 4½ years & yet they did not kill Van der Heuvel."

Dulles was itching to go home and get back to the practice of law, but President Wilson asked him to stay on in Europe. Dulles kept the letter from Wilson, written on the stationery of the Hôtel de Crillon in Paris, in which the President asked him to remain on the job. The letter said:

The Lesson of Versailles

My dear Mr. Dulles:

I hope that you will not feel that I am imposing a too onerous or too unwelcome duty upon you if I beg very earnestly that you make arrangements to remain in Europe for the present to handle the very important and difficult matters with which you have become so familiar and which you have so materially assisted in handling. My request is justified by the confidence we have all learned to feel in your judgement and ability, and I am acting upon the opinion of the men with whom you have been collaborating, as well as upon my own, in making this earnest request.

Cordially and sincerely yours,

Woodrow Wilson

Mr. J. F. Dulles
American Commission to Negotiate Peace

As a result of this appeal, Dulles stayed on as American representative on the Reparations Commission. Still a young man, he found it exciting and stimulating business to be dealing with such prominent men of other countries as the finance minister of France, with Hughes, and with Lord Sumner, the chief justice of England. There were still treaties to make with Austria, Hungary, and Turkey. But his service ended in the fall of 1919 when the Senate Foreign Relations Committee, under the pressure of the postwar isolationists who wrecked Woodrow Wilson's plan for American participation in the League of Nations, passed a resolution expressing the sense of the committee that the United States should not be represented on the reparations group.

8 .

. . . .

Luck and Adventure in Law

THE Senate resolution which caused President Wilson to with
draw American representation in European reparations affairs
reflected the domestic disputes of a troubled political year which
resulted in a turnover of national administration and a return to
"normalcy" under Warren Gamaliel Harding. It served incidentally
to free Dulles to return to his law career, beginning a phase lasting
two decades during which he was soon catapulted into the senior
partnership of his firm and commanded fees which made him a
wealthy man, though not a millionaire. Before he gave up active
practice his income ranked him among the ten or twelve most highly
paid lawyers in the world.

The dry technicalities of the law have their own fascination for
those who devote their lives to it, even though to laymen the work
seems dull and uninspiring. Dulles, however, had been inoculated
by his previous experience with a hyperactive bug of adventure
which enriched his scope of interest and led to an exciting life

in which he was constantly shuttling about the world indulging his personal absorption with the yeasty ferment of human events as well as earning big fees. Janet Dulles recalled the period as an active one in which "we never knew when we might be leaving for Europe on two hours' notice, so we kept our passports up to date all the time."

At Versailles Dulles had been one of five men who acted as Wilson's principal economic advisers. Another member of the group was a Morgan partner, Thomas W. Lamont. Lamont was so impressed with the young lawyer's ability that he arranged to have a Morgan law firm offer him an attractive partnership, carrying three times the pay of his Sullivan & Cromwell job. Dulles considered it and turned it down without using the offer for trading purposes. But he let his superiors know about his decision, and they responded to the hint by giving him a substantial raise and, shortly afterward, taking him into partnership.

Nineteen-twenty was an unsettled year not only in the United States but in the world. Almost as soon as he resumed legal work Dulles found himself back in Europe considering professionally some of the problems he had been working on as an official. The French, charging violation of reparations terms by the Germans, had occupied the Ruhr and created a tense situation.

The German government asked Dulles to represent some of their reparations officials who had been jailed by the French. Dulles preferred not to accept a retainer, but at his own expense he went to Europe to see what could be done. He tried to work out a settlement which would induce the French to withdraw and the Germans to resume payments. He came close to success, winning the tentative agreement of the German chancellor, but was blocked by the opposition of the German foreign minister and the effort came to nothing.

Illustrative of the kind of double life he led as a lawyer were his side activities at this time. In March, 1920, Dulles was in Prague when the director of the German Agricultural Institute, a man named Kapp, joined with General von Luttwitz in an abortive attempt to seize the government in a right-wing putsch. Dulles promptly traveled to Dresden and Berlin to see for himself what was going on, and on his return to Prague gave the American minister, Crane, a concise and penetrating report assessing German public characteristics in the face of the postwar crisis. Two weeks later he found himself in Frankfurt with a couple of days to spare from law business, so he decided to take a look at a Communist revolt which was taking place in the Ruhr. His vivid personal impressions of this early Communist attempt to seize power in Western Europe were set down in a letter to his wife from Cologne on April 3, 1920:

Dearest Janet:

It is rather a gloomy Easter Sunday here, away from you and the children. I slept late this morning as I was rather tired, and then went into the Cathedral for a few minutes. Since then I have been in conference with the rest of our group about the textile matters . . .

I had been at Frankfurt as I wrote you last Sunday, working on the copper proposition, and left there on Wednesday morning by motor. It was a beautiful ride down the Main to the Rhine and then down the Rhine to Coblence. The fruit trees are just getting in blossom and the scenery naturally is of course wonderful. . . . At Coblence I figured that it might be interesting and useful to go up into the Ruhr region of which great stories are being told, so I got a letter from Noyes (the U.S. Rhineland commissioner) introducing me to the British authorities at Coln and telling them to help me to get to the Ruhr.

On getting to Coln Wednesday afternoon I found that the balance of our party would not get to Coln until Thursday evening or Saturday morning, so I decided to devote Thursday to investigating the Red coup in the Ruhr as an interesting contrast to the reactionary coup which I had witnessed at Berlin. The British authorities here said that there was no use trying to get any kind of a pass and that the best thing was merely to go as far as I could and when irrevocably stopped to come on back. Incidentally that is the system which works pretty well over here these days and with a little ingenuity and money you generally get through.

So I got another auto here and Thursday morning Hoskins and I started off. We only told the chauffeur that we were going to Dusseldorf as I don't think we could have gotten a car ostensibly to go further. At Dusseldorf everything appeared quite normal and we told our chauffeur that we thought we would go on to Duisburg. This city is supposed to be the head of the Red government, and the chauffeur was very much alarmed and almost refused to proceed. A combination of threats, milk chocolate and talk about what important people we were finally persuaded him, and we left on the Duisburg road.

The first sign of anything unusual was just outside of Dusseldorf where we found a couple of workmen with rifles who were guarding the road and who stopped us. After pulling out our American passports and letters signed by Hoover, etc., we were allowed to proceed. As we approached Duisburg we were again stopped, this time by a small squad of reds who were guarding the approaches to Duisburg. They all had red bands around their arms and red cloth stuck in their hats, and carried rifles. They were not of course in uniform.

We had more difficulty there in getting through as they were rather suspicious of us. I think that they suspected us of being there in the interests of the French. Eventually we told them that we had to confer with their leaders at Duisburg and they then gave us an escort of a rather ugly fellow who was one of the higher officers in the Red army and he got into our car and went on with us into Duisburg.

We had to pass nearly a dozen guards, I should say, in getting into the interior of Duisburg, but our escort carried us through all right on the strength of his Red Army Commission. The Red committee of five which was attempting to govern the region had its seat in the city hall. That was surrounded by a cleared area rather heavily guarded and with barbed wire entanglements in the streets. It was tremendously interesting to compare the situation with the same thing at Berlin two weeks before.

We got into the city hall and I never saw such bedlam in my life. Despite the guards the building was all full of people clamoring for everything under the sun. Passes were chiefly wanted, but also red officers trying to get instructions, women with baskets trying to get food, etc., etc. The governing commission had shut themselves up in a room which was besieged with people who were supposed to await their turn to get in.

I soon saw that it would take us a couple of days if we waited our turn, so I got hold of an armed guard and explained to him the "importance" of our mission and he finally used his rifle to poke a way for us through the mob and into the sacred precincts.

The sight inside was really pathetic. The supreme committee of five was there, all right. They had a few attendants and were chiefly engaged in violent altercations among themselves. They were uneducated workmen, looking as one pictures Trotzky, unshaved for days, dirty and I imagine not having gotten much sleep since they started to govern!

There was a miserable looking typewriter in the middle of the room and occasionally one of them would sit down and attempt laboriously to tap out some order of the revolutionary government. By the time it was written it would apparently be decided to modify it to the disgust of the writer. I don't think that I have ever seen a more interesting scene than that of these poor people trying their hand at peoples government.

After a while we got the attention of one of the Commissioners, and asked him for a pass to permit us to go to Essen and other cities within the control of the Revolutionary Government. He spoke quite a little English of which he was very proud and after we had impressed him with our harmlessness he agreed to give us a pass.

We were particularly anxious to have something to protect our

74

auto as all automobiles were subject to requisition by the Reds and any guard was likely to stop us and take our car away from us. The Commissioner then sat down at the one typewriter and painfully picked out the letters, taking about ten minutes to write out twenty-five words. In giving the pass to us the Commissioner explained, apologetically, that he could not guarantee how good it would be, as the revolutionary region was so divided among itself and their differences were so acute that their pass might not be generally recognized.

The pass itself, which I still have, will be an interesting souvenir. It is signed by "The Commission of the Peoples Revolutionary Government." We didn't dare ask many questions for fear of seeming unduly inquisitive, but they admitted that they were extremely short of food, and disrupted among themselves and it was obviously only a question of days before they would surrender even if, and particularly if, no military forces were sent against them.

Armed with our pass we then started on our way, going to Mulheim and then Essen. Despite the doubts of the Commissioner the pass served us well and all we had to do was to show it to get through the red guards which were relatively few and quite harmless so far as I could judge. There were no signs anywhere of any violence to persons or property. Of course business was at a good deal of a standstill, although most of the shops were open and in some places the street cars were running and a good deal of public work, road improvement, etc., was going on.

Most of the factories were closed up and coal mining was curtailed, but not entirely stopped. Coal deliveries for France were continuing and Rhine river navigation was uninterrupted. Conditions were really far more normal than the newspaper reports would indicate and I was again surprised, as at Berlin, with the indications of orderliness under most unusual conditions. There were of course no police whatever and no authority except the disorganized Red Commissions and the scattered red guards who were under no real discipline.

Taking into account that here was a concentrated population of a rough class, miners, steel workers, etc., who had been underfed, only partly employed and underpaid for a long time and who were now, through red guards who had the only arms, in entire and unopposed control of the situation, the order and respect for property which was displayed was remarkable.

I have, however, by this philosophizing broken the thread of my story. We motored on to Essen, arriving about 1 o'clock, and we stopped for lunch. We got very good food at the best hotel there, although their menu was limited to two dishes. They said that the food shortage was exceedingly serious and was sure to compel some quick peace with the rest of Germany.

One thing of interest was that the Red Commission had forbidden the sale of any liquor except beer, presumably to avoid drunkenness among the idle workers. After lunch we looked over the Krupp works which were idle. It appeared that the workmen had presented themselves for work that morning, but had been scared away by a few armed red guards.

From Essen we motored back to Dusseldorf by a less populated route and found that in the country areas there was very little disturbance and that the men were working about as usual. There were a few Red guards still about but they were very far from being ferocious, talking readily and allowing us to take and examine their guns. I should have explained the willingness of our chauffeur to go on by saying that after we had interviewed the commission at Duisburg and come out, not only with our lives, but with a pass which seemed to work, he began to think that we really were people immune from danger, and he became quite cocky, so much so that he got into an altercation with one of the red guards which was the only occasion for any ugliness on the part of the latter which we saw. But on that occasion we had to call down our chauffeur very quickly . . .

On the basis of such personal observations, as well as talks with German bankers, Dulles formed judgments about the future of reparations which caused him to write from Dresden on April 11 to Norman H. Davis predicting failure for this part of the treaty unless Germany got economic freedom and a definite obligation to pay. The way in which the reparations clauses were being applied by the Allies, he wrote, was having a deadening effect. The history of reparations bore him out.

It was on one of these early postwar trips to Europe that the man who as Secretary of State was to establish an amazing record of air travel for a Cabinet official took his first ride in an airplane. He and Janet were driving on the outskirts of Paris one day when they came to a field where sightseeing flights were being offered at a small fee. The craft was a biplane with two open cockpit seats. Janet objected that it was too risky and refused to go up, but Foster took a brief flight over Paris and found it exciting and enjoyable. He began using air travel to get about in the United States as soon as commercial flying began to develop, and first flew the Pacific in 1938.

The world's postwar economic dislocations had their unsettling effect in the United States as elsewhere. Wall Street was prematurely under the impression that the financial capital of the world had moved from London to New York. There was a great interest in foreign loans, many of which later came to a bad end. In the spring of 1921 there was a short, severe depression known as the "inventory panic." Many corporations were going through reorganization in the effort to stay in business, and it made a lot of work for lawyers.

Royall Victor was then active senior partner of Sullivan & Cromwell. Under his direction, Dulles worked on some big reorganization cases for clients, including those involving American Cotton Oil and Chicago & Indiana Coal Railway. He took part in a prominent proxy fight for control of the Remington Typewriter Company.

At the same time Germany was undergoing a tremendous inflation, with the mark's value dwindling to nothing. The Socialist government was having great trouble trying to rehabilitate the country and meeting the load of reparations. Various committees were put to work to reorganize the system. One of them, headed by Charles Gates Dawes, the Chicago banker who later became Calvin Coolidge's vice-president, worked out a reorganization plan which was conditioned on a $125,000,000 private loan from the United States. The underwriter for this loan was J. P. Morgan & Company. Lansing Reed, one of the Morgan lawyers, retained Dulles as special counsel with respect to the Dawes loan on the lien of reparations. Work on this loan took Dulles to Europe frequently and kept him deeply involved in the economic side of foreign affairs.

In addition, the firm had been counsel, long before he joined, for many investment banking firms which were floating loans in this country for German public utilities and other corporations which needed capital to rehabilitate their war-ruined properties. Sullivan & Cromwell had provided legal representation in many such underwriting ventures, although Dulles was not personally involved in very much of it.

During this period he was suddenly elevated to the senior partnership. Normally it takes a lawyer about thirty years to work up to the directing partnership of a great law firm. Dulles, however, had been working closely with Victor and also with Alfred Jaretzki and Henry Hill Pierce, the other ranking senior partners. Jaretzki, who had been a member of Sullivan & Cromwell since 1881, died suddenly in 1925, and the following year Victor died. Pierce had been ill since 1923 and was forced to retire because of his health.

Thus in 1926, just fifteen years after he joined the firm as an "associate" at $50 a month, with two years out for war service, Dulles found himself, at the age of thirty-eight, directing partner of a law firm of immense prestige. Cromwell himself remained nominally the senior partner, but he had not been active since 1912, and Dulles ran the shop with the help of Edward H. Green, Eustace Seligman, and Wilbur L. Cummings.

That same year Dulles was hired as counsel for American underwriters involved in arranging a $62,000,000 loan for Poland under a stabilization plan designed to put the country on a sound economic footing. This involved him in revaluation of the zloty, a coinage unit which had started out well but which had later skidded to 45 per cent of its original value. Later on, after the gold zlotys were stolen by Nazi Germany in World War II, and received by Dulles for Poland in legal proceedings, he received a memento of this episode, a gold zloty which he encased in plastic in his private conference room at the State Department.

Poland's financial problems, when the country was reconstituted after the First World War, were different from Germany's, Austria's, and Hungary's, all of which had to undergo fiscal doctoring of one kind or another. As a new nation inheriting three depreciated currencies—German marks, Russian rubles, and Austrian crowns—Poland had to use a wholly new monetary system. She was relatively free from external and internal debt, and her world trade was sufficiently in balance not to be a problem. She created the zloty on a gold basis with a value corresponding to the gold franc. Unlike the other three countries mentioned, her stabilization efforts were entirely voluntary, since she was not under the same obligation to outsiders on account of war reparation. But a disastrous crop failure had required the country to become a heavy importer of foodstuffs, and the gold reserves back of the zloty proved insufficient. The fall in the zloty's value was accelerated by inflationary note issues, by the government and by banks of issue.

With fiscal advice from New York banks and with technical advice from the Federal Reserve, a stabilization plan was worked out under which the zloty was revalued on a standard of .187546 grams of 9/10 fine gold, a value of approximately 11.22 cents. Central or government banks of fourteen countries participated in the $62,000,000 loan involved, which was secured by the issuance of Polish stabilization bonds. Handling the legal side of such a transaction took a high degree of economic, legal, and fiscal knowledge.

There was a sequel to the Polish connection when the Second World War broke out. The Bank of Poland, in advance of Hitler's invasion, had turned over $64,000,000 worth of gold in cases and bags to the Bank of France for safekeeping. When the Nazi armies began their drive into France the next spring, the Bank of France sought to protect its own gold reserves—together with those which it held for the Bank of Poland and also similar gold reserves entrusted to it by the Bank of Belgium—by flying them to North Africa and the United States. When the Hitler-collaborating French government was set up at Vichy, the Germans began flying back what gold had not gone beyond Dakar. The Banks of Poland and Belgium hired Dulles to save their funds if possible.

At that time the Bank of France had some $250,000,000 in gold bars and bullion on deposit with the Federal Reserve Bank in New York. Dulles, on behalf of the Polish and Belgian banks, filed an attachment on the French gold in New York City. The statute under which he filed suit was an old one, passed in the days when attachments were normally used on a burgher's cow or horse to recover a small debt, and when the sheriff was not paid a salary but depended on "poundage" fees. The law carried a sliding scale of fees for the sheriff, and also provided that the plaintiff's lawyer was personally liable for the fees if he lost the case. The risk to the lawyer was not much if the object of attachment was a horse or cow, but in this case it meant that Dulles was personally liable for $640,641.41 if he lost. It was the kind of risk to give a lawyer pause, but Dulles went ahead. He won the case and was thus incidentally relieved of the liability. The denouement came when Dulles accompanied counsel for the Bank of France to the subterranean vaults of the Federal Reserve Bank in New York and watched Federal Reserve officers break the seals on padlocks earmarking French gold and install new padlocks and seals stating that the gold belonged to the Banks of Poland and Belgium. It was the culmination of two years of the most intense litigation. One personal irony of the case was that the French bank's counsel was Frederick Coudert, one of the established lawyers who in 1911 had turned down Dulles' application for a job because he learned his law at George Washington University instead of at Harvard or Columbia.

It was less than two years after the Polish stabilization operation that depression struck in the United States, signaled by the stock market break in October, 1929. Between then and 1932, when it hit its low point, bankruptcies occurred on all sides and innumerable companies went through reorganization. Sullivan & Cromwell was one of the firms kept busy on reorganizations through this period, seeking to save client firms from bankruptcy in some instances, representing bondholders in other cases.

Among the bankruptcies of the period was one of the most

spectacular in history, that of the international firm of Kreuger & Toll, which followed the suicide of Ivar Kreuger, the Swedish match king, in a Paris hotel. Dulles took a leading part in that case, as attorney for a group of American holders of Kreuger & Toll bonds. He had nothing to do with the original Kreuger loans, and was called in on the salvage job.

The bonds held by his clients were selling for 8 cents on the dollar when he took the case. With Kreuger's suicide his whole match empire collapsed. Picking up the pieces was an enormously complicated affair. Kreuger had juggled his assets between Kreuger & Toll, International Match, Swedish Match, and other companies. He had used the assets of one company to get credit and then shifted them to another. Each had different classes of security holders. Match concessions in France, Germany, Poland, Turkey, and South America were involved. Added to the problem of salvaging local assets was the dispute between the different companies as to which was entitled to the assets. Lawyers and accountants had to be hired in each of the countries and compromises had to be made, but in the end, after several years of the most detailed international financial and legal work, Dulles' clients got 80 cents on the dollar for their bonds.

Meanwhile signs multiplied that the United States might go off the gold standard. Since a top-flight Wall Street law firm such as Sullivan & Cromwell seeks to keep abreast of world economic trends and the outlook for its corporation clients, Dulles and his partner, Arthur H. Dean, who succeeded him as directing partner of the firm, devoted an enormous amount of their time to studying gold coin obligation cases all over the world. When President Franklin D. Roosevelt's gold proclamation came, the firm felt reasonably well prepared to cope with the problems it raised in the financial community.

From the 1920's onward the firm had been working with some troublesome cases involving the New York Life Insurance Company, which had operated in Russia under the Czars. Under Russian laws of that period the company was required to keep its reserves in Russia in rubles. After the Kerensky government fell, the Bolshevik government confiscated all assets of the company, together with its reserves. The Communists organized a scheme of getting hold of policies held by Russians, assigning them to U.S. citizens, and then suing New York Life in the New York courts for collection. These cases were quite complicated because the defense was hampered by the nonrecognition policy of the United States toward the Communist government, which prevented Soviet laws from being used, in effect, as a legal bar to having to pay twice. Also there was dispute whether the ruble should be valued according to the date of the insured person's death, the date the claim was presented, or the date of the confiscation of the reserves. The cases dragged along until President Roosevelt entered into the Litvinov agreement recognizing Soviet Russia in 1933.

Dulles did public-service legal business in this period also. In 1933 he was selected by a group of American creditors who had lent money to German companies represented in the *Stillhaltung* agreements—a moratorium seeking to work out an orderly reorganization of the short- and long-term debt. The payment which the German debtors offered the American creditors was partly in cash and partly in a scrip known as *Konversionskasse*. It turned out that under the newly enacted Securities Exchange Act the scrip had to be registered with the SEC, so Sullivan & Cromwell effected the registration, also without fee. The creditors were given free legal service because they were underwriting firms which, having been clients in the past, were currently operating at a loss. The registration was performed for nothing because, having represented the creditors, the firm did not consider it cricket to take money from the debtors.

Late in the 1920's the firm had been taking on representation of American companies, and bankers having European activities, and opened offices in Paris and Berlin. Dulles visited these capitals on the average twice a year, dealing in Berlin with Hjalmar Schacht, president of the Reichsbank. On one trip, shortly after Hitler came to power, as a result of the negotiations Dulles was conducting with his bank official, Hitler invited Foster and Janet Dulles to attend a Walter Gieseking concert with him. It was the only time Dulles ever met Hitler. Because of Hitler's persecution of the Jews, and the increasing difficulty of determining which German firms were involved with the Nazi government, Dulles discussed with his partners the advisability of getting out of business in Germany. The Berlin office was closed in 1934 and German firms still on the list of clients were notified that Sullivan & Cromwell wished to sever further connection.

Despite its extensive European business, the firm never represented cartels. One of its clients, International Nickel, had a British subsidiary, Mond Nickel, which belonged to various cartels; another, American Radiator, had a French subsidiary with cartel connections. In both cases Dulles represented the American parent companies and not the foreign subsidiaries. Specifically he never had anything to do, directly or indirectly, with the great German chemical cartel firm, I. G. Farben. The charge that he did was made against him after the war. Dulles traced its origin and found it was first printed in a Russian publication, Moscow's *New Times*, in the spring of 1947, apparently in retaliation for an article Dulles wrote for *Life* magazine in 1946 entitled "Soviet Foreign Policy and What to Do About It." The Russian charge was parroted by party-line writers over here without attempts to verify it, and was dredged up in his 1949 campaign for the Senate by his political opponents.

As the Second World War approached, European governments sent purchasing missions over here. Dulles helped organize the British mission, and acted as its counsel; also the Dutch. When the Nazis invaded the Low Countries in the spring of 1940, Sullivan & Cromwell drafted various of the decrees-in-exile of the Dutch government, and handled cases here which established their validity. Around Pearl Harbor time a clearinghouse for war charities known as the National War Fund was set up with Winthrop Aldrich as chairman and Dulles as its counsel. This was another of the firm's public-service jobs. The fund financed such wartime organizations as the USO and military services of the Salvation Army. But the time had come when Dulles' interest in world affairs was no longer satisfied by such sideline activities.

9

. . . .

The Quest for a Just and Durable Peace

A^s THE Second World War approached, two influences were
at work drawing John Foster Dulles away from primary
devotion to the law. The more successful he became as a lawyer the
more he was able to indulge his consuming intellectual interest
in world affairs, and his transition was gradual rather than abrupt.
However, this growing preoccupation with the problems of war
and peace which he had started thinking about at The Hague
was one pull that made him find the law a bit irksome. He was
active head of a firm which had about twenty partners and eighty
lawyers, with a corresponding force of stenographers, clerks, and
messengers. He was director of fifteen corporations. He begrudged
the time it was taking to work on Sullivan & Cromwell's administrative details: questions like the splitting of partnerships and
making salary adjustments each year.

But in addition to a growing boredom with the routine of success,
he began to get the feeling that he had neglected the potential

for moral development implanted in him by his religious upbringing. True, he had remained a prominent Presbyterian layman. He attended church regularly; he taught a Sunday-school class at various periods. Like his father, who took the liberal side in earlier controversies, Dulles identified himself with the liberals in the dogmatic schisms of the 1920's which manifested themselves in such disputes as the Presbyterian Assembly and the Scopes "monkey" trial in Tennessee. Nevertheless, the feeling grew on him in the late 1930's that he had been concentrating too much on making money and working to help clients make money and not paying enough attention to the possibilities of public service.

One event which reawakened his interest in moral betterment occurred when John D. Rockefeller, Jr., asked him to head a task force which appraised missionary activities throughout the world. He was unable to undertake the Rockefeller assignment, but his consideration of the project resulted in his first trip to the Far East, in 1938.

Never a man to neglect the opportunities for personal observation along the way, Dulles made use of the trip to pay a visit to Chiang Kai-shek. China's war with Japan had already started and the Chinese government was seated in Hangkow. Flying to Hangkow was dangerous business at the time, and Foster left Janet behind in Hong Kong when he made the trip. Adding to the danger was bad weather and lack of even the most rudimentary kind of instrumental aids to soupy weather navigation. As one who always took an attitude of Presbyterian predestination toward the hazards of flying, Dulles felt uneasy on that trip as the airplane bucked and reared through fog and turbulence toward the primitive landing field on the bend in the Yangtze in China's interior, with the thought always in mind that Japanese fighters were roaming China's skies. Oddly enough, however, the uppermost thought at the time was that if the plane crashed he would never get to finish the book he was then working on, *War, Peace and Change,* about which he had been thinking ever since Versailles.

His visit to Chiang gave him an appraisal different from that prevalent in the period. With American interest focused primarily on Europe until the Second World War, U.S. opinion generally paid little attention to the nature and motivation of what was stirring in Asia. Chiang, as a man who had broken bloodily with Communism in 1927, had by that act become a Tito, in Communist eyes, long before Josip Broz was ever heard of. He was more than a Tito, for in the break he oriented his country's policy toward the West and toward the United States. But with no appreciation of this fact in the United States, the Communists had unparalleled opportunity to heap vituperation upon him and create a propaganda image unattractive to our democratic traditions. The really intensive propaganda campaign, which began after United States entry into the war and continued until the United States permitted China to slip from its side into Communist alliance, was still to come; but even at that time the stage was being set.

Dulles concluded that Chiang was a sincere Chinese patriot in the grip of forces beyond his control in the light of the conditions of the country with which he had to work. This appraisal proved positively shocking to some of his intellectual acquaintances, who felt qualified to make strongly emotional judgments on the basis of what they read without satisfying themselves as to the factual basis of them.

To the accumulation of experiences such as this trip were added events in 1937 and 1941 which proved to be the main turning points compelling his attention away from legal affairs.

In 1937 Dulles attended a Conference on Intellectual Co-operation in Paris, under League of Nations auspices, which was called to study the possibilities for peaceful change in a world which seemed to be moving inexorably toward war. Although the men who gathered there were supposedly the most brilliant nongovernmental minds of their respective countries, Dulles was dismayed by the fact that in seeking to cope with the problems posed by Hitler they were inhibited by narrow nationalistic considerations and conventional thought patterns. They had no answer, even on the theoretical plane, for the clash of interests that was mounting in intensity; they exhibited a static smugness toward the status quo and a timidity toward new courses.

Shortly afterward Dulles attended a Conference on Church and State at Oxford, England, which brought together church figures and laymen from all over the world. Always impressed by intellectual imagination and constructive thinking, Dulles was enormously struck by the scope and range of the ideas the churchmen had to offer. More than any other event, this conference swung his mind to reflection on the importance of the religious aspects of life and convinced him that the effort to create conditions favoring peace could not go forward without the moral dynamism potential in the man of religion.

Dulles plunged into work with the churchmen on the side of constructive efforts for peace. He devoted five years of intensive effort to it, making speeches in all parts of the country and taking part in study groups and public discussions. When he was Secretary of State he looked back on this period as one of the most satisfactory of his life, feeling he had taken a leading part in a missionary movement which had profound influence on American public opinion.

The advent of war tended to sharpen the focus of organizational activity. It narrowed the problem: the present was in a sense taken out of consideration in the fight for survival, and peace-building efforts could be concentrated on the future. The Federal Council of Churches, before which Dulles made an address in 1940, decided to create a Commission on a Just and Durable Peace. Dulles was named its chairman, and spent months at a time away from his office traveling the country to make speeches promoting the organization's ideas.

During this campaign, in August, 1941, Roosevelt and Churchill held their famous meeting at sea and issued the Atlantic Charter declaration. As a student of world affairs, Dulles found the Charter lacking in several important respects, particularly in its failure to provide for a world organization.

In a critique on the eight points of the declaration, prepared for the commission, Dulles said:

"Taken as a whole, the joint declaration must be regarded as a tentative and incomplete statement. . . . Certainly the collaboration of the United States and the British Commonwealth of Nations is a precious thing and the unity of our peoples is something to be fostered. But this in itself will not assure a just and durable peace. The danger is that we should think so. . . . The end of the present war, if it is fought through to military victory, will find an overwhelming concentration of power in one or two nations. That power, of course, will be a reality, the implications of which we cannot avoid.

The Quest for a Just and Durable Peace

"Our task will be to make it a beneficent reality. This requires that we use our power, not to perpetuate itself, but to create, support and eventually give way to international institutions drawing their vitality from the whole family of nations."

On the ground that criticism should be constructive and not merely negative, he made some suggestions for addition to the Charter aims: (1) preparation to supply medicine, food, and clothing during the period of chaos sure to follow the war; (2) "we should seek the political reorganization of continental Europe as a federated commonwealth of some type"; (3) assurance to Japan of access to markets and raw materials, preservation of China from political domination by Japan "or any other alien power"; (4) placing of all nonself-governing colonies under international mandate in accordance with Woodrow Wilson's original conception, which was perverted at Versailles.

Speeches by Dulles and other leaders of the movement were printed in booklet form and circulated among study groups to stimulate discussion. Missions were organized to visit the states. The commission's views on long-range objectives were distilled into 12 "guiding principles" and summarized in *Six Pillars of Peace* and widely propagandized. The intensive campaign began to pay off when the "B2H2" resolution was introduced in the Senate, taking its name from its four authors, Senators Ball, Burton, Hatch, and Hill. It was a manifestation that public support for a postwar peace organization of world scope was taking root. Roosevelt, who had resisted Churchill's desire to include a postwar organization in the Atlantic Charter because of Woodrow Wilson's unhappy experience with the League of Nations, became convinced that American opinion would support another try and he set Secretary of State Cordell Hull to work on plans which led to the Dumbarton Oaks conference and eventually to the United Nations.

Meantime, at an extremely dark point of the war for the Allies—in January, 1942—Dulles made his first flight across the Atlantic which he was to travel so often as Secretary. With Dr. Walter Van Kirk, an official of the Federal Council, he traveled to England to attend a meeting called by the Archbishop of Canterbury to define the spiritual bases of peace. The archbishop at that time was Dr. William Temple, and he sought to bring together Catholic, Anglican, and nonconformist views on the problem. Dulles and Van Kirk traveled to England by military airplane, arriving at Limerick Airport, Ireland, in a blackout, and transferred there to a British military aircraft which had drumskins over the windows. Taking off without knowledge of their destination, they landed at Bristol, from where they were taken by car to London and Oxford. It was against the dramatic background of a wartime England under heavy air attack that they sat down with others to discuss peace.

Dulles, in addressing the conference, argued that unless Great Britain and the United States recaptured a dynamic sense of purpose they would certainly "lose the Third World War." This thought impressed Arnold Toynbee, another speaker, who commented that it was possible to get rid of war at many different prices. Hitler, he said, had made the most practical and workable offer: at the price of German domination and repressive conditions of life. Whenever large parts of the world had been held in peace for a number of years, that was the form it took: thralldom. Had Hitler been as generous in his terms as the old Romans, Toynbee suggested, he might have had his offer accepted.

The Quest for a Just and Durable Peace

Dulles contended that past difficulties of taking the just and durable road to peace were due to exaggerated nationalism but also, particularly, to economic barriers. Each country acted to suit itself without regard to the suffering and injury to others. The solution, he suggested, seemed to be the creation of agencies which would have international foundation and authority and which were charged with particular tasks more than national in scope. Inhibition of state boundary lines would be broken down most readily in that way and would be done without any particular challenge to the authority and prestige of the state, provided the specific task of the international agency was defined quite clearly.

It was clear from what he said that already formulating in his mind was the proposal, mentioned in Chapter 2, which he made two months later in a speech at Ohio Wesleyan University at the time the commission held its study conference. Entirely apart from the substantive aspects of the supranational executive organ he outlined is its revelation of a mind capable of discovering possible mechanisms for modern adaptation in such odd, out-of-the-way places as the Hudson's Bay and British East India companies, from which he drew ideas.

"The thing that Dulles did at the Oxford conference," said a churchman who attended it, "was to convince these church people that it was not enough to inveigh from their pulpits on abstract principles but to get down into the gutter of international politics and fight for your principles. Nobody disputes that war is evil and un-Christian. What's necessary is to understand why it persists and the problem of applying spiritual motives to its eradication."

It seems clear from examination of this phase of Dulles' life that the church movement for peace and the energy of the lawyer who had made the study of peace his passion were elements that complemented each other. Others might have written off the religious leaders as men who lived in an other-world, freed from the practical, not responsible to the pressures of politics. Dulles looked on them as the stuff of politics—a force for exerting pressure in politics and exerting it in the right directions. He saw the opportunity for taking the pressure, some of it no more than simple-pacifist in motivation, and combining it with a lawyer's feeling for the practical and the attainable, and producing results with it.

10

· · · · · · · ·

Bipartisanship

IN THE spring of 1937, Sullivan & Cromwell felt the need of a
good trial lawyer on its staff. The most prominent in New York
City at that time was a young man named Thomas E. Dewey, who
was making a national reputation for himself as special prosecutor
in an investigation into New York rackets. Dulles knew him casually through a mutual acquaintance, George Z. Medalie, an eminent
Republican lawyer and former U. S. attorney whose chief deputy
Dewey had been. Dulles invited Dewey to luncheon and after looking him over offered him a partnership as senior trial attorney with
his law firm. Dewey agreed to join after he had completed his
racket-busting inquiry.

But during the summer public approval of Dewey's success in
convicting Lucky Luciano and other underworld characters led to
demands that he run for district attorney. The pressure was strong.
After party strategy conferences in which Dulles himself participated, Dewey asked to be excused from his commitment and ran

for the prosecutor's office instead. He was easily elected, and thus launched on his political career.

This was the beginning of an association between Dulles and Dewey which brought them both onto the national political stage. They saw a good deal of each other in following months, and when in 1939 the Gallup Poll showed that Dewey was a surprisingly strong public favorite for the Republican presidential nomination, Dulles was one of three close Dewey friends who helped plan his preconvention strategy. The others were Medalie and Roger W. Straus, chairman of American Smelting & Refining. Straus was also one of three cochairmen of the National Conference of Christians and Jews, an organization which joined with the efforts of the Federal Council of Churches to propagate the bases for a just and durable peace.

At the 1940 convention in Philadelphia, although Dewey led for two ballots, Wendell Willkie got the nomination. But in 1944 Dewey won the nomination and Dulles became involved politically in the national campaign as his foreign policy adviser.

Just after the 1944 convention the Roosevelt administration was preparing to hold a conference at Dumbarton Oaks, an estate in Washington, to prepare a postwar peace organization in consultation with Great Britain and Soviet Russia. Public opinion in favor of some sort of regulated world order, stirred up by the campaign in which Dulles had had a leading part, had encouraged action of a kind to which President Roosevelt had not been willing to commit himself at the time of the Atlantic Charter.

Both Dewey and Dulles were perturbed over the character of the Dumbarton Oaks planning, as represented in sketchy information appearing in the press. It appeared to them that the proposed organization smacked too much of big-power control of the world, without adequate representation for the little nations. Dewey issued a statement criticizing it on that basis. He said reports indicated that it was planned "to subject the nations of the world, great and small, permanently to the coercive power of the four nations holding the conference"—the fourth being Nationalist China, although originally only the wartime Big Three were involved.

The White House issued a denial, saying that the Administration sought to organize all peace-loving nations and was thinking in terms of the creation of a council which would be elected annually by the fully representative body of all nations. The statement added: "We are not thinking of a superstate with its own police force and other paraphernalia of coercive power."

Secretary of State Cordell Hull held a press conference the next day and the Washington press corps turned out in force to determine whether a campaign issue was developing on foreign policy. Hull was asked whether he would welcome a conference with Dewey to straighten out the dispute, and replied that he would. It is not generally known that next day Hull got a private dressing down from Roosevelt for this move, which F. D. R. regarded as a political slip which permitted the Republicans to move in on an activity in which the Democrats were taking leadership.

Having committed himself, Hull could not readily withdraw the offer. On August 18, 1944, Dewey sent him a telegram accepting the offer to confer and designating Dulles to represent him.

At the time Dulles was suffering from a severe nerve ailment in his foot. It was extremely painful for him to get about. So difficult was it for him to walk that the most practical way of getting about was to go by auto from his front door to the front door of wherever he was going. Accordingly, Dewey arranged for a state car to pick Dulles up at his home in New York and drive him to Washington. Dulles was using crutches for what little walking he had to do. Wartime gasoline rationing was in effect at the time, and Washington columnist Drew Pearson made a point of the auto trip in one of his Sunday night broadcasts. He said Dulles had not needed to use scarce gasoline, for he had seen him on the street a week later and he looked quite fit. The fact was that after his sessions with Hull, Dulles returned to the home of the friends with whom he was staying and literally crawled upstairs on his hands and knees to lie in bed between his meetings with Hull. A few days later he had an operation on the foot, which kept him in the hospital for some weeks. Nerves in his heel and ankle were crushed and he had no further trouble.

Hull was most anxious not to let the issue of a postwar organization become a part of debate in the political campaign, remembering the results of such dispute in the 1920 campaign, which confirmed the Senate's repudiation of Woodrow Wilson's League of Nations. Dewey was not averse to keeping the issue outside politics, but he did want assurance about the character of the organization.

Hull's account of the conference is contained in his *Memoirs*,* in which he says:

Our conversations began in my office on August 23. At the outset I handed Dulles a copy of our latest draft on the postwar security organization, dated July 18, and a copy of a four-page summary of its major provisions. One page of this summary dealt with the position of small countries in the United Nations organization, and contained six

* Published in 1948 by Macmillan.

references to the draft of the UN charter showing that participation of the small nations was fully provided for.

I said to Dulles that the word "nonpartisan" rather than "bipartisan" should be used to describe the correct approach to the problem of keeping the United Nations organization out of domestic politics. "Bipartisan," I explained, meant that both parties would be involved on a political basis in policy toward the United Nations organization. "Nonpartisan" meant that neither party would be involved in that policy on a political basis.

Dulles argued warmly for "bipartisan." His thought apparently was that his party would thereby be recognized as being equally involved in the formulation of the United Nations agreement and could obtain some political advantage thereby.

I explained, however, that under our constitutional structure we could not have both parties sharing the responsibility. The party in power had the responsibility for the execution of foreign policy. This responsibility could not be delegated. The opposition party, in my opinion, had the moral responsibility not to base its opposition, if any, to our proposals for the United Nations organization on partisan grounds.

I went to the dictionary and studied the definitions of the two words. "Nonpartisan" seemed to me ever more right. I called Dulles' attention to the fact that "bipartisan" referred to two parties, and there might come a time in American history, as there had come in the past, when three parties would have to be considered.

After a discussion that literally lasted hours, Dulles agreed to adopt the word "nonpartisan." Dulles, in his own account of the talks, remarked: "The Secretary seemed to me very stubborn. Perhaps I seemed that way to him." His slant on Hull's quibbling over the word "bipartisan" was that Hull feared, "or at least Mr. Roosevelt's political advisers feared, that the word 'bipartisan' might concede the Republicans an equal status in a project that was now presumed to be politically profitable."

Hull's account of the conferences continues:

When he came back for our second discussion, on August 24, Dulles said he had studied the draft of the proposed United Nations charter and the four-page summary memorandum I had given him, and he considered the draft excellent. He appeared to think it amply took care of the small nations. . . .

During our third and final meeting on August 25, I went over with Dulles successive drafts of a statement we might issue. On the morning of the third day Dulles came to my office and said, in a tone of much satisfaction, that Dewey and he—meaning all the Republicans for whom Dewey was speaking, therefore the Republicans generally —were prepared to go the entire distance with me. We had been talking out differences very earnestly for two days, and we were both immensely pleased at this outcome. I was particularly gratified because at about the time of our conferences some leading Republicans close to Dewey had asserted their right to discuss during the campaign any foreign policy, including the postwar organization.

Dulles said he and Hull never came to complete agreement. Hull wanted to cover all subjects relating to the future peace, including such details as to what arrangements might be worked out with Russia on Poland, which was then a live issue in Polish-American communities. Dewey was adamant against any agreement so sweeping, and Dulles agreed with him emphatically. Hull and Dulles did agree, however, that the effort to create a world organization would be kept out of the political arena; that the two camps would continue to confer on developments as they arose; and that there must be "full public 'nonpartisan' discussion of the means of attaining a lasting peace."

Two days later Dewey submitted to Hull a memo suggesting several changes in the proposed UN charter. One was to give non-member states an equal right to call peace-threatening situations to the attention of the General Assembly or the executive council; another was to provide that treaty conditions might be included in the subject matters that the Assembly or council might consider. Hull forwarded the suggestions to Undersecretary Edward Stettinius, who was in charge of the Dumbarton Oaks negotiations, and with British and Russian consent they were written into the draft.

Republican-Democratic co-operation continued as the charter negotiations proceeded. Other Republican suggestions were submitted. Hull kept Dewey advised of subsequent changes in the charter. During September he warned the Republicans that there was a movement in Congress to require that all applications of force under the security organization be submitted first for Congressional approval. In telephone conversation with Dulles, Hull indicated fear it would stir controversy with the British and Russians, leading them to believe the United States would not be in a position to carry out an agreement with the organization. This requirement was successfully kept out of the charter.

These activities made Dulles the active agent of bipartisanship in subsequent dealings with the Administration, as Senator Arthur Vandenberg of Michigan was the active leader in formulation of legislation passed by Congress. It led to Dulles' appointment as a senior U. S. adviser at the San Francisco UN founding conference and to most of the four-power conferences in the series of meetings from 1945 to 1949, as well as to his appointment on official U. S. delegations to the UN. Dulles did not get the San Francisco appointment, however, until pressure was brought to bear on President Roosevelt by Vandenberg and, through Stettinius, by Bernard Baruch. "It seemed that President Roosevelt then held a certain rancor against Republicans who had been actively identified with the Dewey presidential campaign," Dulles wrote later. When Roosevelt finally relented, Stettinius announced the appointment immediately so as to make sure the President would not change his mind.

Dulles remained a believer in what, with due respect to Hull, he continued to call bipartisanship. He regarded it as hard to define and hard to accomplish. "In time of war," he wrote in *War or Peace*, "we practice a large amount of bipartisanship. Victory is so desperate a need that the Administration in power usually seeks help from qualified persons without regard to their political party, and members of the opposition party gladly respond. Congress votes almost as a matter of course for what a war administration says is necessary. Everyone concedes that there must be a large measure of national unity to meet grave national peril from without.

"Winning a war is important. But winning peace is equally important. Also, the winning of a 'cold' war is as important as the winning of a 'hot' war. In each case our liberty, our free institutions, are at stake."

At two of the postwar conferences with the Russians Dulles demonstrated the specific benefits of bipartisanship.

One was at the first meeting of the Council of Foreign Ministers in London in 1945. It was at this conference the United States learned that Russia was not willing to carry wartime big-power unity over into peace at the price of compromising its interest and ideals with those of Great Britain and the United States. As Dulles described it in a radio report following the conference, "the Soviet delegation believed, and rightly believed, that the United States attached great importance to preserving the appearance of unity among the Big Three. It also knew we were anxious quickly to conclude peace with Italy. It wanted to find out how much of our principles we would sacrifice to attain these goals. It did find out. It found out that the United States was not willing to sacrifice its principles or its historic friendship with China and France."

The then Secretary, James F. Byrnes, refused agreement to questions adversely affecting France and China, and initiated the "no appeasement" policy which the United States followed thereafter. But by doing so he was forced to accept failure in the underlying objective which the American people expected of him: peacetime unity. Without the Republican support represented by Dulles, Byrnes would have had to return home to face Republican charges that the conference was a failure; instead he was able to make a momentous decision involving a new attitude toward the Soviet Union, with confidence that most elements of both parties would support him in the national interest.

While there were other instances at subsequent conferences, the value of bipartisanship was most strikingly demonstrated again in 1948, when Dewey was making his second race for President and the Russians had instituted the Berlin blockade. Dulles was called to the State Department for confidential briefing on the situation, on the basis of which he was able to advise Dewey, who issued a statement firmly backing the Administration policy of resisting the blockade and countering it with the airlift.

As the election approached, the problem of bipartisanship became even more acute. Polls indicated more strongly every day that Dewey would win, and Europe became jittery over the prospect of a Republican administration in the moment of crisis, remembering the isolationism that followed the last previous transfer from Democratic to Republican control. The UN was meeting in Paris and Dulles was a member of Secretary George C. Marshall's delegation. Foreign Ministers of Allied nations were quietly conferring with Dulles, rather than Marshall (but with Marshall's knowledge and consent) in an effort to assure their governments that Dewey would not leave them out on a limb in their attitudes toward Russia. Dulles kept in constant contact by transatlantic telecom with the Dewey campaign train, aboard which his brother Allen was handling liaison, and even flew back to New York October 3 for a one-day conference with Dewey. The importance of a united American front in the face of Communist threat at the time cannot be underestimated.

After Dulles took office he attempted to maintain the principle of bipartisanship by confidentially offering Adlai Stevenson, who as the defeated Democratic candidate was the titular party leader, an appointment to the UN delegation. Stevenson, for reasons of his own, chose to decline, and the practice was not put into effect with an important Democratic figure until Senator Walter F. George was named special ambassador in connection with the Dulles plan to expand the scope of NATO. Democrats continued, however, to be appointed regularly to the UN delegation.

Despite this record, Dulles has left the impression of rather strong partisanship in political campaigns. The reason appears to be that the public generally fails to understand that at no time have the Republicans waived the right of debating whether policy is well executed—in short, the right to treat foreign policy as part of the totality of an Administration's conduct in office.

The dividing line between what is open legitimately to partisan discussion and what is not lies in subjects where domestic division shakes the confidence of our friends or encourages our enemies on questions of basic national interest. It is a hard line to define, and in a campaign year necessarily must be subject to definition by the conscience of the men engaged in politics. At a press conference early in 1956 Dulles was reminded that just before he took office he apologized for some Republican oratory in 1952 by saying that in a campaign year speakers tend to use extravagant terms they might not use under other circumstances. This led him to give his own definition of what is proper by way of "constructive discussion" of foreign policy.

"There is a danger point," he said, "which I think all patriotic citizens should observe, and that is not to shake confidence abroad in the solidity of the United States position on basic matters. We do have a basically bipartisan position which has evolved over the last ten years, which involves the committal of United States prestige and honor to various other countries and various places in the world. If there should grow up any doubt about our determination to stand on those commitments, it would be a very sad day for the United States and in my opinion would greatly increase the risk of war."

11

· · · · · · · ·

Four Months a Senator

AFTER the Paris meeting of the Council of Foreign Ministers
in May and June, 1949, Foster and Janet Dulles had gone
to Duck Island for one of their periodic solitary vacations. On
July 6 the island's lighthouse keeper and radio operator came
to their cabin with a message: Governor Dewey wanted Dulles
to go to the mainland and call him by telephone. The Dulleses were
temporarily stormbound, and it was not possible to leave the
island that day. The water south of Duck is filled with reefs and
ledges, making it extremely dangerous for an amphibian airplane
to land in it. When the wind is from the south, as it usually is,
the pilot can land into it, off the north shore, and taxi into the lee
of the bluffs. When the wind comes from the north, however,
landing becomes a tricky and dangerous operation.

The following day the wind shifted and moderated sufficiently to
permit the Dulleses to be taken off by a lighthouse tender, which
landed them at Picton, Ontario, to make the phone call. Dewey

told Dulles that Senator Robert F. Wagner, Sr., had resigned because of a lengthy illness, and he was appointing Dulles to fill the seat until the November election. Dewey said he would send a State Conservation Department airplane to pick him up. Without returning to Duck Island, the Dulleses flew to New York, wearing the old clothes they were dressed in when their vacation was interrupted. With wardrobes replenished in New York, they continued to Washington that night. Dulles told reporters on his arrival he had "no expectation" of standing for election. Next day—July 8—he was sworn in as a member of the United States Senate. The same day he resigned from the firm of Sullivan & Cromwell.

He had occupied the Senate seat only four days when he made his first speech. It was in support of the North Atlantic Treaty, which was then up for ratification. Vandenberg had urged him to get into the debate before it ended. It was fitting that he did, for the treaty had its inception early in 1948 at a secret meeting at Blair House attended by Marshall, Undersecretary of State Robert Lovett, Vandenberg, and Dulles.

An old senatorial tradition, violated more and more as time goes on, is that a newcomer waits a year or so before venturing to presume on his seniors with his advice in a floor speech. Dulles paid his respects to it, remarking that he felt robed in swaddling clothes rather than a senatorial toga, but with that out of the way he plunged into the thick of debate. His close association with the various steps which had led up to submission of the treaty was of course known to his new colleagues, and they listened to him with interest and respect. It was significant of his effectiveness that before he finished speaking Robert Taft, a very senior senatorial authority and leader of the opposition, felt obliged to take part in the debating duel.

Dulles laid out the historical background of the treaty with his usual clarity of exposition.

At San Francisco's UN founding conference, he recalled, "we had already begun to realize that Soviet ambitions conflicted with the ideals for which our nation had fought and which were expressed in the Atlantic Charter. Also, it there became apparent that a UN organization could not be expected to reconcile these conflicts by coercive machinery of its own. That would not have established peace, but would have started new war. So the plan of Dumbarton Oaks was changed at San Francisco so that those nations which had common values could organize their own collective defense. . . .

"It was that action, taken over four years ago at San Francisco, that made possible—I go further, and say it indeed foreshadowed—the defensive organization, first of the American states, and now of the North Atlantic community. . . . Far from being a step backward, NATO is a step forward. It is apparent now, as it already had begun to be apparent at San Francisco, that security could not be achieved at a single step through a single world organization. It is going to be necessary to advance progressively through a series of organizations for collective self-defense. The North Atlantic Treaty is one more such organization. The treaty can, and I believe will, lift from the UN a burden and anxiety which it was never designed to carry."

He traced the origin of the Western scheme of defense to the 1947 Moscow conference, where he had been an adviser to Secretary George C. Marshall. It was there, he said, the idea originated that the United States would out of its own strength encourage the still-free peoples of Europe to find a new strength out of unity, and "there came, in quick succession, the European Recovery Plan, the Brussels Pact, the uniting of the British and U.S. zones of Germany, and, shortly, adding to them the French zone, making possible the creation of the Bonn government of Western Germany, internationalization of the Ruhr, the joint U.S.-British airlift which held Berlin against the Soviet blockade, the Council of Europe, and now the North Atlantic Treaty. . . .

"With all due reservations, I feel that we are on the way peacefully to resist, and I hope, eventually, to throw back Soviet Communism in Europe. But if we have found a way, we have not yet gone down that way far enough to find a place where it is safe to stop. . . . In any great enterprise there are risks and possibilities of abuse. Such risks have to be taken to defeat the dynamism of Soviet Communism. The greatest risk of all is the risk of doing nothing, for the dynamic always prevails against the static. When I say that I do not say it as an apology for recklessness."

But there was still more to NATO than common defense, he argued. "Admiral Mahan said that the function of force in human affairs is to give moral ideas the opportunity to take root. NATO can provide the opportunity for our spiritual faith to reassert itself in practices that will enlarge men's opportunity to develop morally, intellectually, and materially."

Opposition to the treaty was not based on isolationism, though it numbered in its ranks many of the prewar isolationists. The opposition's chief worry was that ratification of the treaty would itself commit the United States to supply arms to European countries with which the treaty allied it. The grudging converts from isolationism were willing to accept the principle of collective defense with Europe but not willing to pay for the arming of Europe. Taft asked Dulles whether he considered there was a legal or moral obligation to this effect under the treaty. Dulles said no.

Dulles was now debating from a more prominent position politically than he had ever spoken before, and in a forum under wider public scrutiny than any he had used. His statement that ratification of the treaty carried no additional commitment was supported by President Truman's message to Congress on the subject, and also by the report of the Senate Foreign Relations committee. But the treaty's opponents were directing their main efforts to proving that it did.

As debate went on it became clear that on the legal point Dulles was taking a strictly legal position; he admitted under questioning that if the Senate approved ratification he knew that the Administration planned to ask immediately for an authorization bill to provide the funds for arming Europe. On the question of moral obligation, his answer was that military assistance did not necessarily mean arms or a European force in being—which was Vandenberg's position too. He told Senator Forrest Donnell of Missouri that perhaps the best military assistance the United States could give France, for example, would be "to have an atom bomb somewhere in the United States," or that France's best way of aiding the United States would be to provide a base on her territory.

Basing a position on the distinction between "arms" and "military assistance" was drawing it too fine for political debate. It was typical of a mental agility permissible in dealing with technicalities of law, but not acceptable in dealing with public questions. Approval of the North Atlantic Treaty came not because the Senate was assured it involved no additional commitment, but because a majority not only accepted its principle but were prepared to vote tax funds as well, knowing that money would be asked for arms. There were other occasions later when Dulles' legal mentality led him to make flat statements which were equally unacceptable as political positions.

The Administration did, indeed, follow treaty ratification immediately with a Military Defense Assistance Program authorizing a $1,440,000,000 appropriation. Perhaps because of the wartime habit of seeking and obtaining from Congress the broadest kinds of power grants, the bill was worded so as to give the President enormous powers in perpetuity, subject only to repeal by Congressional action over which he would have had the veto.

As such, it was opposed by Republicans and could have been defeated. However, Vandenberg and Dulles, believing in the purpose behind it, elected to co-operate with the Democratic administration to achieve its purpose. They discusssed their objections with Secretary of State Dean Acheson, and a substitute bill was introduced. This bill, after hearings, was further changed to include safeguards proposed by Vandenberg, Dulles, Senator William Knowland, and others. Knowland sponsored addition of a $125,000,000 fund for Nationalist China, which had not been included at all in the Administration bill. Dulles supported him on it.

"As things now are," Dulles argued in Senate debate of September 21, "our Pacific front is wide open to encirclement from the east. Stalin himself wrote some twenty-five years ago that the West was most vulnerable to attack through the east, and the Soviet government has been supporting Communist revolutionaries in China ever since. I saw that support with my own eyes in Hankow in 1938, and it is somewhat surprising that our government seems to have been totally unprepared to meet the danger. Today the situation is critical." It was just as the Nationalists were being driven off the mainland. Dulles noted, however, that Congress could not "impose" foreign policy on an Administration unwilling to carry it out. This was precisely the case with the Truman administration as to China policy.

As a senator, Dulles also supported the Administration bill to aid displaced persons, recalling Molotov and Vishinsky's attempts at various conferences to get Western governments to agree to send back refugees from Communism. He opposed the nomination of Leland Olds for a third term as member of the Federal Power Commission. He joined with several other senators in introducing a bill to permit the Quartermaster Corps to set up a research laboratory and sponsored a large number of private bills to aid individual refugees. The Senate assigned him to serve on the Post Office and District of Columbia committees.

His senatorial service did not last long. Wagner's resignation, making possible his appointment, had occurred early enough in the year so that Dewey's replacement would, under New York law, last only until that November's election gave the voters a choice. Dulles, though he discovered he liked being a senator because he had a better forum for his speeches than ever before, had no desire to wage a political campaign himself. But Herbert Lehman, former governor and one of New York's biggest vote-pulling Democrats, announced for the seat and other Republicans proved reluctant to tangle with him. Because of the failure of any other prominent Republican to come forward, Dulles eventually was forced to make the race.

Dewey lent him experienced campaign help in such persons as Tom Stephens, who later served as President Eisenhower's appointments secretary, and Jim Hagerty, who later became Ike's press secretary. Stephens taught Dulles to simplify his public speeches. He objected one day to the unamplified phrase "North Atlantic community." Stephens claimed that the average person would not understand what he was talking about. Dulles demurred. Stephens proved his point by going out in the hall and pushing the elevator button. When the car arrived, he asked the operator if he knew what the phrase meant. The man said no.

With practical tutelage of this type, Dulles toured New York State by bus on a handshaking campaign in the familiar U.S. political tradition, interrupting it as necessary to fly to Washington on important Senate votes.

The two main themes of the Dulles campaign were "anti-Statism," by which he meant opposition to federal encroachment on private enterprise fields such as medicine, and anti-Communism. He accused Lehman of accepting Communist support, and also argued that his own defeat, since he symbolized bipartisan support of a Democratic administration which opposed Communism, would permit the Communists to "chalk up another victory in their struggle to get into office here." The greatest rejoicing in such event, he contended, "will not be in New York or Washington but in Moscow."

Lehman replied by accusing him of using the tactics of "the glib, resourceful, tricky lawyer," though he refused the challenge of a face-to-face debate when they both happened to be making speeches in the same city one day. Lehman was able to turn the anti-Communism theme into a charge of "bigotry" against Dulles on the basis of a speech at Geneseo, New York, on October 5. Referring to the Communist strength in New York City, Dulles told his upstate audience: "If you could see the kind of people in New York City making up this bloc that is voting for my opponent, if you could see them with your own eyes, I know you would be out, every last man and woman of you, on election day."

The New York *Post,* only one of the metropolitan dailies supporting Lehman, called the voters' attention to it in an editorial entitled "Death of a Statesman." It also carried a layout of pictures of New Yorkers supporting Lehman—seventeen citizens, including six women and one Negro, all with at least passably honest, and in some cases handsome and intelligent, faces. "This is the first time a major candidate has introduced beauty as a voting qualification," said the *Post,* "or suggested that upstate Republicans have nobler features than their fellow men." Lehman called it "a diabolical and deliberate insult to the people of New York City." Lehman defeated Dulles by 196,293 votes.

On election night, when the decision was known, Dulles went around his Hotel Commodore headquarters thanking each worker for his help, accepting the outcome stoically. Next day, when he was cleaning out his desk, one of his staff entered his office to find him speaking by telephone with his brother Allen, his feet up on the desk as he talked, and waving to some young ladies in the window of a model agency across the street. Startled to discover a frivolous side to the sober lawyer, the man inquired: "Did you wave first, or did the girls wave first?" Without answering the question, Dulles remarked with a grin: "It's too bad we have to move out of here, isn't it?"

12

· · · · · · · ·

Pilot Operation: Peace with Japan

AFTER the unexpected Dewey defeat in 1948, while Dulles was in Paris, President Truman magnanimously permitted him to serve as acting head of the U.S. delegation during an absence of Secretary Marshall. It was a gesture which Dulles greatly appreciated, helping to restore his morale after his and his party's prestige had been struck a heavy blow. Presumably it was in appreciation of the Republican foreign policy support that Dulles had been rendering when Truman's own political fortunes seemed at a low point.

But after Dulles' defeat in the senatorial race by Herbert Lehman all debts had been wiped out and Dulles was in the Truman dog-house. In November of 1949, with three years to go before the Republicans had another crack at seeking national control, it seemed that his days as an adviser were over. Probably he would have remained on the sidelines for the rest of Truman's term if Arthur Vandenberg had not insisted that bipartisan co-operation could not continue unless Republicans were given posts where they could keep party leaders informed of developing policy and carry back Republican suggestions. Vandenberg nagged sufficiently so that in March, 1950, Dulles and former Kentucky Senator John Sherman Cooper were given State Department posts as consultants.

In this job Dulles masterminded the writing of a treaty of peace with Japan, though not by design at the time he was named. He was assigned to the job chiefly because his restless energy galled at sitting around without something definite to do. It came about this way:

One day he said to Secretary Acheson: "You'll never get anything done unless you select someone in whom you have confidence, give him a job to do, and then hold him to results. Look at the Japanese Peace Treaty—the department has been discussing it for four years without result. Why don't you give someone one year in which to get action, with the understanding that if he can't do it, he fails? Give him a target and enough authority to get there."

It was a fact that since early 1947 the department had been fussing intermittently over the treaty. The United States proposed a conference at which the majority of Far Eastern Commission nations would decide treaty disputes. Russia countered with a demand for a four-power conference. Russia's use of the veto had brought negotiations over Germany and· Austria to a complete standstill and in the light of this it seemed useless to go ahead on Japan. Nevertheless, various State Department committees held meetings and drafted possible treaty clauses—some eighty single-spaced foolscap pages of them. By late 1949, although the obstructionism of Russia remained—in the State Department view—as a potential roadblock, the need for a treaty became more and more urgent.

Pilot Operation: Peace with Japan

Acheson was impressed by Dulles' suggestion, and soon afterward he assigned him to take over the handling of the treaty. The government had not yet decided, however, whether as a matter of national policy there should be a treaty. The Pentagon was reluctant to give up the command relationship it held over Japan through SCAP. Dulles discovered that, even before deciding what kind of treaty to write with Japan, it was necessary to achieve peace between the State and Defense Departments.

In pursuing this task he made his first trip to Tokyo. His aim was to make sure it was time to make peace, and formulate the principles which should guide it. General Omar Bradley, then chairman of the Joint Chiefs of Staff, happened to be in Japan at the same time, and in three-cornered discussions with General MacArthur the groundwork was laid for an agreement based on the practical logic of the times. MacArthur supported the contention that after several years any occupation was bound to show diminishing returns. The Japanese had behaved admirably for five years and were beginning to feel they had earned the right to regain their sovereignty. If cheated of this goal, sullenness and resistance could be expected to rise, and once a nation of 83,000,000 souls decided to fight further subjugation it would be hard to handle. The time to act was before this stage was reached.

Scarcely had an informal meeting of minds taken place on this basis when the Communists attacked in Korea, introducing a new fact into the postwar world: the totalitarian countries were ready to use military force, and risk world war, to achieve their ends. For a few weeks the treaty had to wait while the United States took stock. But assessment of the new situation convinced American officials that peace with Japan was even more necessary than before.

The islands had been denuded of troops for Korea, and the occupation was scarcely more than a name.

The issue was brought formally to a head after Dulles' return to Washington. The two departments came to a political decision when the Secretaries of State and Defense signed a memorandum which was endorsed by President Truman the next day, September 8, 1950. The President made Dulles his official representative, with the rank of ambassador, to handle the matter.

The decision was to seek peace. But what kind? Dulles' approach stemmed from his experience as a young man at the Versailles Peace Conference of 1919, when he had seen the vindictiveness of men like Clemenceau corrode the ideals of Woodrow Wilson.

"You can have one of two kinds of peace," Dulles said. "One is a Carthaginian peace, which is cruel, ruthless, inflexible, and must be enforced with military strength for a long time. It is a peace that can tolerate no infractions whatever. The other is a peace based on the belief that human nature is capable of regeneration; that if it fails at times, it is capable of better ways of life. This kind of peace is one of magnanimity based on power.

"There is no half way between these two kinds of peace. You must have one or the other. We want the kind of peace that has a good chance of making Japan and the United States close associates in the future. It cannot be done without the free will of the conquered. It must be a peace of reconciliation."

It was with this philosophy that Dulles approached his task. The next problem was one of procedure. How to go about writing a treaty? The traditional way was to call an international conference —but that would involve Soviet Russia with her built-in veto. Moreover, during the years of inaction, a new complication had been added to the Far Eastern power situation: Communists had conquered the Chinese mainland and set up a government recognized by seventeen nations, though not by the United States. It raised seemingly insuperable problems of recognition for a conference. Dulles decided to proceed "through diplomatic channels," which meant that the United States, taking the lead, would confer separately with the other interested nations. This made it possible for Dulles to talk to Great Britain's Sir Oliver Franks in the morning and Nationalist China's Dr. Wellington Koo in the afternoon when it would have been impossible for the three to meet formally at luncheon for the same purpose. It enabled Dulles to invite Russia's Jacob Malik to his house in New York of an evening for a frank, hair-down talk about the treaty—although it never prevented Malik from using every propaganda cliché in the Soviet repertoire in the halls of the United Nations next day.

By November, 1950, discussions had proceeded far enough so that the United States circulated among the nations of the Far Eastern Commission, including Russia, a seven-point memorandum embodying the main principles which it sought to write into the treaty.

Almost immediately the progress was upset by full-scale Chinese Communist intervention in the Korean War. Planning was shelved again until the effects of this development could be assessed. By late January it was apparent the Chinese attack had not been decisive. Dulles, eager to get things rolling again, made a second trip to Tokyo.

From his discussions up to this point Dulles knew the problem that had to be solved to get a treaty written was the problem of security. "Security," said Dulles, "has not been, and never is, automatically solved by victory." Security meant looking in two directions. It meant some sort of guarantee for Japan, which faced the prospect of being turned loose in the polarized world of 1950-51 without army, navy, or air force to defend its regained sovereignty. The United States had positive reasons for not wanting her industrial potential gathered within the Iron Curtain, integrated with the resources of Manchuria, and thus made available to help provide the Communist world with the kind of economy which could underwrite a long war and possibly win it. In view of this, the United States could be counted on to supply the sea and air power needed to protect Japan; but after peace her troops would have to get out and leave the task of land defense to Japan's 75,000 policemen.

Security also meant giving assurance to nations which had been occupied or threatened by Japan that the late enemy would be prevented from rebuilding an aggressive military machine. This problem was not so acute in the Philippines, which had granted American base rights and arranged for an American Military Assistance Advisory Group, but it was a politically live issue in Australia and New Zealand. Although Dulles was personally convinced that the war-depleted Japanese economy could not support an aggressive militarism in the foreseeable future, he recognized the political psychology of it.

Dulles devoted his second Pacific trip to clearing up the security problem. With President Truman's approval he made a speech in Tokyo offering the Japanese American troops as garrison forces after conclusion of the treaty—provided the Japanese wanted them. Details could be worked out later and a special treaty consummated after the peace pact. The Japanese willingly accepted. To Australia and New Zealand Dulles offered a mutual-assistance pact, pledging that the United States would regard an attack on either of them as an attack on itself. This was announced later in Washington. It is noteworthy that every time a major step was agreed on, Dulles made a public statement or a speech about it.

After security, the big problems were economic, particularly reparations. It was only natural that the Philippines, whose cities had been bombed to rubble, should feel that Japan must pay something toward the damage—a feeling shared by other victims also. Dulles recognized the justness of this attitude, but he also knew that if Japan were to take her place in the Western line-up she had to be assured a healthy national economy. He knew that the United States, which had already poured into Japanese rehabilitation two billions of the tax dollars she had collected from her own citizens, and had sent thousands of them to help in the task, would have to underwrite the payments indirectly if the treaty exacted heavy cash reparations. He knew too, from the experience following Versailles, that if Japan, like Germany, knew her earnings would be taken away, it would rob her of any incentive to rebuild.

On the subject of economic restrictions, therefore, Dulles marshaled his strongest arguments for a forgiving peace. Those who worked with him in the negotiations say he was never more forceful and eloquent than in stating the case against binding Japan with economic fetters.

"If you use the lash," he told the statesmen so inclined, "if you exact reparations, if you constrict Japanese economic opportunity, if you act as jailer and master of slave labor, if you drive Japanese shipping off the seas and shut down her textile mills, you will create a peace that can only lead to bitter animosity and in the end drive Japan into the orbit of Russia."

This argument won out. The treaty provides that Japan pay

reparations in the only way economically practicable: by providing free services, technical assistance, and manufacturing facilities to the nations she had injured. As an island nation she was allowed all the shipping she could create, and in the other elements of a viable economy she was left free to rebuild herself without artificial hindrance.

Steadily the treaty was taking shape; steadily, but not smoothly. One crisis centered on General MacArthur's removal as Supreme Commander. Dulles had been most careful from the start to keep the treaty out of partisan politics, and for some days he did not know whether the political furor would engulf his work. He made a third trip to Japan—in all he flew 125,000 miles during the treaty-making year—simply to assure the Japanese that General MacArthur's departure did not mean the end of the world. When General MacArthur's subsequent blast at Administration policies omitted mention of the treaty, Dulles knew it had steered clear of the ruckus.

There still was the job of reducing all the agreed principles to a treaty draft in legal language. The United States had circulated a draft in March and asked for suggestions. Dulles wanted to keep the treaty readable and, ignoring the eighty pages of clauses which had been gathering dust since 1947, produced an eight-page initial draft. In the accretion of suggestions from other nations it inevitably grew longer, but it remained a relatively short document.

In June there were enough points of dispute still at issue with Great Britain to make Dulles feel it necessary to take a flying trip to London. The British had worked up a draft of their own. The knottiest dispute was over which China to recognize.

Great Britain had face to maintain in its recognition of Red

China—face that could be backed by rather cogent arguments about the "reality" of the situation, with Mao Tse-tung in practical control of the great bulk of Chinese territory. From the American standpoint, dealing with Red China was simply out of the question.

In diplomacy you look over a treaty to see what points you are not interested in and then seek to use those points for bargaining. Examining the British suggestions, Dulles and his State Department deputy, John Allison, found what they sought in a pact called the Congo Basin Treaty, written at St.-Germain-en-Laye in 1919. Under its terms all countries had freedom of trade in Africa's Congo Basin, and five nations—the United States, Britain, and Japan included—were given certain customs concessions.

Prior to World War II, Japan had cornered 90 per cent of the area's textile trade, seriously undercutting Britain's business. The United States had no interest in the concession, but it was important to the British, who wanted Japan deprived of her favored position. The American negotiators held out until the last minute on this point, but finally yielded. Although the yielding was not a specific horse trade on the China issue, it created a graceful opportunity for Britain to accept the proposed American compromise on China: that neither China sign the treaty. This might look like unnecessary finesse to a Congress which tends to think in terms of "Do what we say or we'll cut off aid"—but the fact is that it is far more effective with any nation endowed with an ounce of spunk. The London *Economist*'s Washington correspondent, commenting on Dulles' tact in this matter, wrote: "Had Mr. Dulles insisted that the Chinese Nationalists should sign the treaty, he would have been acclaimed in Congress . . . [he] chose instead to seek a solution which would not offend the countries of the Commonwealth." The compromise left it to Japan, after regaining sovereignty, to decide which China should sign peace with her.

The result of the trip to London was joint sponsorship of a revised treaty text by Britain and the United States. The text was revised once again after that, embodying changes proposed by almost every nation which made suggestions, but its main outlines were unchanged.

The steadiness of progress, however, began to alarm the Russians. After several protesting notes and *aide-mémoire,* the Soviet Union unloaded a major objection in a note on May 7. Although the Russians had been sent every memorandum and draft which was generally circulated, they proposed starting the job over again from scratch, with a four-power conference. Dulles read the note and started drafting a reply immediately in longhand.

After his reply to Russia had been typed and sent the rounds of the State Department and submitted to the White House, it came back with a handwritten notation in Mr. Truman's angular script: "This is a jewel." Secretary Acheson, himself a top-flight lawyer, hefted the document before his staff at next morning's briefing and remarked: "This is one of Sullivan & Cromwell's $25,000 briefs."

The Russians claimed the Potsdam Agreement had specified that four nations—the United States, U.S.S.R., Great Britain, and China—draw up a treaty for Japan. Mr. Dulles replied that Japan was not mentioned in that connection, adding: "This was natural, for the war with Japan was then in full vigor and the Soviet Union was then neutral in that war."

The Russians pointed out that the Cairo agreement specified the return of Formosa and the Pescadores "to China." Dulles noted that it also mentioned Manchuria and that what it said was "The Republic of China," which was not the Soviet-recognized "Chinese People's Republic." Deadpan, he wrote: "The Government of the United States inquires of the Soviet Union whether it in fact now desires that Manchuria, Formosa, and the Pescadores should be restored to 'The Republic of China.' "

As for Russia's pretended concern about a future offensive military threat from Japan, the note's dry legal language did not fail to make a very sharp point: that the United States certainly was much more concerned about it than Russia, since it "bore the burden of Japan's war of aggression for nearly four years as against six days of Soviet Union belligerency."

When, in spite of all its protests, Russia accepted the American invitation to the treaty conference at San Francisco—an invitation put on a take-it-or-leave-it basis—most people following the treaty progress were surprised. The State Department's professionals were not. They knew that Japan was one of the two great prizes of the postwar world in the struggle between Russia and the United States—the other being Germany. They could not imagine the Soviet Union letting the island empire slip out of reach without fighting to the last.

At approximately the mid-point in the negotiation of the Japanese treaty, Assistant Secretary of State Dean Rusk, then in charge of the Far East, looked back over the steps which had taken place and was struck by the thought that here was a model operation for future American diplomats to study. He considered detaching a foreign service officer to "live" with Dulles just to record the story so that budding statesmen might profit from learning how a master performed. Regretfully he concluded that the process was by then too far advanced to make such a project successful, but it was a tribute to the craftsmanship of the job.

Although Dulles had been thrust on the department, State did not begrudge him his success. It gave him complete co-operation and saw to it that he was detached from all other duties to perform his assigned task. It supplied him with a top-flight career officer, John Allison, as deputy (Allison flew around the world in the interests of the treaty), and wherever Dulles traveled, American Embassy officials were at his beck.

When the show reached San Francisco, it became a team operation. Secretary Acheson called the signals, Dulles carried the ball, and Rusk organized the interference. There was work still to be done.

While most of the free governments went to the conference inclined toward the treaty, many of them had misgivings based on political situations back home. There were groups in every important country opposing the treaty and their influence had to be taken into account. It was important that the United States should understand what these domestic considerations were, and have a chance to offer its suggestions for coping with them. The obverse of this was that some would-be signers had doubts about the constancy of the United States, particularly in the light of Congressional moves which periodically threatened to undo executive action in the foreign policy field. Was America getting them into combined commitments from which it would later withdraw, leaving them unable to carry on against Russia by themselves? Such delegations had to be reassured. The backstage story of San Francisco, never spectacular, was one of patient back-and-forth communication which steeled both sides to the task ahead.

Pilot Operation: Peace with Japan

The over-all result was a remarkable demonstration of how the United States can win response if it accepts its newly achieved responsibilities and applies intelligent leadership to them. It was a diplomatic maneuver in which America seized the initiative and kept always ahead of events. It was hardheaded, based on American interests first because the United States was the responsible power, both in the Pacific war and afterward, and the contributor of her substance to the vanquished; but it was also tactful.

It was imaginative in the execution, for the Russians never got nearer than the sidelines, although they could have had a full partnership in it had they been willing to accept the democratic principle of compromise and majority rule.

Most of all, it was making peace in the open. No major pillar of the peace was erected without a public display of it. Each time Dulles developed a new concept in the treaty making, his procedure was to plumb its appeal with all interested parties, and then to tell the public about it in a major speech or policy statement. This often had the effect of creating political controversy while the public educational process went on. "I believe in open covenants," one of Dulles' aides remarked irritably during one period of troublesome dealing on the reparations question, "but I think they should be secretly arrived at." He was expressing more pique than conviction, because the publicity created additional work. Those who took part in the treaty making conceded that, despite such irritations, the open way gives peace a broader, sounder base.

Dulles met his own deadline in the operation—the one-year limit he had proposed to Acheson. The San Francisco treaty signing ceremony was held one year to the day after he accepted a special commission from President Truman, though the commission was preceded by several months of exploratory work to convince himself the job was possible. Later, when Dulles was appointed Secretary of State, his critics conceded him a good job on the Japanese treaty but pointed out that he had been free to concentrate on the one task. Therefore, they contended, it proved nothing in establishing his ability to handle an administrative position as complex as that at the State Department.

The Japanese treaty assignment was not followed by any other, and after a few months Dulles resigned his consultant's job at State so as to be a completely free agent in the impending campaign.

13

. . . .

The Call from Ike

O<small>N MAY</small> 5, in the presidential campaign year of 1952, Dulles made a speech on Indochina to the French National Political Science Institute in Paris. In it he spoke of "Deterrent power" and the need for fighting the enemy at "times and places of our own choosing." The actual purpose of the trip, however, was not to advocate policies he later adopted as Secretary, but to plumb for himself the mind and personality of the man commanding the North Atlantic Treaty forces, General Dwight D. Eisenhower.

The visit to Eisenhower was suggested to him by Lucius Clay. Dulles, as a Dewey strategist in 1944 and 1948, knew his friend was not a candidate in 1952. Dewey had declared flatly and firmly for Ike in 1950. Taft's foreign policy views, in Dulles' opinion, left a lot to be desired.

Dulles had two long talks with Eisenhower at SHAPE headquarters. Having recently concluded the Japanese peace treaty, Dulles talked to Ike about the Far East; Ike talked about Europe, with whose affairs Dulles had been so intimately connected since Versailles. To his pleasure, he found Ike's views about Europe coincided closely with his own. They agreed on the need for firm opposition to Communism, and on the NATO principle of collective defense; they agreed heartily on the need for promoting Western European unity through the European Defense Community. They both felt it was highly important to keep alive the hope of eventual freedom in the Communist satellite nations.

Dulles returned home feeling committed in his own mind to support Eisenhower against Taft. His friend of Japanese peace treaty days, General Douglas MacArthur, visited him to urge support of Taft, and told Dulles he could be Secretary of State in Taft's Cabinet. Dulles had no such offer from the Ike camp, and he could not tell if MacArthur was speaking with Taft's specific authority, but in any case the offer did not tempt him. He decided that Ike was his man, and he told Herbert Brownell about it.

Brownell and the Ike strategists asked him not to make a public announcement. They wanted him to help draft the foreign policy plank for the Republican platform, and thought he would be more effective if he were not publicly committed.

Dulles was willing, but he felt he should let Taft know where he stood. He made a trip to Washington and had a talk with the senator, informing him that he intended to support Ike but would, at the request of Ike's backers, avoid committing himself and would advise on foreign policy if that was satisfactory to Taft. Taft said it was. Accordingly, arrangements were made, since Dulles was not a delegate, to have him serve as adviser to Senator Eugene Millikin of the platform committee. The arrangement was satisfactory to both sides. He was not involved in the bitter intraparty infighting before and during the convention at Chicago.

The Call from Ike

Foreign policy was the first plank of the Republican platform, following immediately after the preamble. To political laymen it must have seemed a strange example of work for a man dedicated to bipartisan foreign policy. It was a hard-hitting indictment of Democratic administration, containing such vigorous statements as these:

"The present administration, in seven years, has squandered the unprecedented power and prestige which were ours at the close of World War II.

"In that time, more than 500,000,000 non-Russian people of 15 different countries have been absorbed into the power sphere of Communist Russia, which proceeds confidently with its plan for world conquest.

"We charge that the leaders of the administration in power lost the peace so dearly earned by World War II. . . . Communist Russia [has] a military and propaganda initiative which, if unstayed, will destroy us. . . .

"They required the National Government of China to surrender Manchuria. . . . Thus they substituted on our Pacific flank a murderous enemy for an ally and friend. . . .

"In South Korea, they withdrew our occupation troops in the face of the aggressive, poised-for-action Communist military strength on its northern border. . . . With foresight, the Korean war would never have happened. . . ."

There was considerable of the pleading lawyer's extravagance in these statements, and, in the remark about foresight on Korea, what seemed to be a case of 20/20 hindsight. Dulles did have something definite in mind, however, as he later demonstrated when he had to deal with Indochina: the belief that wars come about mainly through miscalculation, and that if the enemy were put squarely on notice what his action would lead to, he would think twice before taking the risk.

The lawyer's right to subordinate personal views to plead a client's case is something understood but not necessarily fully accepted by the lay public. That Dulles, a professed believer in bipartisanship and an adviser under Democratic administrations, should be involved in authorship of so vigorous an attack on Democratic foreign policy was a matter that attracted attention in various quarters, including that of the Washington columnist of *The New Yorker*. "The life of a platform writer is hard and onerous," wrote Richard H. Rovere, pointing out that it was not necessarily a dishonorable job to get two factions of a party to submerge or bypass their differences. A man engaged in such a task, Rovere suggested, should be allowed "a moral discount" when he is clearly speaking for others. On this generous basis, Rovere went on to tell how he had taxed Dulles at Chicago with differences between his own previous utterances and statements in the 1952 platform. Rovere said: "He replied that as an individual he could not [subscribe to some of the statements] but that as a platform writer he was merely stating the Republican case against the Democratic Party, which was committed to the principle of liberation by the Atlantic Charter." He remembered that Dulles added, with respect to the Communist-dominated nations, "They *weren't* liberated, were they?" Rovere's comment reflected the layman's attitude of understanding without accepting: "Of course the facts were on his side."

The lawyer's trait of drawing fine distinctions to explain his advocacy of another's cause is not one that endears him to the other side, and its appearance in Dulles when he began to emerge as a public figure was one quality that tended to build up dislike for him. "When is Dulles Dulles?" Rovere inquired. To those who, like Rovere, had not plumbed the combination of traits embedded in the Dulles character—the moral upbringing with the lawyer's requirement of "getting things done"—the question remained a perplexing one.

After the party platform was adopted, and just prior to Ike's nomination, Dulles declared himself for Eisenhower on one of the numerous spot TV pickups the national networks put on. It was, of course, the endorsement of an individual, a member of the Dewey forces, and one whose position was privately known; it had, therefore, none of the significance of an announcement by a politician controlling a bloc of delegates—such as the decisions of Michigan's Arthur Summerfield and Pennsylvania's Governor John Fine.

During the Republican campaign he made speeches in twenty states, mostly under nonpartisan auspices, although a few were before Republican organizations. Dulles felt that there was not too much point in speaking to Republican groups, already planning to vote for Ike. Nonpartisan meetings presumably attracted some people whose minds were not yet made up and who therefore were open to persuasion.

On election eve he made a speech in Decatur, Illinois, and then took off by air for Duck Island to have a rest. For the first time in his retreats into the island's refreshing solitude he took along a small battery-powered portable radio in order to hear the election returns. Thus he learned Tuesday evening that the Republicans had finally made it after twenty years.

Foster and Janet stayed out the week on the island, and when they returned to New York the President-elect had gone to Augusta, Georgia, for a postcampaign period of rest and golfing. But Lucius

Clay and Herb Brownell called on Dulles immediately, with Eisenhower's offer of the State Department job in the Republican Cabinet.

Dulles had expected the job in 1944. He had almost tasted it in 1948, when everyone believed Dewey was sure to win. This nearness to the office, this quadrennial assumption about Dulles which revived in 1952, built up to myth proportions the popular impression that his one goal in life was that particular office.

The opening words of this book, qualified only by phrasing designed to conceal the writer's reservations, pay tribute to that myth since it had become too formidable to dispose of casually. Like most myths it had foundation in fact; Dulles had, at times, thought of himself as Secretary of State. But it is equally a fact that Dulles was not ambitious for the job per se. His ambition was to achieve a position in which he could apply his own ideas to the job of peace-making—ideas which rejected some past techniques as having proved unsuccessful and which offered some new approaches. He had never really resolved in his own mind that the job of Secretary of State gave him the best opportunity for doing it.

Thus when Ike's victory put the plum within his grasp—in fact, even after he had been offered the job—Dulles still seriously questioned whether it was what he wanted. He did not look on it, as a politician might have, as a reward in itself or possibly as a steppingstone to the Presidency. His career had not been in politics, and his outlook was based on the goals of his career. He wondered if the extra duties of Secretary would prevent him from concentrating on policy making. Analyzing the duties of the Secretary, he found there were fifteen distinct requirements of the job aside from the one of making long-range policy. The memorandum he prepared at the time set them out as follows:

MORE IMPORTANT DUTIES OF SECRETARY OF STATE

(1) Protocol. Meeting, on arrival and departure, foreign Chiefs of State and Foreign Ministers visiting Washington.

(2) Receiving Ambassadors of foreign countries and hearing their statements regarding matters affecting the two countries.

(3) Attending international conferences in connection with UN, NATO, Pacific security, etc., and visiting foreign countries.

(4) Selection of top-level personnel in Department and abroad in foreign missions.

(5) Relations with Congress, receiving Congressmen and testifying before the several Senate and House Committees.

(6) Preparation and delivery of public addresses for self, and for President if dealing with foreign affairs.

(7) Press conferences and private press-radio commentator and like relations.

(8) Consultation with top-level associates, as necessary to maintain Department morale, and seeing U.S. diplomats back on leave or for consultation.

(9) Dinners, receptions and social functions of diplomatic corps and as given by U.S.

(10) Settlement of policies and controversies with independent and co-ordinate agencies, such as Defense, Mutual Security Agency, Treasury, Commerce, Ex-Im Bank, Board of Psychological Strategy (VOA) CIA (positive program), etc.

(11) Approval (initialing) of important outgoing cables and reading important incoming cables and memos of conversations with important personages.

(12) Handling the percentage of correspondence that requires personal attention.

(13) Seeing important private persons who demand and are entitled to see a top official.

(14) Attendance at Cabinet meetings and general White House talks. Briefing and consulting with the President.
(15) Dealing with current crises arising around the globe and calling for immediate reactions.
(16) Making long-range policies.

Under the Truman administration, in legislation intended to unify the armed services into one Department of Defense, a National Security Council had been set up which in practical effect had replaced the President's Cabinet as the top-level policy-making body of the federal government. It seemed to Dulles that the job of executive director of the NSC would be one in which he could devote his energy more single-mindedly to what he wanted to do.

All of this he talked out with Brownell and Clay. "It's only the Secretary's foreign policy function I'm interested in," he told them. "You can have all the rest of it." But in the end he agreed with them that the thing to do was accept the nomination as Secretary.

There were three considerations in the decision. One was that he had no assurance of being able to influence policy effectively through the NSC without risking the possibilities of major conflict with whoever was named Secretary of State. A second was the Clay-Brownell contention that he had more widespread backing from all factions of the Republican party than any other single individual the President might name, and thus his selection would promote party unity. Finally, he recognized that the tradition of the job, its prestige rank abroad, was something he wanted despite what he regarded as its handicaps; that what he said as Secretary, regardless of what it was, would be harkened to simply because he spoke as the official voice of American foreign policy.

Later, looking back from the vantage point of three years in the office, he felt confirmed in his decision. In the spring of 1956 he made a speech to the fiftieth annual meeting of the American Society of International Law on "the institutionalizing of peace." He remarked to a friend at the time: "There is nothing in this speech that I have not believed for a long time. The views are views I have set forth in other speeches and in articles before I became Secretary. But saying them in this capacity gives them a permanence in history."

Having overcome his doubts with Clay and Brownell, Dulles was not surprised that as soon as the President-elect got back to New York he summoned Dulles to the Hotel Commodore, where a preinauguration headquarters had been set up for the incoming administration.

Mr. Eisenhower made the offer official, and Dulles replied he had certain reservations about the job.

"I thought you talked them all out with Clay and Brownell," said Eisenhower.

"I have," replied Dulles, "but I wanted you to know about them."

"Well," said Ike with a grin, "now I know." On that basis it was settled. His appointment led the first batch of the new Cabinet members to be announced, followed by those of General Motors President Charles E. Wilson as Secretary of Defense and Oregon's Governor Douglas McKay as Secretary of the Interior.

14

· · · · · · · ·

Administrative Troubles

DULLES took office with an impressive background for the policy and diplomatic sides of his job, but he was untested as an administrator. The State Department had grown to a vast establishment with 32,000 employees in Washington and in its 290 embassies, legations, consulates general, consulates, and consular offices abroad. It ran a propaganda program which spent $86,000,000 out of its total budget of $240,000,000, and supervised a military and economic foreign-aid program which was then running at the rate of $6,000,000,000 a year.

He smacked head on into a series of difficulties. Some of them stemmed from his distaste for administrative work, but to a larger extent they were inherent in political turnover after twenty years, and in the climate in which it took place.

Employee morale was at a low point to begin with—not only with respect to the civil service workers but the Foreign Service as well. While the Democrats were in power both groups were under attack by Senator McCarthy but they had a feeling of protection in the fact that Secretary Acheson spoke as their defender, and President Truman's policy was not to give Congress access to personnel files. Now that protection was gone, as far as they knew.

The call for "positive loyalty" which Dulles issued on his first day in office, of which we took note in Chapter 1, was the opposite of reassuring. Dulles was not thinking in terms of "McCarthy loyalty," having in mind the need for wholehearted dedication of the department to vigorous American policies as articulated under President Eisenhower's direction. But McCarthy had succeeded in implanting the idea that he had patented the word, and by association the phrase "positive loyalty" conveyed the idea of McCarthy.

In his book, *Eisenhower: The Inside Story*, Robert J. Donovan recounts how Ike entered office much concerned about good relations with Congress. Donovan notes that the question of Congressional relations came up at the first two Cabinet meetings.

After the second Cabinet meeting, Dulles, on return to the State Department, called in the head of the executive secretariat and told him, "By direction of the President, I want you to inform the officers of the department that he wants one hundred per cent co-operation with Congress."

"Does that mean with McCarthy, too?" inquired the chief clerk. "Yes," said Dulles.

As a result, State Department officials down to assistant secretary level were officially notified of the President's wish. But when McCarthy gave evidence that his vendetta with the State Department had not ended with the change in administration, Dulles was the first Cabinet officer to tangle with him.

The relative naïveté of the new administration was illustrated by the fact that virtually the first piece of legislation asked of Congress by President Eisenhower was a bill providing the Secretary of State with two undersecretaries instead of one. The incumbent was to be retained as No. 2 man in the department for the political side of foreign affairs, and the new man was to handle administration—the routine appointments, budget problems, and other housekeeping details. Ike asked for the additional official because Dulles wanted it, and Dulles wanted it because he believed it would free him of much of the non-policy aspects of his job.

In theory it should be possible to find a man capable of handling an administrative job of this type, but the bureaucratic and personal rivalries inherent in government operations make it all but impossible to make practice fit theory. The man chosen for administrative undersecretary was Don Lourie, of Chicago, president of the Quaker Oats Company. Lourie was a friendly, personable man, but totally inexperienced in the ways of government. One of his duties was to oversee departmental security. Lourie asked one of his Chicago neighbors if he knew anyone in Washington he might pick for the job of security chief. It happened the neighbor knew two people in Washington. One of these Lourie hired—Robert Walter Scott McLeod, a one-time Iowa newspaperman who had later worked for the FBI in New Hampshire and subsequently joined the staff of New Hampshire's senior senator, Styles Bridges, in Washington. It may seem incredible that Lourie happened so casually on a man who turned out to be identified with the McCarthy wing of the Republican party, but that is the way it came about.

McLeod's background was good qualification in Lourie's eyes because he firmly believed the new administration needed someone to make a critical examination of the department's personnel from the security standpoint, and it seemed likely to keep McCarthy and his allies off the department's neck if someone in McCarthy's confidence was in charge. The compound of suspicion and appeasement in this assessment was typical of the attitude of the whole Eisenhower administration when it first took office. Dulles, for example, was quoted by State Department officers as having said: "I'm not going to be caught with another Alger Hiss on my hands."

McLeod attacked his job with what might charitably be called an excess of zeal. His men discovered, for example, that members of the department's policy-planning staff were receiving copies of the Communist newspaper, the *Daily Worker*. They questioned staff secretaries to learn what officers were represented by the initials on the list to which it was circulated. Reading Communist publications is, of course, an essential job for anyone seeking to follow the twists and flipflops of the party line, and especially so for a group charged with advising on formulation of policy to combat it. Had McLeod's men invaded the Secretary's office they would have found not only Stalin's *Problems of Leninism* within reach of Dulles' desk, but numerous other pertinent writings and speeches by Soviet figures. Dulles had devoted one entire chapter of his book, *War or Peace,* to the high importance of "knowing your enemy." But Communist publications were not the only target of McLeod's underlings. When they began inquiring which members of the planning staff read the *Reporter,* a non-Communist liberal periodical, the staff chairman, Robert Bowie, protested to Undersecretary Walter Bedell Smith, who put a stop to it.

The Eisenhower administration was engaged during that initial period in conducting FBI recheck of the entire government working force and at the same time making heavy reductions in personnel in all departments for budgetary reasons. At the State Department, "RIF" (for reduction in force) separations occurred simultaneously with loyalty and security separations. The availability of RIF procedure was a weapon in the hands of McLeod and his men for use in cases where they were threatened with frustration in security cases. How many individuals were done injustice in the process is something known only to the men in charge of the personnel records. The effect was to make a shambles of morale for several months. The London *Economist* commented in a report from Washington: "A McLeod, considerably bigger than a man's hand, hangs over the State Department."

McLeod's soaring zeal was quenched only after he tried to interfere in the appointment of Charles E. ("Chip") Bohlen as ambassador to Moscow. His move aroused the highest echelons of the Foreign Service, which resented the fact that it had been put under the authority of an outsider, and posed a question whose answer was nervously watched by foreign diplomats: were McCarthy standards to guide selection of the men sent to represent the United States abroad?

McLeod, with information which by his standards he considered derogatory to Bohlen, went over Dulles' head to the White House with his protest. He cooled off after learning from a close aide of the President's that Bohlen, who had been a golfing partner of Ike's at SHAPE headquarters in Paris, was Ike's personal selection for the job. McLeod's explanation was: "I just wanted to be sure they knew what they were doing."

McLeod's insubordination was so flagrant that Dulles spent one whole evening discussing what to do about it with several advisers he called to his home. Still undecided next morning, he was skimming the papers when he ran across a story about the Bohlen case in the Washington *Times Herald* containing information which could only have come from McLeod. Dulles went to work feeling the proper course was to fire McLeod. The only thing that saved him was the fact that Undersecretary "Beedle" Smith dropped in to see Dulles that morning before McLeod arrived at the department, and argued Dulles out of taking the action on the ground that it would embarrass the new administration to fire so quickly a man who in his opinion should not have been hired in the first place.

McLeod, though he never knew how close he had come to being bounced, realized he had to take other judgments than his own into account. Eventually he got a new perspective on his job and did well supervising the refugee relief program through an operating deputy.

Sometime later there was a similar flurry when it was learned that derogatory information had been filed to prevent the nomination of Mrs. Mildred McAfee Horton, wartime chief of the Navy's WAVES, as U.S. representative to one of the United Nations bodies. The circumstances were different, however; in Mrs. Horton's case the determining consideration was the fact that the deadline for the appointment was too short to give her adequate time to answer satisfactorily questions raised about various of her associations, though in Dulles' absence Undersecretary Smith himself vouched for her loyalty. There was no such deadline in Bohlen's case, and the Administration was prepared to fight it out.

McLeod was not involved, however, in the more spectacular cases involving career officials John Carter Vincent, John Paton Davies,

George Kennan, and Paul Nitze. The cases of Vincent and Davies were holdovers from the Truman administration, when both had undergone loyalty investigations. Vincent's case had gone through all stages except final decision by the Secretary when Dulles took office; Davies' case, while well advanced, was acted on later. In both instances the Secretary ruled against the officers, forcing their retirement on pension. In both cases he insisted on reading the voluminous record himself, rather than accepting summaries prepared for him, before acting.

George Kennan's case did not involve loyalty or security considerations. He had been the last Truman ambassador to Moscow, recalled after objections by the Soviet government to his continuance in the post. One-time chairman of the policy-planning staff, he had articulated the so-called "containment" policy of the Truman administration toward the Soviet Union. As such he was a psychological liability to an administration which proclaimed that "containment" was too static a policy and was on record as favoring a policy of "liberation."

Kennan might have been offered another foreign assignment had he not made a speech at Scranton, Pennsylvania, in which he cautioned the government against doing anything official that purported to affect the governmental system in another country. At approximately the same time Dulles, in testimony before a Congressional committee, was contending that the United States should use moral pressure and the weight of propaganda to weaken the Soviet hold on its satellites. It was a demonstration of quite different philosophies as to the course the government should pursue, and although Kennan informed Dulles by way of explanation that he prepared his speech without knowledge of the Secretary's testimony, it illustrated a frame of mind which Dulles considered of little use in the new scheme of things.

As a career minister awaiting reassignment, Kennan was in and out of Washington during this period. Each time he came back he found he had been shifted to a different office in which to work. It was after Stalin's death and he ranked as the No. 1 "Russian expert" because of his training in the service, but no one consulted him officially. A Foreign Service officer not reassigned within a specified period automatically is retired, and this is what happened to Kennan.

Paul Nitze, who had succeeded Kennan as chairman of the policy-planning staff, was an independently well-to-do official whose brains Dulles wanted to retain in the government. Since he had been a key official in the Acheson administration, it was decided to use him in another job. One of the Defense Department's retiring officials recommended him to Secretary Charles E. Wilson to do policy planning for the Pentagon. This was satisfactory to the Administration, but the shift aroused the opposition of McCarthy and others on Capitol Hill.

All these cases of prominent officers contained elements of unwillingness on their part to accept higher level decisions on policy with which they did not agree. Kennan's speech brought the issue out in the open with respect to his own case. Nitze's differences remained a family secret, but were no less pronounced.

Dulles had entered office hoping that the two big operating functions of the department could be divorced from it so as to confine State more purely to its policy and diplomatic functions. The old Mutual Security Administration was turned into an independent Foreign Operations Administration under Harold Stassen, and the former information program was given autonomy as the United States Information Agency under Theodore Streibert, in both cases under State Department policy guidance. Nitze believed it would dilute foreign affairs authority to set up such activities—specifically the foreign-aid function—outside State. In meetings of the National Security Council staff Nitze argued against it.

In April, 1953, when Ike was preparing the basic foreign policy pronouncement which he embodied in his speech to the American Society of Newspaper Editors on April 16, the President transmitted the third draft (out of eleven which the speech went through) to Winston Churchill for his information. The British Prime Minister replied with a number of suggestions to the effect that Ike was being tough on certain points that called for flexibility, and fuzzy on points where he should be tough. Dulles was out of reach at Duck Island, and Nitze was summoned to a meeting which discussed Churchill's suggestions. In general, he supported the Churchill argument. Ike remarked, "That's not what I've been hearing from your boss." Nitze replied, "Perhaps not, sir, but you asked my opinion and I gave it to you." Nitze, after one week at Defense, quit in disgust over the White House attitude toward right-wing attempts on Capitol Hill to get rid of him.

To a degree it was such attitudes, more than questions of loyalty or security, which basically also tipped the scales against Vincent and Davies. Critics complained that by these "firings" of prominent officers the new administration was demanding slavish, unquestioned obedience of its slightest whims. This was not the case. Dulles did feel the serious need for having his high-ranking officers thoroughly behind his basic policies; he expected intelligent criticism in the formulation of decisions, but he could not brook continued opposition based on a frame of mind which, for one reason or another, was unwilling to accept that the men newly put in charge of policy were entitled to try new operating methods and stand or fall on the result.

McCarthy's influence on the department, while reflected for some time in McLeod's initial approach to his job, was surprisingly ineffective considering the fact that as a result of the Republican victory he had been elevated to chairmanship of the investigating committee in which he conducted his celebrated TV probe of the Army in 1954. For several months the President's White House advisers sought to avoid either outright appeasement or head-on clash in coping with McCarthy, and his influence atrophied in the face of responsible handling of executive authority. During this period McCarthy clashed directly with the State Department in two instances.

The first concerned the information program, presided over by a Dulles-selected official, Dr. Robert Johnson, president of Temple University. McCarthy had discovered that books by Communist or Communist-line authors were on USIS bookshelves around the world, and he set up a hue and cry about it. Johnson's reaction was to order removal of the books, a move done with so abject an air that at least one USIS overseas office literally burned the proscribed volumes, raising memories of the Nazi "book burning" during Hitler's regime. Dulles was drawn into the controversy at a press conference and was obviously at a loss for adequate explanation.

"I thought I had appointed someone to take care of things like this," he remarked testily to aides afterward. It was a practical lesson in the difficulties of delegating administrative authority and a reminder that the head man remains responsible for the blame in any case. Eventually the controversy petered out, partly as the result of the creation of an independent USIA under Theodore Streibert and partly because some of the authors whose works were involved showed up to disadvantage in Congressional hearings by invoking the Fifth Amendment in refusing to answer questions about Communist affiliation.

The other McCarthy incident occurred when the senator announced one day in March, 1953, that he had accomplished something the State Department had been unable to do. He said he had "negotiated" an agreement with Greek shipowners to keep their ships from carrying goods to Communist ports in the Far East. Then he summoned Stassen for testimony on free world-Communist trade. Stassen, describing the efforts by which the U.S. government had made agreements in consultations with the governments of Greece, Great Britain, France, and other countries, which effectively restricted trade with Communist China, accused McCarthy of having "undermined" the government's objectives. McCarthy demanded an appointment with Dulles; the Secretary invited him to luncheon.

What was said between the two was never publicly revealed. Actually Dulles did nothing more drastic than to quote the senator a few pertinent passages out of George Washington's Farewell Address—passages warning against usurpation of constitutional functions and advising that commercial relations with foreign nations have as little political connection as possible. Incredible as it might seem that these mild words tamed the fire-eating Joe McCarthy, the fact was that Joe joined in a "communiqué" issued after the luncheon which noted the "dangers that would result if Congressional committees entered into the field of foreign relations, which is the exclusive jurisdiction of the Chief Executive." The statement went on to say that McCarthy agreed that if he uncovered information in future about ships which were circumventing the government's trade restrictions he would promptly communicate with the "proper authorities." With that, McCarthy walked out of the State Department's life.

Sidestepping McCarthy with a minimum of notice was, after all, a considerable achievement of tact in view of White House uncertainty about how to deal with the senator. The essential deftness of this performance, however, was more than offset by the fact that administratively and diplomatically the new Secretary seemed to be in hot water all the time.

Washington had not grasped the fact that the new crowd did not feel under compunction to follow the same standards as the old; nor that it was not as timid about expressing itself in public to foreign governments. Neither had Washington adjusted itself to the fact that Dwight D. Eisenhower did not react to newspaper uproar about his Cabinet members as Franklin D. Roosevelt did about his; therefore, the question most frequently asked about Dulles by the government-wise hands during the first three months was based on judgments they did not realize were outmoded. The question was: "Who is going to replace Dulles?" It was not: "Will Ike fire Dulles?" That was assumed. The important point for the "insider" was to learn who would be the new Secretary.

The judgment habits of sixteen years built up under President Roosevelt tended to mislead not only Washington observers but foreign governments. Careless or too-literal press interpretations of supposed foreign policy differences between the President and his chief diplomatic technician led foreign offices, as well as the

American public, to conclude that the President was a more reasonable man than his Secretary.

There was a certain basis for this belief. When he was drawn out at press conferences on foreign policy subjects, Ike sometimes had not considered them in such detail as Dulles, and he was by habit less articulate and less precise in his speech. Besides, Ike's basic desire to be friendly with everyone tended to make him speak more softly than Dulles, who often had to calculate his speech in terms of what he judged would produce results abroad.

This difference in tone was particularly noted during Ike's illnesses, when it seemed that the United States talked tough as long as Ike was in the hospital and soft when he resumed direction of the government. It led some to the totally erroneous conclusion that Dulles was seeking to take foreign policy off on his own when Ike was not around to hold him back, and that Ike had to restrain him on return. The fact is that Dulles operated with an acute sense of the constitutional authority of the President in foreign affairs, and Ike reciprocated with complete admiration for the technical skill of his chief subordinate.

But the idea persisted that Ike was more pliable than Foster, and essentially this thought was behind the visit to Washington in January, 1956, of British Prime Minister Sir Anthony Eden: Dulles was being stubborn about a number of pet British projects, such as the desire to bring the United States into adherence to the Baghdad Pact, and letting Communist China into the United Nations. The British request for a conference was based on the thought that perhaps if Eden could present his arguments directly to the President, in person, without filtering them through Dulles, Ike would see reason. Like other such efforts, it brought a rude awakening.

Ike bluntly told Eden, for example, that if Britain thought the United States was going to support Communist China, he should know that the Peking government's admittance to the UN would be followed immediately by a Senate resolution (1) to withdraw the United States from UN membership and (2) to invite the UN to get physically out of the United States.

Understanding between the President and the Secretary grew stronger the more they worked together. Ike was outspoken on numerous occasions in praising Dulles' handling of his foreign policy problems—and he invariably knew more about the factors that went into the judgments than did Dulles' critics.

Likewise the internal administrative roughness of the Dulles State Department inevitably wore smooth in time. The bureaucrat's major dread is the dread of change. The incumbent boss, no matter how tough he may be on his employee, is a known quantity. Unless his ruthlessness rivals that of Ivan the Terrible, the average employee prefers the comparative certainty of knowing how he will react to the comparative uncertainty of how the new boss will react. But in time the unknown becomes known and is accepted. Such acceptance can take place even if the new administration is not as efficient as the old. In the case of the Dulles State Department, administrative operations at no time were as smooth as under Dean Acheson. The Dulles make-up was not geared to placid, up-from-the-bottom administration. But it was capable of acceptance and of effectiveness.

At the outset Dulles felt uncertain of himself, as well as of the department, for a simple and understandable reason: he did not feel sure he knew everything that was going on in the vast department. It was unsettling, for example, to find on his desk a proposed minor treaty which had been under negotiation for months and was being submitted for his final approval before being transmitted to the White House and the Senate for the ratification process. While he might not find anything objectionable about the treaty, such incidents increased his feeling that activities were in progress of which he was not aware. He corrected this kind of situation by circulating all hands with notice that whenever work began on a treaty he wanted to be informed of the fact. He also ordered careful study first to determine whether the subject matter really deserved treaty handling or could be covered in some less formal fashion. In connection with his study of the German situation he learned there was no compilation of all existing treaties with Germany; it took the department about two months to bring them all together. By such moves, but more through the mere passage of time and routine absorption of knowledge about the manifold business that necessarily had to originate below him, he gained confidence in himself as administrator and in the men who were working for him.

15

• • • • • • • •

Life in an Airplane

IT WAS less than ten days after he assumed office that John Foster Dulles took off on his first transatlantic trip by air. President Eisenhower had wanted him to visit Europe between election and inauguration, but Dulles postponed it on the ground that his first task was to put together an official team at the State Department. The initial European trip ushered in a series of air journeyings around the world which acquired such a hectic pace they intruded on the public consciousness and led to humorous and sometimes derisive comments on what seemed to be a travel mania of the unusual individual who had become Secretary of State.

At one of the dinners of Washington's exclusive newspaper club, the Gridiron, members put on a skit depicting a meeting of the Joint Chiefs of Staff at Washington Airport—the only spot where they could nab Foster for conference between trips. Dulles, winging in from Asia, came onstage wearing an aviator's antigravity suit and a space helmet; after disposing of the Joint Chiefs' problems, he emplaned for Europe. The satire was not too farfetched, and Dulles enjoyed it as much as anyone present.

The fact remains that Dulles traveled farther, visited more countries, and personally got to know more world statesmen well than any other diplomat in history. Each trip had a definite purpose: fact finding on the original trips to Europe and the Middle East and when he went on through Southeast Asia after the 1956 SEATO conference at Karachi; or knitting together the threads of some specific policy, as in the case of his hurried shuttling to Europe and back in the effort to win acceptance of EDC, Western European union, and unity of action on Indochina. Behind them, too, was the firm conviction that you can get infinitely more results out of face-to-face discussion with a man, talking candidly about your problems, taking his measure and grasping how his mind operates, than you can learn in a year of exchanging cables. "Nowadays," Dulles said on a TV broadcast when asked about his travels by a member of Congress, "when you can by overnight flight talk face to face with the foreign ministers of other countries, it's silly to go at it the old-fashioned way of exchanging notes, which take a month, perhaps, before you get as good an understanding, and not then as good as you can get by talking a few minutes face to face. I don't think we'll ever go back to the old-fashioned way."

A good illustration of this came not long after he had made this TV appearance. Dulles had gone to Panama with President Eisenhower to attend the meeting of American presidents, and continued on to two other South American capitals. While he was in Lima, Peru, Egyptian President Nasser seized the Suez Canal. The British and French wanted Dulles to fly immediately to London to take part in a conference; Dulles declined, but assigned Deputy Undersecretary Robert Murphy to represent the United States. Dulles returned from Lima at 12:10 P.M. on a Sunday, without any plans to go to London. The following Tuesday, overnight cables from Murphy made it plain that Britain and France were bent on headlong use of force, a course which Dulles thought was ill-advised. He went over to the White House to talk with Ike about the situation. The President decided it was necessary, after all, for Dulles himself to go over. Returning to the State Department at 11:30 A.M., Dulles alerted two officials—Legal Adviser Herman Phleger and Assistant Secretary Carl McCardle—and two members of his personal staff that they would be leaving for London at 2:00 P.M.

Dulles himself did not have time to pack, and Mrs. Dulles was at the hairdresser's, getting a shampoo and set because she was planning to entertain Dame Pattie Menzies, wife of the Australian Prime Minister, at luncheon next day. Eric, the Dulles butler-valet, packed for the Secretary. At 1:58 P.M. his airplane—borrowed from Defense Secretary Wilson for the trip—lifted its wheels from Washington Airport. Despite all the speed, the secretariat arranged the thousand and one details that an international conference requires—all but one. They couldn't find the "bed board," a board Dulles used under his mattress for spinal support. It turned out that someone had left it in Panama.

Between Washington and the lone stop at Argentia, Newfoundland, Dulles drafted a document which with only slight editing became the communiqué issued by the three powers two days later. He spent two nights in the air, two days and one night in London, and was back in Washington a few minutes under seventy hours from the time he had left, knowing that, whatever happened at Suez, he had bought at least two weeks' time in the struggle to avert a military clash—for the communiqué had postponed action until after an international conference.

Anyone who flies as far as 559,988 miles is bound to encounter some dangerous moments, but because of the supersafety precautions which are followed by Military Air Transport Service for VIP's, they were relatively few for Dulles. On his way back from the Geneva Foreign Ministers' Meeting in November, 1955, he and Mrs. Dulles were eating breakfast in their cabin when a piece of metal broke off one of the engines, struck the window beside them and cracked the glass. The Constellation continued to Bermuda on three engines and, since the window had a double thickness of glass, the cabin pressure was maintained. On a Far Eastern trip his plane had to make three passes at the field before being able to land safely at Taipeh. On the same trip, arriving in Laos, his airplane had to be kept circling for some time while water buffaloes were shooed off the landing strip at Vientiane. Once he woke up at night to find himself suspended horizontally in the air, as if by levitation. The plane had hit an air pocket.

For official trips of the Secretary of State the Air Force provided a plush Connie. Sometimes it was President Eisenhower's airplane, the *Columbine III*. If that was busy, it often was the *Dew Drop,* famous for having been prepared in 1948 for Thomas E. Dewey, in anticipation of his election, as a replacement for President Truman's DC6, the *Independence*. A mustache cup, presented by Truman, is exhibited with an appropriate plaque under glass in the *Dew Drop's* cabin as a satirical comment on the Air Force's election judgment.

Life in an Airplane

The official State Department party generally consisted of ten, including the Secretary's top aides for the area being visited, his confidential assistant, his chief secretary, and Mrs. Dulles. Janet Dulles skipped only a few of Foster's trips. Though her husband's transportation charges were paid for out of departmental travel appropriations, her fare was paid for personally by the Secretary.

The State Department secretariat, bearing in mind the personal idiosyncrasies of an incumbent Secretary, generally assists the Air Force in stocking the airplane with appropriate provender. Dulles was understood to like having peanuts around to nibble; in flight, stewards have been known to put peanuts in front of him as early as nine o'clock in the morning. He usually ate a Spartan luncheon, generally an apple and cottage cheese salad, so this also was an item —but he concluded that thoughtfulness was being carried too far after cottage cheese salad was put on the menu for dinner, too. For two years after he started his travels a bottle of Johnnie Walker red label was always put in his cabin before the start of each trip, even though it always came back unopened. The bottle traveled the equivalent of ten trips around the world before a newsman informed the secretariat that the Secretary preferred rye or bourbon, anyway, ahead of Scotch, and that he was carrying his own bottle.

In flight his practice was to change to slacks, sweater, and carpet slippers as soon as the craft got aloft and settle down to work conferring with his aides or dictating to his secretary. But he knocked off business for dinner, which was always completely social. He generally joined the rest of the party in cocktails beforehand, having a rye on the rocks, topped with a little water, which he stirred with his index finger. Dinner conversation was light and easy. Perhaps because he ate and drank lightly, his stomach seemed to adjust to overnight changes of six hours in eating schedules, and his brain to the difference of sleeping times on the two sides of the Atlantic, better than most of his fellow travelers'.

One of the oddities of being a high government official is that you don't need to carry money around. Dulles developed the habit of going without ready cash because he found he had no call to spend it. Plane fares were taken care of by vouchers signed by subordinates; there were never any porters to tip because his security men saw to his luggage. He never had to shell out taxi fare because an official limousine was always waiting for him; there was never a hotel bill or a luncheon check to pay. He was never even asked to show his diplomatic passport, No. 2, but on his first trip to Japan as Secretary he insisted on presenting it and getting it stamped to emphasize symbolically to the Japanese his respect for their independence as a result of the treaty he negotiated.

One of the secrets of his amazing stamina which allowed him to take the punishment of heavy travel and changed eating and working hours without visible effect was Dulles' ability to relax as completely as he concentrated. At the office or on a diplomatic trip his mind was constantly on his work. But just as he knocked off for a pleasant, social dinner aboard the airplane, he pulled down a curtain on work in Washington when he left the office. He may have had reason to return to work, at home later in the evening, but he invariably relaxed before and during dinner.

No matter how crowded his schedule, he invariably took time for a private chat with his wife before the evening meal. Even if he was scheduled to attend an official stag dinner he took the time to drive home and see Janet for a few minutes first. Usually the two went out to dinner together, or entertained at home or officially, for the Secretary's social duties are heavy. And when he finally got into bed he had a stack of paperback detective stories for light reading to clear his mind of official worries before he went to sleep.

Another trick of relaxation was to soak in a warm tub for about ten minutes after he got home. Two members of his staff learned about this habit when he reached Paris on his first official visit. They needed some information from him for a cable they were drafting to Washington, and since he had left for Ambassador Dillon's residence to get ready for an official dinner, they followed him there.

On arrival they were told the Secretary was in his bedroom, changing to black tie. They knocked on his door and heard a muffled voice telling them to come in. They entered, but found no one inside. From the bathroom the voice directed them: "In here."

Solemnly they entered the bathroom. There they found the Secretary of State stretched out full length in the tub, his arms folded across his chest as if he were Edward the Confessor posing for his tombstone in Westminster Abbey. Deadpan they asked their questions; with equal gravity he replied, and they left him to finish his relaxing soak. He was not a man for diplomatic "side."

He concentrated as completely as he relaxed—sometimes with disconcerting effect. Once during the negotiations leading up to the Korean truce, a conference was being held in his office. As talk proceeded, he reached over to pull the wastebasket near his chair, and taking a penknife out of his pocket, leaned back and began to sharpen a pencil. He seemed completely absorbed by the task, wheeling around occasionally to blow the shavings off his vest into the wastebasket. But suddenly he interrupted with a suggestion which showed he had followed the whole discussion most carefully.

Without his penknife he used to feel that something was missing. He contemplatively whittled many a pencil down to a stub while listening to Molotov in four-power meetings—an action which Molotov found quite irritating.

At the Geneva Foreign Ministers' Meeting of 1955 he had another reaction to Molotov's long propaganda screeds. The conference was being held under the "simultaneous and consecutive" translation systems, meaning that as Molotov spoke in Russian, interpreters were rendering his words in English and French over the earphones; but periodically the Russian paused so that his own translator, Oleg Troyanovsky, could make a consecutive translation into English. Dulles developed the habit of listening to the earphone account of what Molotov was saying, holding a receiver up to one ear rather than putting on the headset. Then, when Troyanovsky took over, Dulles put down the earphone, shut the words out of his consciousness, and turned his attention to a folder of the nonconference business of the State Department which was always pressing on him. He seemed to have no difficulty turning his mind from one to the other.

It would be too much to expect, however, that his mind never wandered while he was concentrating or relaxing. He quickly became bored when, during business hours, he was confronted with something he considered unimportant. One day he was being briefed by a staff group when he buzzed for his secretary. She entered the room and said, "Yes, sir?" He inquired, "Do I need a haircut?" She looked him over critically and replied that she would make an appointment with Charley, the barber who cuts hair for busy men by appointment and who also cut Acheson's hair. Dulles habitually relied on his wife or secretary to remind him that his hair needed trimming. The nonplused briefing officers lamely concluded their task and withdrew as quickly as possible.

Regardless of the tightness of his schedule, Dulles was never too busy to attend to personal and family amenities. The same quality of attention to the little niceties which caused him to present his passport in Japan for stamping also caused him to take the time to attend funerals of State Department employees, including that of a long-time messenger; to call personally on his secretary, Miss Phyllis Bernau, when she was in the hospital; and to drive to Richmond, Virginia, when the daughter of Assistant Secretary Walter S. Robertson was married. The solicitude which caused him to make sure he and Janet had a few minutes alone each day extended also to such things as picking out her birthday and anniversary presents personally—a task some busy men leave to their secretaries —and arranging for cake and champagne. Despite the primitive communication from and to his island, he went to the trouble one year of sending his sister a birthday wire while he was vacationing there.

His sister Eleanor, an expert on Germany and on economics, had been working for the State Department for some years when, at the start of the Korean War, she was transferred to the National Production Authority. By the time of the Truman-Eisenhower interregnum the economy was taking in stride the needs of the armed forces and the agency was headed for its windup. Eleanor happened to mention to her brother that she wanted to go back to the State Department. Somewhat to her surprise he remarked that he would do nothing to help her. She promptly went to work to get transferred before he took office. Dulles was not sensitive to criticism, generally speaking, except when he thought it might have some justified basis other than difference of opinion, and he felt he might be open to the charge of nepotism despite her previous record with the department. But since she was back on the payroll by the time he had charge of it, he let the reappointment stand. Professionally she had as much difficulty seeing the Secretary as any of his subordinates, having to go through his staff for a claim on his time, but socially she saw him once a week on the average. Foster and Janet might dine with her one weekend or invite her over the next. The Secretary saw more of his brother Allen, of course, since as head of the Central Intelligence Agency Allen had frequent official business with the department and often was invited to the same official social functions.

Dulles did not see a great deal of his eldest son, since John Watson Foster, the engineer, lived in Mexico with his family. But each time he went to New York he tried to arrange for dinner with his daughter Lillias. His younger son Avery, a Jesuit priest, sometimes visited him in Washington. When Dulles made a speech before a Jesuit audience he asked Avery to read it beforehand and make comments; in June, 1956, when Avery was being ordained, the Secretary was devoting the weekend to preparation of an important foreign policy speech and he moved operations to New York so that he could attend the ceremony.

Many have been unable to understand how Avery, coming from a Presbyterian family, could have become a Catholic and a Jesuit without straining family ties. At Harvard some of Avery's classmates, making a cruel pun of his name, called him "a very dull ass."

Life in an Airplane

Avery was anything but dull; he was a student of exceptional brilliance with a strongly philosophical turn of mind. Some members of the family believe that his college experiences and companions, followed by a long period of hospitalization when, as a wartime naval ensign, he was recovering from an attack of polio, led him introspectively to his independent conclusion. Avery's decision to train for the Jesuit priesthood was, of course, a surprise to his parents, but it did not result in strained relations. The Dulles clan had always felt closely knit as a family, and had tolerance for intellectual differences.

16

· · · · · · · ·

The Unpopular Man

O F THE sixteen duties of the Secretary of State which Dulles listed at the time he was considering his role in the Eisenhower regime, all but one were official or semiofficial. The lone exception was No. 7—"press conferences and private press-radio commentator and like relations." There is nothing in the government manuals requiring a Cabinet member to hold press conferences. Some hold fewer than others—Ike's first Secretary of Health, Education, and Welfare, Oveta Culp Hobby, held the record for avoiding press conferences up to the time she left—but all are forced to deal with the problem of public relations either directly or indirectly through aides.

Dulles worked harder at this job than any of his colleagues. He held more public press conferences, which were open to any accredited U.S. or foreign correspondent, including the representatives of TASS, the official Russian government news agency. He also provided more private guidance sessions for U.S. correspondents. As we have seen, he had past experience with public relations in such episodes as the Commission on a Just and Durable Peace and the Japanese treaty negotiations. Newsmen who got acquainted with him in those days found him an excellent source of news and guidance but only when they took the initiative. His own system of dealing with the positive aspects of it was making speeches. In analyzing his needs on this score as Secretary, he decided he needed a newspaperman to help him, and he selected his best friend in the Washington press corps, Carl W. McCardle, to serve as Assistant Secretary of State for Public Affairs.

McCardle had been a top-flight correspondent for the Philadelphia *Bulletin,* with wide experience in international reporting. He became acquainted with Dulles at the San Francisco Conference of 1945 at which the United Nations was founded. The friendship which began there continued at other conferences where Dulles was adviser and McCardle was covering as a newsman, particularly the Moscow Four-Power Conference of 1947, when George Marshall was Secretary. Each nation used a briefing officer to inform its own correspondents of the ministerial sessions. The American briefer was Chip Bohlen. His instructions limited him to telling the correspondents only the bare facts of what was taking place, without intepretation as to meaning, without color, without going behind the scenes. To flesh out the bare bones they were getting officially, individual newsmen cultivated other delegation members. Dulles and McCardle developed the habit of walking the streets together while they talked about the conference, incidentally taking in such sights of Moscow as Lenin's tomb. The close association that developed between them, which continued through the Japanese treaty-making phase, was not generally known to McCardle's colleagues. Because of this, McCardle's selection was a surprise to the Washington press corps. They were accustomed to assistant secretaries who were more in the diplomatic mold.

McCardle brought two valuable qualities to the job: (1) a newsman's outlook on the public's right to have the news within the limits of national interest and (2) the personal confidence of his chief. Dulles relied on him completely in the handling of press and radio. As a result of the sound basic belief of the Secretary in telling the public what he was undertaking to do, and a shrewd knack in McCardle for picking the ways to do it, the State Department's business was explained to the public more fully than ever before.

Curiously, although scientific poll sampling of public opinion over the intervening period showed an upswing and steady maintenance of public support for Dulles and the U. S. State Department, this did not endear Dulles to the Washington press corps. Usually the reporters dote on the man who makes news for them, and Dulles made more news, publicly and in private guidance sessions, than any other Cabinet member. But most of the large group who write about foreign affairs, and the smaller group who cover the department's doings more intensively from day to day, developed a cordial dislike of Dulles. A small minority of both regarded him favorably.

The explanation of this phenomenon was partly personal and partly symbolic. With some it reflected personal pique. One correspondent who had been able to get Dean Acheson on the phone when necessary found that with Dulles his calls were shunted to McCardle, and McCardle was not always agreeable to putting him through to the Secretary. With some it reflected failure to dig into

Dulles motivations and discover what objectives he was working for; the habit in some of placing Dulles moves against the background of Acheson operating methods caused them to misinterpret and misunderstand what was going on. With some it was emotional, resulting from personal feelings about the department's handling of loyalty and security cases. One radio commentator, Eric Sevareid of CBS, became so incensed over the firing of his personal friend John Paton Davies that he demoted the Secretary in his broadcasts by disposing of him as "J. F. Dulles."

The dislike could not be attributed to poor social relations. Dulles met with newsmen for off-the-record dinners far oftener than did Acheson. Acheson was polished and one of the most urbane of men; Dulles was a man of vast, controlled intellectual energy; but both were capable of friendly social conversation with newsmen. Dulles did not find it the least embarrassing or inhibiting to sit down at the dinner table with E. Sevareid or with anyone else who criticized him in print or on the air. He was not, as we noted, sensitive to criticism based on difference of opinion; he defended his own viewpoint with logic and vigor and managed to bear up if someone disagreed with him. Once when an aide told him the *New York Times* had a column condemning about every aspect of his foreign policy, Dulles brushed him off with "I couldn't care less."

The more general explanation was that Dulles, more than any predecessor, personified U.S. foreign policy, and there are usually about as many ideas about what the United States should do in its foreign relations as there are men writing about it. In the field of domestic affairs people accept the fact that the Democrats cannot do everything they would like because there may be strong Republican opposition, and vice versa; in foreign affairs there is not the same conception of the frustrations of international politics. Does Eisenhower want flexible farm price supports? People understand that because the opposition wants rigid supports the President has to accept something else. Does a British-Greek dispute over Cyprus threaten the stability of NATO? Editorial writers tend to look at it from afar as something that can be settled by having Britain turn Cyprus over to Greece. Frustration is never popular, and frustration is the rule rather than the exception in free world dealing with allies, where results must come by common consent and not by vote of a governing body. The State Department is never popular, and when the head man becomes the personification of it, the dislike of those who want to do things differently centers easily on him.

One element in the dislike we noted in a previous chapter: people don't cotton to the legal mind in action on problems involving emotional reactions. Dulles took office with the brand of the corporation lawyer on him, and "corporation lawyers are twice as crooked as the other kind," one State Department official solemnly told his fellows at the time.

Probably more telling, however, was the fact that Dulles was a dedicated man, and such individuals are not easy to understand or deal with. His ambition was complete when he achieved the office. He was not seeking to please politicians or get a good press in order to ingratiate himself for further advancement. He had an acute sense of pleasing the people necessary to his plans for getting things done—Congress, and his boss, the President—but primarily his conduct as Secretary cocked an eye toward the moral judgment of history. His days were incredibly busy, and he had to have a sense of what was important and what was not. Also, while his stock was sturdy American and his upbringing genteel, he lacked the kind of prestige attached to being born to the purple of a *Mayflower* name in American society, so that in one sense he was a self-made man with some of the rough edges of one who perforce has had to assert himself to get recognition. This element may account for the persistent feeling in some that he was vain. The quality might more precisely be described as a combination of pride and self-confidence; his ego was a healthy one.

A final, and probably controlling, reason why Dulles was not popular with the people who write most about foreign affairs is that there is a tremendous difference between pointing out a problem and coping with it. This was also part of the explanation why Dean G. Acheson was unpopular as Secretary of State, for it is a basic dilemma of the State Department, sharpened by the growth in importance to the world of U.S. leadership. As the source to which so much of the free world looks for solution of its problems, the United States is constantly confronted with diametric clashes of its own interests in dealing with its allies. The easiest part is to point out the problem. Editorial writers and columnists make a comfortable living out of it.

A good deal of the time the foreign affairs writer contents himself with identifying the problem to his fellow citizens. Often he seems to assume that the Secretary of State is not aware of it. On occasions when he ventures to solve the problem, too, he invariably sweeps casually away any facts which get in the way of his proposal.

How devastating such writers can be, writing separately about separate parts of a problem! Columnist Joseph Alsop, investigating the Middle East situation for his readers in the spring of 1955, gave a good illustration. From Cairo he wrote on April 18: ". . . the primary question for the Western policy makers is not what to do about the Arabs and Israel or the Arabs and the Soviet Union. The primary question is what to do about the new Arab nationalism. Any Middle East policy that is not squarely based on a clear, positive answer to that question of what to do about the new Arab nationalism is a cheap fraud and feeble delusion." After visiting London he wrote two summing-up columns from Washington, in one of which he said: ". . . a firm, clear, and united Anglo-American policy, if it can ever be worked out, may yet save the day in this critical area. . . . The oil enterprises in the Middle East are not only vital to Britain because Britain desperately needs oil. They are mainly vital because the profit from British ownership of the Middle Eastern oil enterprises in effect pays for all the oil Britain consumes. . . . What does it matter if Britain's struggles to defend her own jugular have become pretty convulsive, compared to the hard fact that the same Britain also happens to be the jugular of the United States?"

Forgetting that in Cairo he had swept the Arab-Israeli dispute under the rug, Alsop came up with a conclusion that the minimum terms for dealing with the Middle East required the United States to (1) prevent the destruction of Israel and (2) conserve the Middle East oil supply which is Britain's lifeblood. This could be done, Alsop suggested, if we "made" Britain "stop being neo-colonial" and gave her a "solemn guarantee" that we would not permit the oil to stop flowing. His conclusion happened to coincide, generally, with the State Department's, but his proposal as to how to accomplish it seemed rather on the amateurish side to the officials dealing with the problem.

The Secretary of State's job picks up where the editorial writer leaves off. Having had the requirements pointed out to him, the Secretary needs only to meet them. It's not a simple task, since in carrying out what may be the most enlightened theory he must cope, on one side, with what Congress and public opinion (not always so enlightened) will accept; and, on the other, face frustrations abroad from nations who don't derive their enlightenment from the same sources.

The chief complaint publicly voiced against the Dulles State Department—and indeed against the Eisenhower administration—with respect to its public relations was that it "played favorites" and tried to sell an official line. Favoritism among news sources is a practice of every administration to some degree, and has to do with the confidence of the source in the writer and his editorial slant. The loudest squawks about it came from writers who fared better under the Democratic administration. Can the politician be blamed for trying to peddle his own line? The journalist who complains about it reflects on his own acumen as a man free to detect and resist it if he wants. No journalist with enterprise and integrity needs to toady to it, for the politician likes to see his name and his news in opposition as well as in administration papers.

Despite the press corps feeling about Dulles, the fact is that in press conferences and in other ways he made himself more accessible, and therefore did more to propagate, his department's views than any other official of his rank. He revitalized the press conference as a forum for putting out news by being very forthright in answering questions. His weekly sessions, normally at 11:00 A.M. on Tuesdays when he was in town, developed a drawing power second only to the President's. He invited controversy by being candid.

A time-honored rule at the Secretary's press conferences was that the Secretary could not be quoted directly, only in the third person.

The reason for this was that it was not deemed wise for an official whose words were often of great importance to foreign governments to talk "off the cuff." But the same consideration applied, in even greater degree, to the extemporaneous words of the President, and when Ike, despite this fact, began authorizing direct quotations from the transcript of his conferences, Dulles followed suit. McCardle arranged for correspondents to get mimeographed copies of the transcript as soon as possible after the session. Finally, taking the process a step further, the Dulles press conference was thrown open to full and regular television coverage, also like the President's.

One curious fact about these publicly recorded sessions with press and radio, in which his answers were off the cuff, is that with all his reputation for foot-in-mouth talk, no true "blooper" came out of a press conference. Dulles could handle himself on his feet as a trained lawyer should without getting into trouble. Controversies over his remarks there were; an example was the press conference at which, on the eve of the 1953 nation-wide elections in Germany, he spoke in favor of the Adenauer coalition. It was unprecedented for an American official to speak so candidly in public about the internal affairs of a friendly country, and criticism boiled up on that basis. Dulles, who knew he was capable of making mistakes, felt later he had erred on that occasion, but the point of the criticism—what will the Socialists think if they win power?—was lost when Adenauer was returned to office with a better majority than before.

It was on the prepared statements and the prepared speeches, on the documents which have been passed up and down the line for official comment and suggestion, that he ran into trouble. Most celebrated example was his reference to Portugal's "provinces" when he issued a joint communiqué with the Portuguese foreign minister after a Washington visit by the latter.

Statements of this nature, involving considerations affecting two or more of the department's geographical divisions, often run into a tug of war between them. In this case it involved the Bureau of European Affairs, headed by Assistant Secretary Livingston Merchant, and the Bureau of Near East, South Asian, and African Affairs, headed by Assistant Secretary George V. Allen. Each regional chief is expected to think over the implications of a statement in terms of how it will affect the interests of the United States in the area over which he has charge; he is not concerned about its effect elsewhere, for that is the duty of his colleague. In the case of the Goa statement, Merchant, bearing in mind Portugal's NATO role and Atlantic island bases, approved a reference which remained in the statement which Dulles finally sponsored without personally having gone into all possible implications.

The sin of the phrase lay in oversensitive Indian interpretation that this signified an American decision to back Portugal in its dispute with India over Goa. Dulles had no such intent and American policy had not in fact changed from impartiality between two friends in a quarrel in which we were not involved. As a pragmatist Dulles realized that, since India had chosen to put the worst possible interpretation on it, the reference had done harm and was therefore an error. At his next press conference he defended the communiqué's wording as factual, not editorial, for Goa is described as a province, not a colony, in the Portuguese constitution. Then he added the explanation that he had not intended to take sides in the dispute. He made no attempt to shift the blame to faulty staff work.

An amusing sidelight on the bloopers or supposed bloopers in staff-produced papers was that on two occasions Undersecretary Herbert Hoover, Jr., sponsored them for the department at times when Dulles was out of reach on Duck Island or on a trip. One related to official reaction to a statement of Chou En-lai during the Asian conference at Bandung in 1955, the other to a shipment of tanks to Saudi Arabia. In the sputterings of the more rabid critics there was unconsciously satiric reflection of their frustration at not being able to alight on their usual victim.

Another aspect of Dulles' press and public relations was his desire, amounting almost to a mania, not to be party to secret negotiations with the Communists. He recognized, of course, that the actual sessions could not be held before the eyes of the press, as the UN conducts its business. What he sought to avoid was keeping any major secret from the public—as, for example, the three-power agreements at Yalta which awarded the Japanese territories of Southern Sakhalin and the Kuriles to Russia, which was not made public until after President Roosevelt's death; or the arrangements for Russian interests in Manchuria, which were passed along to Chiang Kai-shek as a *fait accompli*. The reason for this obsession was that, regardless of wartime justification for secrecy, or for big-power action affecting smaller powers, Dulles believed the only course in peacetime was to do things in the open.

Accordingly, at each of the international conferences Dulles took part in, McCardle arranged extensive post-session briefings of correspondents, in which virtually the entire day's proceedings were recounted. This function was brilliantly performed until his death by Henry Suydam, chief of the State Department's news division, who larded what inevitably had to be a tedious account with an old reporter's eye for the color of the occasion and an urbane feeling for mood. Competition forced the other nations to go in for similar "tell-all" briefings. Many of the American reporters, shopping around, preferred the British briefing, since it was organized to provide a quick summary first and then the full account. But at Geneva's Asiatic conference in 1954, an Australian reporter who sampled the various offerings remarked: "The Americans are the only ones who are honest about it. They're just dumb enough to tell what they really think."

Each nation supplemented the official briefings, open to all accredited comers, with private briefings for its own nationals, as was the custom previously. Within weeks of each conference the State Department published the verbatim record of the principal conference speeches, removing any trace of mystery about events behind the guarded doors.

The obverse of this same obsession with telling the public what went on was the publication in March, 1955, of the complete record of the Yalta conference. The State Department had compiled the papers for historical purposes and Congressional Republicans, during their period of control, had voted funds to print them and speed up issuance. By the time they were ready, talk of a "summit" conference was in the air.

Bit by bit the major secrets of Yalta had come out. There was nothing sensationally new in the complete record, as publication proved. It did not reveal proof of perfidy by Alger Hiss, as some Republicans suspected. Its value lay in depicting the accumulation of small motivations which went into the major decisions, enriching and illuminating the understanding of what took place. Only in its entirety, only in its filling in of the chinks, would publication add to public knowledge.

Because of high-flown Republican campaign charges about Yalta, issuance of the papers was somewhat delicate politically. Theoretically they were prepared for Congress, and by this time the Democrats were in control. During a period when the British were raising certain limited objections to publication, Dulles offered to give the text on a confidential basis to the members of the appropriate committees, but Senator Walter F. George, chairman of the Foreign Relations Committee, refused on the ground that the contents would be sure to leak.

McCardle, as an experienced newsman, knew there was only one publication which he could be sure would print the whole text: the *New York Times*, which makes a practice of printing complete texts of important official documents. McCardle arranged to give one copy to James B. Reston, its Washington bureau chief. Since the record comprised two volumes the size of big-city telephone books, the job of transmitting such an enormous record to New York was detected by rival publications. News security was breached on Reston's exclusive, and knowledge of it created a clamor which forced general release of the documents. Thus in outcome the "favoritism" to the *Times* was nullified; but the press condemned McCardle for the intent, even though his intent was based on professional shrewdness in gauging how best to assure printing of the whole record. Very probably the furor over the "leak," which was as great a one-day sensation as the Yalta papers themselves, caused the story to get much wider attention than it otherwise would have received. McCardle hadn't exactly planned it that way, but from the State Department's standpoint the attention it got for the Yalta Conference was all to the good.

17

· · · · · · · ·

Korea: The End of a War

THE first substantive foreign policy move of the Eisenhower
administration occurred within two weeks of inauguration. It
initiated a course of action designed to end the Korean War which,
before four months had elapsed, succeeded in producing Communist agreement to sign a truce. But before the truce could be
consummated there came a final moment of crisis during which
Dulles awakened President Eisenhower in the middle of the night
to inform him of a development that threatened not only to torpedo
the truce but to cause renewed fighting on a scale that could have
led to a new world conflict. It was the first of three now-celebrated
occasions when the United States was brought to "the brink of
war."

The initial move, however, did not appear on the surface to
have direct connection with the Korean conflict, nor was it possible
for the Administration to make its significance clear lest it betray
information to the enemy. This inability to let domestic critics

know that a specific move is part of a larger plan is something that plagued Dulles—and indeed plagues any Administration—throughout his service. The chess player may expose a pawn or a knight as part of an involved gambit; the kibitzer can see only the chesspiece in danger, and assumes the player doesn't know what he is doing. The player cannot stop to explain without exposing the whole move to his opponent.

This first Korean move was the so-called "unleashing" of Chiang Kai-shek. In his first "State of the Union" message to Congress on February 2, the President said the free world could not indefinitely remain in "a posture of paralyzed tension" and that his administration intended to adopt a "new, positive" foreign policy.

"There is no longer any logic or sense in a condition that required the United States Navy to assume defensive responsibilities on behalf of the Chinese Communists," said the President. "This permitted those Communists, with greater impunity, to kill our soldiers and those of our United Nations allies, in Korea. I am, therefore, issuing instructions that the Seventh Fleet no longer be employed to shield Communist China. Permit me to make crystal clear, this order implies no aggressive intent on our part. But we certainly have no obligation to protect a nation fighting us in Korea."

The order provoked a sharp but brief uproar which set a controversial tone for Republican foreign policy at the outset which persisted in almost everything Dulles did afterward.

It was interpreted almost universally as presaging an attempt by Chiang's forces to reconquer the mainland of China. On that assumption, many Americans and most foreign allies feared that Chiang would embark on a reckless adventure from which he would have to be rescued by the United States, and that this in turn would bring on a third World War. The word "unleashing," not used by the President, was a journalistically invented (and inaccurate) description of the order. The fact is that no one in the Administration expected Chiang to respond to it by attacking the mainland. He did not have the capability, unassisted, for anything more than commando raids, and the United States had no intention of backing any assault-with-intent-to-conquer.

When this subsequently became apparent, the criticism changed its tone. Since Chiang did not attack, the critics decided that the Administration was trying to be "positive" with words when it could not be positive in deeds.

But if the Administration did not expect Chiang to attack, there was still a benefit to be reaped from the move. No enemy with regard for his own security can ignore a threat on his flank, regardless of what low-ranking estimate he might give it. The uncertainty it created—uncertainty about his intelligence information as to the size of the threat, uncertainty about U.S. intentions in backing it up—forced him to dispose some of his strength to cope with the unknown. While the Korean War lasted it remained a point of pressure against the Peking regime, and to this day it is a source of worry to Chinese Communism.

Only one foreign government, however, protested the Eisenhower move, and that not formally. The British Embassy's Far Eastern expert, F. S. Tomlinson, telephoned the then Assistant Secretary of State John Allison at his home, after regular hours, to express his government's "misgivings" about the course Ike had taken. The Allies generally were nervous. Like the holdover employees of the new Administration, they were in a period of dread-ing change itself. They had grown accustomed to American policies and usually could guess how the United States would respond to foreign stimuli. Here was a move outside the set pattern and they were fearful where it might lead.

There was more than psychology and nerve warfare behind the order to the Seventh Fleet, because other moves were to come later. The whole problem of ending the Korean War had been discussed aboard the *Helena* when Ike was returning from his trip to the battle area.

Truce had been under negotiation for a year and a half. For almost a year only one issue stood in the way—the UN Command's refusal to turn back to the Communists those prisoners of war which it held who did not want to go back. It had polled the POWs and learned that 46,380 of them—the big majority—never wanted to see Communist rule again.

Historically, return of war prisoners was an accepted thing among the nations until the end of the Second World War. Always before, when fighting stopped, the captured men wanted to go home, whether in victory or defeat. Only in the aftermath of the war in Europe came the discovery that Communism tended to destroy this age-old loyalty to country, for significantly large numbers of Communist prisoners, both Russian and satellite, resisted repatriation.

By the time of the Korean War it was an established U.S. principle that no one unwilling to return to Communist subjugation should be forced to do so.

Aboard the *Helena*, the men who later belonged to the presidential Cabinet and the National Security Council decided to press for peace, but they recognized that something more than desire for it was needed to bring it about—something that would make the

Communists desire it, too. The military stalemate suited Communist purposes well; it pinned down the bulk of U.S. land forces and tied up heavy air and naval strength.

The something needed to change this Communist complacency, it was decided, was the prospect of defeat. If the Reds refused to negotiate sincerely for a truce, the United States must have an alternative, and that alternative had to be victory.

The UN war machine was capable of it, being like a powerful motor running at cruising speed. There were tactics available which the UN Command had denied itself. Air attack could be carried behind the Yalu into Manchuria, destroying the bases and supply sources of the Chinese armies. Tactical atomic weapons could be used to provide a tremendous beef-up in the UN punch. The China coast could be blockaded by the U.S. Navy, and Chinese mainland targets bombed. The decision aboard the *Helena* had been to press for truce; but if that failed, to fight the war to win.

It was from the latter alternative that the previous Administration, heavily influenced by its allies, had shrunk. The fifteen allies whose representatives took part in seeking to mastermind the war's political strategy from Washington feared to push Communism that hard lest Russia react as the Western world's military power approached its Siberian borders. Britain, Canada, and others had counseled against it.

The Eisenhower order to the Seventh Fleet marked the end of town-meeting indecision and embarked the United States on an independent course. It was in fact the beginning of a "positive" move, and it was not a reckless one to present the Communists with a threat of unknown proportions on their flank as a starting gambit.

The second element of the maneuver was diplomatic, and was entirely concealed. Some way had to be found—some convincing way—to convey to the Chinese Communists the information that the United States was determined to get peace, by negotiation if possible but, if not, by victory. Dulles found a way when, on May 21, he visited New Delhi during the course of his first trip to the Near East and India. Feeling that the Communists put credit in Nehru's information and judgments about the West, he privately impressed the alternatives on the Indian leader during two days of talks. He felt reasonably certain the Communists would hear about it from the Indian ambassador in Peking.

They did. Apparently Ambassador Panikkar conveyed the message convincingly, for not more than two weeks later—June 4— the Communists made a move which marked the end of stalemate on the prisoners-of-war issue.

Proposals and counterproposals had been made back and forth over the months. On May 25 the UN Command made a new one suggesting transfer of both North Korean and Chinese repatriation holdouts to neutral custody for a limited period, after which they were to be given civilian status and released, or voted on by the UN General Assembly, which was sure to vote their release. The Communist move of June 4 was to come in with a counterproposal which closely paralleled this, although it was vague on the principle of nonforcible repatriation. Within four days the UN Command, in discussions on the point, succeeded in pinning it down so that the Communist could not abuse the principle, and on June 8 a prisoners-of-war agreement was signed.

The nearer peace came the more bitter Syngman Rhee became about it. "We cannot accept any armistice as long as the Chinese remain in Korea," he proclaimed. He was all for fighting, but was powerless to do so without UN Command backing. Instead, on June 18, before the armistice procedure had begun to operate, he released some 27,000 of the prisoners who were under guard by ROK troops.

It was an enormous breach of the UN Command's agreement with the Communists to let the prisoners be questioned under neutral auspices, but one which the UN Command was not consulted about in advance and powerless to stop once the men began streaming out of the prison compounds and disappearing into the Korean countryside. Word was flashed immediately to Washington, where it was 2:00 A.M.

In his home, Dulles was awakened by ringing of the private telephone beside his bed. The State Department duty officer read him the urgent message. Dulles thanked him, hung up the phone, and lay wide awake thinking for several minutes of the possible consequences of Rhee's willful action. Then he picked up a second telephone, connected with the White House switchboard, and told the operator he wanted to speak to the President.

Briefly they faced the decision over the telephone: if the Communists used Rhee's action as a pretext for reopening the war, was the President still agreed that the United States had to go for victory? Did he still believe, as he had on the *Helena*, that from now on it had to be all-out to win, with tactical atomic bombs if necessary? The President did.

Thus calmly did the two men look war in the face, one in his bedroom off Rock Creek Park, one in the White House, several hours before dawn on June 18. There was no brandishing of threats for the Communists did not even know of the decision. All

Peking had to go on was the steely resolve behind the American attitude which they had sensed earlier.

The "brink of war" decision for the United States, forced on it by action outside its own control, amounted to sticking by the belief that the fighting of the Korean War to victory was a better risk than backing away from it and inviting further aggression.

What telephone calls were made in Peking that day? Did Chou En-lai call up Mao Tse-tung? Did Mao communicate with the Kremlin? We do not know, but we know the Communists faced their own "brink of war" decision. They did it on a more pragmatic basis, weighing the loss of face involved in buckling to Rhee's defiance against the conviction that the United States would hit back hard. The Communists backed away from it.

Before the end of July the armistice breach had been patched up and the instrument signed. The enormous political and economic problems left for a country devastated and torn in half still remained, but fighting in Korea had stopped.

18

. . . .

Berln: A Diplomatic Gambit Opens

Iᴛ ᴡᴀs a year, less one day, after he became Secretary that John
Foster Dulles began officially the particular part of his task
which he preferred and for which he had trained all his lifetime—
the shaping of long-range foreign policy, No. 16 on the list of
duties of the Secretary which he had compiled prior to taking office.

Naturally the move had required preparation. Obviously it could
only be the start of a process which would take years to complete—
perhaps not during his term. Determined to set in motion events
which would break the stalemate of war-threatening tension which
gripped the world, he could by no means feel sure of or foresee the
eventual outcome, except in the sense of his deep conviction that
what he planned was based on the fundamental human motivations
of mankind and would, therefore, win out in the long run.

But when on January 21, 1954, he emplaned for Berlin he was
keyed and ready to tangle with the Russians on what he analyzed
as the core problem of world tension, the unnatural division of

Germany. Though he had gone through many postwar conferences with the Soviets, this was the first time he went to the table as head of the U.S. delegation, with authority to bring into play the immense power of his country, and therefore it was the first opportunity to display his effectiveness as a diplomat.

Winter's cold gripped all of Northern Europe in the early morning of January 22 as President Eisenhower's big airplane bore Dulles and his party to the scene. The *Columbine* penetrated the cold war's tension front over the East German border a few minutes east of Hamburg, leaving behind the bustling activity of the Western Zone to drone steadily over snow-clad country seemingly lifeless by contrast. It flew down "Airways Red 6th Corridor," one of the narrow, invisible lanes through which the Communists permitted foreign access to the old German capital, through broken clouds and occasional snow flurries.

There had been doubts at the State Department when the Russians proposed Berlin as the site for the conference. Was it wise to travel behind the Iron Curtain to a tiny Western enclave? Would security be too great a problem? Dulles had brushed aside the doubts. "That's a good place to meet," he decided. "Berlin will dramatize the whole complex of problems with which we have to grapple."

Although for months Dulles had had the State Department at work on intelligence compilations, political analyses, and position papers on every conceivable angle of what might come up, in his own mind the course of action was simply organized. He wanted to make a genuine try to reach agreement with Russia on reunification of Germany under acceptable conditions. If that failed—and he was under no illusions—he wanted to demonstrate that it was Russia, not the West, which was the obstacle to peace.

There is an old precept of the McGuffey reader era that "it takes two to make a fight." As a student of history Dulles knew the fallacy of this well-intentioned pacifist observation as applied to international relations; as long as nations existed bent on conquest, and as long as the hunger for peace and freedom existed in their potential victims, it would take only one to make a fight and two to make peace.

The world was well aware it took two to make peace, and somehow the Russians were succeeding in implanting the idea generally that it was the West, but more particularly the United States, which was the unco-operative element in the equation. At Berlin Dulles convincingly demonstrated for the first time that the Russians were the real recalcitrants. Later on at Geneva, as we shall see, he and President Eisenhower made a convincing second point with profound effect on world opinion: that, for all the talk of "massive retaliation," what the United States really wanted was peace, not war.

Dulles had enunciated the principle of massive retaliation in a Paris speech and in a *Life* magazine article in 1952. He reiterated it and gave it the label in a speech to the Foreign Policy Association in New York shortly before leaving for Berlin. This time, because his views had taken on a "permanence in history," it drew worldwide attention. It was essentially a defensive policy, vitally necessary for a nation which ruled out preventive war as a means of ensuring against its destruction; Winston Churchill said in a House of Commons debate on March 1, 1955: "There is widespread belief throughout the free world that, but for the American nuclear superiority, Europe would already have been reduced to satellite status, and the Iron Curtain would have reached the Atlantic and the Channel." But world opinion, including considerable American opinion, overlooked the "re" in "retaliation." Most critics spoke of it as if the United States planned to "taliate" against Russia, instead of merely issuing solemn warning that if attacked it would defend itself and its world interests with the utmost vigor.

It is doubtful if many of the critics of the Dulles "doctrine of deterrence," of which "massive retaliation" was a part, bothered to read the complete spellout which he gave the theory in his article for the April, 1954, issue of *Foreign Affairs*, a long-hair publication of limited circulation. Dulles later took to describing his policy as one of "selective retaliation," but it was not second thoughts about the policy, because the article specifically brought out this point. "Massive atomic and thermonuclear retaliation is not the kind of power which could most usefully be evoked under all circumstances," he wrote.

He posed the question: How should collective defense be organized by the free world for maximum protection at minimum cost? His answer was: "The heart of the problem is to deter attack. This, we believe, requires that a potential aggressor be left in no doubt that he would be certain to suffer damage outweighing any possible gains from aggression. . . .

"To deter aggression, it is important to have the flexibility and the facilities which make various responses available. In many cases, any open assault by Communist forces could only result in starting a general war. But the free world must have the means for responding effectively on a selective basis when it chooses. It must not put itself in the position where the only response open to it is general war. . . .

Berlin: A Diplomatic Gambit Opens

"The indispensable need [is] to demonstrate a purpose to resist, and to compel any aggressor to expose his real intent. . . . That does not mean turning every local war into a world war. It does not mean that if there is a Communist attack somewhere in Asia, atom or hydrogen bombs will necessarily be dropped on the great industrial centers of China or Russia. It does mean that the free world must maintain the collective means and be willing to use them in the way which most effectively makes aggression too risky and expensive to be tempting." In short, let the punishment fit the crime and add something to discourage a future attempt.

At any rate, the two diplomatically made points—first, that Russian threats were the real block to peace and, second, that the United States did not want war—later changed the entire character of the world struggle. To follow this change we must begin with the Berlin conference.

One of the preparations for Berlin was the Western Big Three conference at Bermuda, which had been held the previous December. In its original conception Bermuda had not been intended as a pre-Berlin skull session. Churchill, obsessed with the idea of "meetings at the summit" to smooth out world problems, had been pressing unsuccessfully for a conference with the Russians. Dulles objected on two grounds: during wartime, when the burden of fighting falls on a few great powers, it is necessary and useful for them to have high-level co-ordination of their plans, but in peacetime it tends to create the impression that the big powers are trying to run world affairs and slighting the smaller nations; also, he believed it created a false impression of harmony. Ike agreed; he did not think the time had come for meeting again with Russia.

During one of the trips Dulles made to London, Churchill

sounded him out to see if the United States would object if he went to Moscow by himself. Dulles cooled him off by saying that, of course, Great Britain as a sovereign power in charge of its own affairs was entitled to take whatever action it saw fit; however, he added, Churchill should weigh the advantages of a liaison role between the United States and Russia against the danger of softening the base of the Anglo-American alliance, the West's most solid underpinning.

Churchill abandoned his pressure for the Russian meeting, but he kept promoting a meeting with Ike, and finally it was agreed that there would be a meeting. But Churchill suffered a stroke, which caused its postponement. After his recovery it was finally reinstated as a U.S.-British-French conference in Bermuda.

The press of the three nations, who with outsiders numbered over a thousand, found itself baffled by the Bermuda conference. The diplomatic critic of *The New Yorker* described the communiqué as "a document intended to put the best possible face on the fact that no decisions of importance were reached during the four days of talk."

The fact was that France and to some extent Great Britain had come to inform the United States that the European Defense Community treaty had little chance of adoption and to see if the United States had an acceptable alternative. Churchill and the then French Premier Joseph Laniel found both Ike and Dulles adamant on the subject. EDC had been dying when they took office. One of the first acts Dulles undertook was to try to shock France into acting on it, as we noted in Chapter 1.

Dulles had long believed that, unless Western Europe got together in some sort of association that would prevent its nations from going to war against each other about once every generation, Western civilization itself was threatened by a dynamic, aggressive Communism. He had been drawn to Ike as a leader because he learned that Ike felt the same way. Both of them knew that EDC was not the only answer to the European unity problem, but among the practicable answers it seemed to them the best. It was designed to merge German and French troops in a Continental army in such a way that it would be difficult for the two traditional enemies to get at each other's throats. Instead, the strength of both would be devoted to a Continental element of NATO.

The Americans knew also that if they so much as hinted they had an alternative if EDC failed they would kill off what faint chances there were of EDC's passage. Dulles' own estimate, after his return from that first trip to Europe, was that its chances for ratification were only about four out of ten. Nevertheless, the French had proposed it in the first place, and neither he nor Ike was willing that the project be abandoned by default. They refused to be infected by the velleity of their European allies. At Bermuda they insisted that the issue be carried to a showdown, win. lose, or draw, and they won that point even though EDC, as it happened subsequently, lost out as the result of weak-livered French politics.

Dulles gave additional point to the American attitude when he visited Paris for a NATO meeting later in December. He said French defeat of EDC would force the United States into an "agonizing reappraisal" of its European policies unless an acceptable substitute were found.

As he flew toward Berlin, therefore, Dulles knew his basic minimum task in confronting the Russians was to hold the Western alliance together. Bermuda had been reassuring on this point. He had arranged to arrive early—three days ahead of the scheduled opening of the conference—so that he could hold prior meetings with the British and French foreign ministers.

As the *Columbine* established radio contact with Tempelhof airdrome and began its gradual descent under the monitoring of hostile as well as friendly radar, Dulles had good reason to recall his previous experiences in Berlin. He had seen the city as a boy, early in the century, when his chief impression was of the arrogance of the police. He had made numerous visits after the First World War to deal with Schacht and the German bankers on bonding business, and had closed his Berlin office because of the Hitler policies.

Most vividly he remembered two visits after the Second World War. One was in 1946, just after he had been reading historian Arnold Toynbee on "challenge and response." His airplane from London landed amid such incredible devastation ("It was like landing in the Colosseum in Rome," he wrote home) that he thought here, surely, was a challenge too great for response. The next time was two years later, during the airlift. Ruins were still there, but so remarkable had been the job of tidying up the rubble that he felt nothing could keep down a people who had responded so diligently to the challenge of rehabilitating themselves. Because of this he was not assailed by fears when, later on, the Russians agreed to independence for Austria in return for its neutrality and caused the professional worriers to wonder if it was bait for the Germans. He was convinced that the German nation was not destined to be a weak and neutral nation; his job was not to defend Germany against such a fate but to channel its energy into constructive paths.

Berlin: A Diplomatic Gambit Opens

It had been five years since the Big Four Foreign Ministers had met. After 1949, in Paris, the U.S. State Department shied away from East-West meetings. In 1951, because of British and French gropings for some concessions from the Soviets that would ease the pressure under which the Continent lived, the State Department reluctantly agreed to try again—but only if an agenda could be arranged in advance.

The Communists are world champions at pettifogging when it suits their purpose, and dispute over the wording and order of an agenda is one of their favorite devices for giving this warped talent full play. So many fruitless hours had been spent with Molotov by Western ministers with more important tasks on their hands that the device of naming ambassadors to do that part of the jousting was hit upon. The United States sent Philip C. Jessup to Paris in the spring of 1951 to see what he could work out in concert with the ambassadors of Great Britain, France, and Russia. At the Palais Rose they held more than seventy meetings over a period of about three months without reaching agreement on so much as one comma of a proposed agenda. Ever since, the words "Palais Rose" have been synonymous with futility in the glossary of Western diplomats.

The fact was that the United States—and even its partners, though they felt impelled by home public opinion—shrank from tangling with the Russians after 1949. They feared the propaganda buffeting which Molotov handed out. Once engaged, they feared to disengage lest they be accused of "breaking up the conference." This attitude was clear in the halfhearted and abortive negotiations of 1951.

All this was changed in the approach to the Berlin conference.

The State Department, under its new management and with a renewed sense of the justice of its cause, was eager to do battle. Dulles approached the test with great confidence. The Allied position had been carefully concerted by means of a three-power working party in Paris which had sought to anticipate all contingencies and which reached agreement on all fundamentals. There remained some differences on details, but Dulles knew that before the conference ever got to such refinements, basic decisions would have to be taken that would carry great importance and would mean the conference was on the way to success.

He believed the Soviets were arriving with much greater doubts on their minds. Hopes were high in Germany that the country could be reunified, and hopes were high in Austria that independence, promised in Moscow ten years previously, would be granted. The rest of the free world, though not as emotionally involved, yearned for the letup in tension that would follow such moves toward settlement. If those results did not come about, it would only be because of Soviet unwillingness.

Dulles was prepared to make the effort, but he was under no illusions. He analyzed the basic obstacle to be the probability that the Soviets would not dare, by retiring from East Germany and Austria, to permit a salient to be pushed deeply into the Soviet orbit, carrying an aura of freedom close to Poland and Czechoslovakia. He expected that attitude and he expected that Molotov would try to camouflage it. He was determined that if this estimate proved correct he would not let Molotov conceal from the world Russia's real motives.

On the eve of the conference he told his staff: "We in our own minds are prepared for a constructive conference if the Soviets are willing to have it so. The obstacles that we see are not in any respect on our side. If the Soviets are willing to have an Austrian peace treaty, all we have to do is stick a pen in their hands. It has been so for seven years, five at least. If they want to unite Germany, Germany can be united. There is no real obstacle in the way except the obstacles which reside in the system of the Soviet Union and the fact that either the liberation of Austria or the unification of Germany will set up very serious problems for them. If they feel they can cope with those problems there will be no difficulty from our side. If those results are not achieved, it will only be because the Soviet system makes it impractical for the Russians to do what is simple and elemental justice with relation to Austria and Germany."

It took the better part of four weeks to make it clear that Moscow was not ready to retreat an inch in Europe. It also took some new tactics.

The "plot" of a long-range diplomatic maneuver, like the plot of a novel, does not spring complete in its intricate detail from the author's brain. It is built up, bit by bit, in response to the conflicts faced. The author of fiction, on the basis of his thinking about life as he has experienced it, hits upon a central theme. The scores of individual incidents that build up, illustrate, and confirm the theme come only as the writing proceeds and as the author's mind copes with the conflict with which he is dealing. The reader grasps the theme only as the trend demonstrated by the succession of dramatic incidents accumulates in his consciousness.

Similarly, the contemporary news accounts of what happened at Berlin by themselves failed to convey the plot of the new drama that was opening in diplomacy.

There was, of course, realization that conditions were ripe for a new approach since East and West had last met: Stalin's death raised the possibility that his successors might want to use different techniques; in the United States and Great Britain the governments had changed hands. But it is only after new tactics have been employed for some time that their pattern emerges and the significance of their effect can be gauged.

The initial tactics at Berlin were modest ones. The first was a slick undercutting of the old Soviet practice of interminable talk about agenda.

It surprised nobody that Dulles and his Western colleagues, Anthony Eden and Georges Bidault, came to the table with one agenda, and Russia's Vyacheslav Molotov with another. Bidault presented the West's ideas, which were as follows:

1. The problem of German unity.
2. The Austrian State Treaty.
3. Security in Europe.
4. Other matters.

Molotov, at the close of a long speech, said:

"All the foregoing allows me to submit the following proposal relating to the agenda of the Berlin Conference:

"1. Measures for reducing tension in international relations and the convening of a meeting of the Ministers of Foreign Affairs of France, Britain, the U.S.A., the Soviet Union, and the Chinese People's Republic.

"2. The German question and the problems of insuring European security.

"3. The Austrian State Treaty."

The motive behind previous squabbles over agenda order was the desire of both sides for tactical and propaganda advantage. This was avoided at Berlin by an extremely simple stratagem: the West accepted the Russian agenda.

"Mr. Molotov's agenda," said Dulles, "is not the agenda that we would propose, but it is an agenda which we will take for the sake of getting on with our work. We do not want to turn this conference into another Palais Rose. We would have preferred to deal with Austria earlier, but if the Soviet Union prefers to leave to the last what is the easiest to do, then we will accommodate ourselves to their wishes in this respect. The important thing is that we quickly show a capacity to discharge our responsibilities toward others and not try to waste time in recriminations."

Bidault echoed, "I have made up my mind to prevent a three months' debate on the agenda." Eden added, "I came here, like M. Bidault, to discuss our real problems."

One round of Western speeches left Molotov pawing the air, and the conference moved immediately to his Item 1.

When it came to discussing Molotov's proposal for a conference including Red China on the vague issue of "World tensions," Dulles categorically refused to accept. He told Molotov: "The United States rejects the Soviet concept that any so-called 'five great powers' have a right to rule the world and determine the destinies of other nations. . . . If conferences can do nothing better than create new conferences, the whole conference method will become an object of ridicule, and we with it."

Molotov, however, insisted on dragging the issue out for three full days, until Dulles gave him a second nudge. Noting that "reduction of international tensions" was a subject broad enough to include Germany, which was a prime source of international tension, he suggested that the German question could be discussed without waiting formally to take up Item 2. Molotov saw the point and abandoned his filibuster.

Were these no more than parliamentary tricks? Was it of any benefit to the United States, or to the cause of world peace, to have it demonstrated that the American Secretary of State was a more resourceful parliamentarian than the Soviet Commissar of Foreign Affairs? Certainly not, if the only purpose was to show that John Foster Dulles was a smart lawyer. The purpose, however, was to force Molotov to quit stalling and talk substance. This it accomplished. The usual barbed-wire entanglements were cleared away. And once Molotov was forced to talk business on the problems of Germany and Austria, new pressures were applied. It was on the Austrian treaty that the Western Ministers scored their major tactical coup of the conference.

Dulles had hoped that protocol could be worked out so that he would be the first to speak each time Molotov concluded. Such trifles as whether the French or English spelling would be used to list the attending states, and whether discussion proceeded clockwise or counterclockwise around the table, often play an important part in dominating one's adversary. In this case they had worked out satisfactorily. Dulles was in position to make the first response to Molotov each time. It gave him a chance to suggest the line for the other two, and gave them time to think before they had to speak.

Previous negotiations had narrowed Russian objections to the Austrian treaty to five provisions. One afternoon the West offered to accept the Soviet version of all five if Molotov would sign the treaty that afternoon.

Beads of sweat popped out on Molotov's shiny forehead and his round poker face betrayed momentary dismay. By the time his speaking turn came around he had an answer ready: the German question had to be settled first. There were several quick rounds in which the Westerners pounded hard to get the treaty signed forthwith, but Molotov sought refuge in the excuse that it could not be done before some means were found to ensure that German militarism would not again threaten peace. Since he had just demonstrated, in the German discussions, that Russia had no intention of permitting solution of that question, it laid bare Russia's true intentions in a way no amount of reasoned argument could have done. Russia was just unwilling to yield an inch of European territory it occupied.

This was an exposure by maneuver rather than by propaganda, but the propaganda angle was not overlooked. Dulles had a sharp needle for Molotov. Upbraiding the Russian for obstructionism on the Austrian treaty, he recalled the Greek myth of Sisyphus.

"For about two thousand years now," he said, "there has been a figure in mythology which symbolizes tragic futility. That was Sisyphus, who according to the Greek story was given the task of rolling a great stone up to the top of a hill. Each time, when after great struggle and sweating the stone was just at the brow of the hill, some evil force manifested itself and pushed the stone down. So poor Sisyphus had to start his task all over again.

"I suspect that for the next two thousand years the story of Sisyphus will be forgotten, while generation after generation is told the tragic story of the Austrian State Treaty, and how we were repeatedly at the point of concluding it when always some evil force manifested itself and pushed the treaty back again."

There is virtually no sense of shame in the Soviet make-up, and

Molotov clung to his specious excuses down to the bitter end. So the Berlin conference ended in frustration on all three points of the Soviet agenda.

Yet it was not really a draw.

The fight had been sharp, and it had been over substance. Each side had probed the other's intentions and each retired to adapt its tactics accordingly.

Despite the parliamentary outmaneuvering he underwent, Molotov won the immediate substantive advantage.

Molotov, the most battle-hardened of the four ministers at the table, was a skillful diplomatic technician. He was the old master, indicating by his behavior that with Stalin no longer figuratively looking over his shoulder he was enjoying more latitude of maneuver than any Soviet foreign minister had ever had. On Germany, on Austria, he faced a situation which no amount of technical skill could surmount: solid Western unity, for one thing, and a world opinion, backing that up, which had grown more sophisticated about Communist guile—in Europe—in the five years since last they had met. The carefully nurtured British-French-American unity was what held the line against him. But there was one crack in the unity, involving the Far East, and this Molotov exploited.

Molotov got nowhere with his proposal for a five-power conference including Communist China, but he did get acceptance of a proposal to hold a conference on political settlement of the Korean problems. So much the United States wanted, too; the Korean armistice terms had provided for holding such a meeting but the Chinese Communists had stalled it. Molotov's victory was to play on French weariness with the Indochina War and win acceptance of a phrase stating that at the same time there should be a discussion of "the problem of restoring peace in Indochina."

It was more than the mere fact of agreeing to confer that led to the subsequent Western debacle at the Asiatic conference held in Geneva the following April, May, and June; it was Communist military exploitation in the interval, compounded by further breaching of Western unity on the Far East situation. One paragraph in the final Berlin communiqué gave the Communists the opportunity for exploitation after their own fashion, and it is the diplomatic technician's job to provide the opportunity.

But the true importance of conferences such as Berlin is in its by-products. Such conferences are always important and always significant, although the long-range significance cannot always be seen, even by the participants, at the time.

The Moscow conference of March, 1947, dealt with questions like the Saar and the Ruhr, but its most important result, which came almost incidentally, was the aligning of France in partnership with Great Britain and the United States. France had gone to the conference linked to Russia by a 1944 treaty negotiated by General Charles de Gaulle. There were a number of Communists in the French government. Russia, straddling at Moscow between a pro-French and a pro-German position in her effort to keep French friendship and still not let go of the great European prize of Germany, then still divided into four parts, alienated France to the extent that France subsequently eliminated the Communists from her government and lined up with the West.

The 1954 Berlin conference had its by-products, too. One—the armistice which gave half of Vietnam to the Communists—was plainly visible. The other was equally visible, but its link with Berlin was not as apparent. That was the Soviet decision in 1955 that the time had come to sign a peace treaty with Austria.

Soviet concealment habits being what they are, there is no way to prove that the Russian turnaround on Austria stemmed from Russian realization that European opinion had been swung heavily against them by exposure of their unfair and unreasonable stand on Austria at Berlin. Interpreting the Kremlin's motive still takes much long-distance mind reading. On our side we know why our government takes the attitudes it does, because we debate them and examine the reasons in public. No free government ever gets far out of line with the main body of public opinion without getting called back on course.

Soviet secrecy often leads some of the more vocal and more nervous figures of the free world to believe that because the Russians achieve dramatic surprise—a result of their being able to move in stealth—they are superhumanly clever and are leading us into a trap. The responsible statesman, possessed of good intelligence on his antagonist and with a sense of the basic resolve, the brains, and the power behind him, is not deceived; he knows the Russians are not gods, nor are they eight feet tall. He knows they are human, and plagued by the doubts which assail all human beings. Against that knowledge he weighs the visible fact that, without any surface motive that could be considered really convincing, the Russians did decide to yield on an Austrian peace treaty. When they did, they accepted terms less favorable to them than they could have had at Berlin. They conveniently forgot that they had wanted the German question settled first.

Thus Berlin produced movement and change, just as previous conferences had done. The "deadlock" was more apparent than real. Dulles left Berlin without an inkling of what was to come on

Austria, and a realization that the crack in Western unity which Molotov had uncovered in the Far East needed strong intramural repair work. He knew Berlin was not an isolated event ending in frustration, but a producer of change. Having spent a lifetime evolving plans to channel the process of change to the ends of peace and human justice, and having set out at Berlin to force the pace of change, he turned his thoughts to the next move required. It was two years before the full scope of the change initiated at Berlin became apparent. The Russian turnaround on Austria was only a hint, and the Soviets did some more backing and filling before making the new line official before the world in their open denunciation of Stalin.

19

· · · · · · · ·

Indochina: A Different "Brink"

As the Berlin conference came to an end, only those close to
Dulles noted his vague unease after he agreed to the final
communiqué, which provided that "the problem of restoring peace
in Indochina" might be discussed at Geneva. The unease showed
with only a faint shading out of his introspective analysis of what
had happened.

He had refused a five-power conference with Red China; that
had stuck. He had inveighed against devoting one conference to
setting up another—but the United States had been ready ever
since the Korean armistice to sit down with its Korean enemy, Red
China, to settle the political question; so that could not be considered a concession. Most strongly he disliked agreeing to getting
the United States involved in a conference on Indochina—but his
advisers told him that unless he did the Laniel-Bidault government
of France would fall and most probably would be succeeded by
one which would sell out Indochina. He really had no choice, did

he? Was not his first task to preserve the unity which held through Berlin? And wasn't this essential to it?

These were the thoughts with which he reassured himself. Back home there were two views of Berlin. Some felt the conference had been a great success, and others that the Communists had won, because they translated Communist ability to frustrate as meaning Western defeat. None of this affected Dulles. As a lawyer accustomed to pleading his case and as a politician he spoke of Berlin on his return as a "victory," and he spoke his conviction about it; but it was a conviction based not on the superficial propaganda considerations on which his partisans judged it. Nor did the gloomy view impress him. He had started without illusions, and nothing had happened to shake his belief in the fundamental power of the United States, the rightness of its aims, and in free men's capability to accept their rightness. The defeatists defeated only their own interests. The man of action, engaged in the fight, could not waste time looking back. His task was to look ahead and calculate his next move.

He warned Georges Bidault about what to expect from the Communists, based on American experience in Korea. "If you are going to put Indochina on the agenda for Geneva," he said, "between now and then General Ho Chi Minh will make immense efforts to win victories that will gain him political advantage. You can expect fanatical attempts to gain a good political position."

The French were even then under attack in the outpost of Dien-bienphu. Bidault replied that his government believed the fortress could take Ho's fiercest attacks and inflict heavy losses on the Communists.

Dulles came back home with an idea forming in his mind for a grouping of the free powers—not on the NATO pattern, with contributed forces, but paralleling its collective security concept—as a means of backing up the French in Indochina. The friendly Asian nations did not have the strength by themselves, but if France agreed and Great Britain joined with the United States, all of them together could swing powerful help against the Communists. Such an organization might give the French something to bargain with at Geneva; as it was, they faced the conference with a shaky political situation at home and a shaky military position in the field that was made to order for the Communists.

Before Dulles could get his plans under way, the calamity against which he had warned Bidault in Berlin began to loom. On March 20, General Paul Ely, the French chief of staff, visited Washington on his way back home from a trip to Indochina. He told American officials that Indochina would be lost without American military intervention. It was the first responsible estimate from the French that they could not hold in Indochina, and its implications were enormous to U.S. Far Eastern policy. President Eisenhower, at a press conference two weeks later, described Indochina's position as similar to one unit in a row of dominoes, so that if it fell it would carry the rest of Southeast Asia with it.

Ely wanted an air strike from American carriers against the Communist forces surounding Dienbienphu. On the basis of military advice, Dulles felt an air strike alone would be ineffective, and also that it exceeded the President's constitutional power. Ely's request, however, did not represent an official appeal by the French government for American intervention. Governments do not act on questions of such gravity on nothing more than one foreign official's request. Ely was told that it was a political decision for his government whether to make such a request of the United States. Nevertheless, with its own interests vitally at stake, the U.S. government did not propose to await engraved invitations before deciding what to do. At President Eisenhower's request, Dulles called Congressional leaders to the State Department on Saturday morning, April 3, to discuss the advisability of intervention. Admiral Radford and several other officials attended. Under consideration was a proposal for a Congressional resolution authorizing use of American air and naval power in Indochina, not limited to Dienbienphu.

President Truman had ordered action of this type after the North Koreans attacked in 1950, and President Eisenhower had vowed that, except for the requirements of U.S. self-defense in the face of attack, he would consult Congress before committing the armed forces to battle. The proposition put before the Congressional leaders was one later adapted to the Formosa crisis, in which it proved notably successful.

Here the proposal was to apply it on a local scale. Targets had been selected; the aircraft carriers *Boxer* and *Philippine Sea* were in the area with their tactical air groups and atomic weapons aboard. If it came to involvement, the United States knew where it would attack. The airplanes would strike at staging areas where the Chinese Communists grouped the forces they were pouring in behind the Vietminh, but would not attempt to carry warfare to the big Chinese population centers. The plan was to hit where it would be militarily vital.

There was difference of opinion among the group of congressmen who attended the April 3 session, but there was a consensus about the situation which Dulles shared. This was that the United States should not undertake the bailout of the French alone. We had just freed ourselves of one war in Korea; we should not plunge into another unless our allies were willing to give us help. Neither Dulles nor his visitors believed that a crash operation would be of much effect. If the United States intervened, it would have to be as part of a carefully thought-out program of common defense. In Dulles' mind the problem had more than military implications: there was the issue of French colonialism, and his own belief was that if it came to using land armies, the manpower would have to be supplied locally.

This was precisely in line with what Dulles had been formulating in his mind as a development needed to counter the Communists at Geneva. The threatening military situation only made action more urgent. It was in line, too, with Ike's ideas as he discussed them in conferences with Dulles between Ely's visit and the April 3 meeting with Congressional leaders. Accordingly, next evening Dulles went to the White House after dinner and met with the President in his upstairs study. Admiral Radford was the only other person present.

At this Sunday evening meeting a momentous decision was taken: to intervene in Indochina under certain conditions—the conditions talked over with Congress. Britain, Australia, and New Zealand would have to join, because the defense of Malaya was involved; the French would have to agree to stay in and rid themselves of colonial taint by taking further steps toward the complete independence of Vietnam, Laos, and Cambodia.

This was the point at which the United States faced the "brink of war" in Indochino, one of three celebrated "brinks" in the Dulles conduct of foreign policy. Much has been written about the three risks of war taken by the United States since the Republicans took office, but none of it distinguished between the "brink" in Indochina and the other two—the first involving Korea, which we examined in the preceding chapter, and the third affecting Formosa, which comes later.

In the case of Indochina, it was not a simple choice between the United States and the Communists. The question was not: Shall we fight to maintain a basic principle? It was, rather: Shall we go into a French war to save our own and the free world's interests? So the decision was not the same kind as in the other two. It was: Yes, under certain conditions.

In this form, it was something that could—and was—presented with two different kinds of stress. Some accounts described it as a decision *not* to go to war—unless. Some pictured it as a decision to *go* to war—provided. It was, of course, both, since in effect they were one and the same thing. But it was not the same simple yes-or-no decision made in the cases of Korea and Formosa, and therefore its effect was different. In fact, it never did take effect: the conditions were not met.

It did, however, represent the same basic determination on the part of the United States to fight against Communist encroachment. After the Sunday night White House meeting a cable was dispatched to Winston Churchill saying that Dulles would like to fly over for consultation on Indochina. Churchill inquired how soon he planned to come. Dulles replied laconically "tomorrow" if the British were willing. Despite the urgency implicit in this reply, Churchill kept him waiting until the end of the week before cabling that the British would be glad to talk with him. Dulles took off for London literally two hours after getting word. He did not even go home to pack; Mrs. Dulles did that for him.

Spending three days in London and Paris, Dulles came back with what he believed to be Eden's agreement to start work immediately on organizing "united action" in Asia and getting Bidault's reluctant agreement on behalf of the French to internationalize the war and make further concessions to the three native states involved. The talks were not concerned with the American military strike—that was for U.S. decision—but with the fundamental conditions which had to precede it: the sound collective security basis which would make it worth-while to commit the prestige of the United States with some prospect of success.

But in London there had been a change of heart. Foreign Minister Eden had confidentially sounded out his Commonwealth colleague, Prime Minister Nehru, on the Western plans. Nehru reacted strongly against them. The Indian leader was opposed to "blocs" and particularly to seeing them spread to his back yard in Asia. His objections had effect with Eden, but not with Dulles. The American Secretary could see no reason why Nehru should have, in effect, a "veto" over American plans.

After Dulles scheduled a meeting of the appropriate nations for the first Tuesday after his return, Sir Roger Makins, the British ambassador, telephoned him on Easter Sunday afternoon to inform him the British government had instructed him not to attend. Eden's official explanation was that he thought before the West should undertake the contemplated defensive organization it should see what propositions the Communists had to offer at Geneva. The meeting was held anyway, disguised as a session of the Korean allies (who included the nations concerned in Indochina) and the British attended but took no part in the discussion.

Indochina: A Different "Brink"

Plans for united action had to be abandoned. The West's Big Three, who had stood together so well at Berlin, faced the Geneva conference badly divided. France no longer had the will to fight; the United States would fight if others would; Britain did not want to fight. While press dispatches from the three capitals reflected feelings of recrimination on the part of various officials, Ho Chi Minh's armies steadily pressed the attack on Dienbienphu, which by then had become a siege.

Because Geneva would bring most of the NATO members together, the spring meeting of the NATO ministerial council had been scheduled for Paris for the preceding week. On April 23, after a closed session of the council, Georges Bidault sought out Dulles in the meeting room and led him to one side. The situation at Dienbienphu had become desperate, he said, and for the first time officially, on behalf of the French government, he pleaded for a strike against the attackers by U.S. air power. Dulles said he would think about it. Dulles and Bidault dined together that night, and the French foreign minister was greatly depressed. Dulles told him the judgment of U.S. intelligence was that Dienbienphu was doomed, but Bidault insisted that U.S. intervention could save it.

Next morning, in Ambassador Dillon's residence, Dulles summoned his top aides to discuss it with him. For two hours they earnestly considered whether the situation justified unilateral American intervention. They decided it did not. Without telephoning Washington to reopen the question with the President, Dulles called in his secretary and dictated an answer to Bidault conveying the decision not to intervene. His letter laid out the reasons: it exceeded the President's constitutional powers, being warlike and requiring Congressional approval; there was not time for that to be effective, and it was doubtful that Congress would approve, since the American conditions had not been met; and finally our own military judgment was that it would not by itself save the situation. Next day he flew on to Geneva.

Dienbienphu held out until the Indochina conference was well under way. When it fell, it quickly brought the downfall of the Laniel-Bidault government. The French reaction brought into power a man who had offered to settle the Indochina war in four weeks—by June 20—or resign. He was Pierre Mendès-France. Under the circumstances his negotiating power was nil; in effect he had to ask Red China's Premier Chou En-lai what his terms for settlement were.

The Communists surprised the West by settling for partition along the 17th parallel of latitude in Vietnam, instead of taking over the whole country. At the time it was a rather unexpected turn of events, and not easily explained. Even now American officials cannot be positive of their conclusions, but as shifting Communist tactics unfolded afterward and illuminated some of the incidents which had been murky before, a number of Communist motivations came to light:

Two of them are of almost equal importance and it is impossible to judge which predominated. One was that from the viewpoint of the Chinese Communists there was grave danger of American intervention on behalf of Vietnam. Another was that, since this was the key period of the Soviet drive to kill off EDC in pursuance of their European policy, it was essential for them to play up to the French, to be charitable to the French vanity which required nominal retention of a stake in the area; therefore, to be charitable about the settlement.

Indochina: A Different "Brink"

Does it now seem incredible that U.S. policy deterred the Chinese Communists from pressing home their advantage, through the Vietminh, in Indochina and taking over all of Vietnam? Only to those who considered U.S. policy to be vacillating and uncertain when in fact, on the record, it was steadfast, cautious of committing U.S. power, and consistent. One of the cries of alarm uttered by the professional worriers after the Korean War ended was that the Chinese would merely make use of the relaxation to transfer their energies to Indochina. It never occurred to them that the United States might also transfer its power to Indochina—and they were right in that the United States has distaste for plunging into a new fight just after ending an old one. But how did it look to the Chinese Communists? They had witnessed a ballooning of American will to checkmate them; the balloon had been pricked, true enough, in the temporary collapse of plans for organization of what later became SEATO; but how could they be sure they were not pushing the United States too far? As one of the elements incapable of positive proof but in the realm of high probability, Chinese Communist conviction that the United States meant business and could not be pushed too far was the real "brink" for them on the other side of the precipice.

But there were other motives. The French national fiber collapsed much more rapidly than its Indochina armies. Not only were the French undefeated south of the partition line, they were undefeated in the northern delta of Indochina. Dienbienphu was a psychological symbol blown up to mammoth size, entirely out of proportion to its military value had there been any spunk in the French national character. Mendès-France, suing for peace, capitalized on a back-home feeling that all was lost. The Communists, whose intelligence about the amount of American arms available to the French was good, knew that if they had to face determined resistance, it would take them at least a year to conquer the delta alone. There was ample military reason—putting aside the psychological defeatism of France—for being cautious.

Finally, from the vantage point of subsequent perspective, with the Communist shift from policies of force and threat now spread on the record, it is quite probable that Chou's mildness at Geneva was part of an over-all Communist decision to adopt political penetration instead of naked aggression as the way to win in the Far East. No one at Geneva at the end of June in 1954 seriously believed that there was anything left in South Vietnam to prevent legal take-over, in due time, by Ho Chi Minh and the Vietminh under the sordid terms of the settlement.

These were some unspoken considerations which explained why the Communists accepted political settlement in place of military conquest. The final bargaining showed that they had wanted settlement more anxiously than they admitted. But it was another intervention by Dulles, in which U.S. prestige again was used as a power factor, that gave Mendès-France a better bargain than he first had tried to settle for.

Mendès was willing to partition Vietnam on the 16th parallel of latitude. The Communists demanded partition on the 14th. Unable to make headway and fearful (as was Eden) that the United States would repudiate the settlement, Mendès sent Dulles an urgent cable asking him to return to Geneva.

Dulles flatly refused. Vietnam was not his to partition. If the French chose to do it, the United States could not interfere, but he certainly did not intend to give explicit or tacit U.S. blessing to the award of rule over millions of human beings to Communism. If the United States could not accept the result, it would only dramatize the split in the Western alliance to have the Secretary of State return to Geneva.

Mendès persisted. If Dulles could not return to Geneva, could he come to a meeting in Paris? It took Dulles only forty-five minutes' conversation with Ike to decide that there still was opportunity for U.S. power to influence the result at Geneva, and he took off on another transatlantic trip. Mendès flew from Geneva, accompanied by Eden, leaving Molotov fuming over the interruption.

In the Paris conversations, Dulles told Mendès his minimum price for peace was not high enough. If he suitably increased his minimum demands on the Communists, the United States would upgrade its representation at Geneva, but Dulles himself would not return. In return for his moral support, Mendès agreed to insist on partition at the 18th parallel instead of the 16th. Dulles accordingly agreed to have Undersecretary Smith return to Geneva—but, since Smith was suffering from stomach trouble, he first telephoned the White House to ask Major General Snyder, the President's physician, to find out if Smith's health would stand the trip. When Snyder said it would, Dulles wrote out the cabled instructions.

As a result of this tangential intervention, the Communists finally settled on partition at the 17th parallel, instead of the 14th as they had demanded. The difference meant inclusion of one important city, Tourane, in the free part of Vietnam, kept several airbases out of their hands, and left open in free territory the only road from Laos to the sea. Molotov demanded of Mendès, in return for the concession, that the United States sign the agreement, but he had to be content with a unilateral statement by Smith on behalf of the United States to "refrain from the threat or use of force" to challenge it, coupled with a warning that any renewal of fighting would be a matter of "grave concern" to the United States.

The United States simply dissociated itself from the arrangement which gave Communism the upper half of the country. "We can accept such things as a fact," Dulles told his staff. "We can accept them as something we do not consider it right to go to war about, as we have in North Korea, in East Germany, in Austria, and in the satellites. But we cannot endorse it and guarantee to the Communists the enjoyment of the fruits of their aggression."

Criticism of Dulles over his Indochina performance was probably the severest of his career. Most of it stormed around an article in *Life* magazine in January, 1956, recounting the story of the three "brinks of war." This article drew greater attention than any other on the subject, primarily because of a cover-page note calling attention to the story inside. The note said: "Three Times at Brink of War: How Dulles Gambled and Won." Partisan critics and people who do not read beyond the headlines attacked him for risking the safety of the United States. Adlai Stevenson pictured him as playing "Russian roulette."

Dulles' own words, as quoted in the article, told the story more clearly than the headline. "You have to take chances for peace, just as you must take chances in war," he said. "Some say that we were brought to the verge of war. Of course we were brought to the verge of war. The ability to get to the verge without getting into the war is the necessary art. If you cannot master it, you inevitably get into war. If you try to run away from it, if you are scared to go to the brink, you are lost. We've had to look it square in the face—on the question of enlarging the Korean war, on the question of getting into the Indochina war, on the question of Formosa. We walked to the brink and we looked it in the face. We took strong action."

Of all the columns of print devoted to the Dulles theory of taking chances for peace, of "waging" peace as one wages war, the most sensible were those of the London *Economist*, which thought his choice of words was clumsy. Its lead editorial of January 21, 1956, said:

But those who read the whole article with the purpose of getting at its intended meaning, and not simply of finding sticks with which to beat the Eisenhower administration, will have little difficulty in seeing . . . [that] . . . his central thought . . . is of the need for certainty.

He believes that the only risk of total war is as a result of miscalculation by an aggressor, owing to his not knowing how far he can safely go. The aggressor must therefore know for certain at what point he will call down retribution upon himself; there must not be any twilight zones in which he can think that he can get away with a bold forward push. What is more, there cannot be any certainty unless the alliance of the free nations will draw the line clearly and give the aggressor no reason to doubt their determination to defend it. If, when faced with a threat of aggression, the free nations do not stand firm on their chosen line, even to the brink of war, then there can be no certainty and no safety. On that occasion, it is true, the risk of war is reduced—there would have been no war in Korea if Mr. Truman had run away in July, 1950. But the risk of war on the next occasion is increased, since the aggressor has been encouraged to believe that he can safely disregard mere verbal prohibitions. Indeed, what may be called the anti-brink policy—the policy of not threatening to fight if the line is crossed, or of not meaning to carry out the threat even if it is uttered—is almost certain to lead to war. For as step succeeds step, it becomes more and more difficult for the aggressor to believe that any of the threats of action are to be taken seriously, while the other side gets nearer and nearer to the point where it will resist from sheer desperation. . . .

Surely it is the lesson of the years from 1933 to 1939, which should not be forgotten so quickly that a statesman who tries to re-emphasize it, however clumsily, should be held up to obloquy. Let it be repeated over and over again—the danger of war coming through too much bellicosity on the part of the democracies is virtually negligible. The only real danger is that the democracies will allow doubts to arise about their united strength and resolution—doubts which, whether justified or not, will encourage a potential aggressor to have a go. This is the danger that Mr. Dulles was trying to guard against.

20

· · · · · · · ·

Formosa: Deterrence Confirmed

THE third "brink of war" in John Foster Dulles' life as Secretary
involved defense of Formosa, the island off the Asian mainland which the Chinese call Taiwan. In the handling of this incident the Dulles policy of deterrence was formalized in action
approved by Congress and backed by the American people in an
amazing demonstration how U.S. sentiment toward the dangers
of Communism in Asia had shifted in the two years he had been
in office. Communist attack in Korea had been unexpected, and the
U.S. reaction to it under President Truman was instinctive. In
the case of Formosa, Dulles anticipated the action, and the policy
designed to cope with it was deliberate. Being deliberate, it represented an advance in the U.S. ability to be master of its own conduct in foreign affairs.

The formalizing of the policy of deterrence, putting the Chinese
Communists on notice that it would mean war with the United
States if they attempted to conquer Free Chinese territory, occurred

in the passage by Congress in January, 1955, of a resolution authorizing President Eisenhower to "employ the armed forces of the United States as he deems necessary" to prevent it. The resolution was approved by the House of Representatives on January 25 by the lopsided vote of 409 to 3; by the Senate on January 28 by 85 to 3.

So complete was American public support for the proposition that the only real debate centered on the question whether the United States intended to defend the islands of Quemoy and Matsu, in addition to Formosa and the Pescadores Islands. The resolution granting authority to use the armed forces extended the U.S. protection "to include the securing and protection of such related positions and territories of that area now in friendly hands and the taking of such other measures as he judges to be required or appropriate in assuring the defense of Formosa and the Pescadores." Were Quemoy and Matsu such "related positions" and were they also covered by the U.S. pledge?

It was a question only President Eisenhower could answer. It has not been answered publicly to this day. Both Dulles and the President resisted pressure, which lasted for months, to force an unequivocal Administration statement answering it yes or no. At one Dulles press conference about three months after other crises had completely distracted American attention from Quemoy and Matsu, a news correspondent began a question about them by saying, "Mr. Secretary, we haven't heard anything about Quemoy and Matsu for a long time—" Before he could finish, Dulles emitted one of his hearty guffaws. "Maybe that's a good sign," he said.

Indeed it was. Advocates on each side of the argument which raged over the "offshore islands" question thought they knew the only way to preserve peace, although they could not possibly know all the facts on which Dulles and the President based their actions and commitments. It was not known, for example, that Free China's President Chiang Kai-shek received a personal letter from Mr. Eisenhower satisfying him that the United States would help defend Quemoy and Matsu, for that fact has not appeared in print until now.

The advice which poured in on the government as to what to do about the islands was of two types. One group, represented by such figures as California's Senator William Knowland, believed that the best way to prevent the Communists from taking Formosa was to help Chiang fight them at Quemoy. Others argued that the islands were too near the mainland—within easy shot of big guns, in the case of Quemoy—for effective defense, and that peace could be assured only if they were given to the Communists, thus putting ninety or a hundred miles of blue water between the Communists and the Free Chinese on Formosa.

The fact that neither course was taken, and still the islands remained in Chiang's possession without war, either big or little, was a tribute to responsible and hardheaded diplomacy. Perhaps it also was an indication that the well-meaning amateurs don't always know what they are talking about. Had the Chinese Communists forced the issue by attempting to conquer Quemoy at the time when the issue raged, the U.S. response would have been the one advocated by Knowland. This the Chinese Communists became convinced of, and this was the knowledge that deterred them. This was the "brink" in Formosa.

Like a relay runner who was getting an extra baton to carry every lap instead of passing his baton on to a fresh runner, Dulles picked up the Formosa problem on his way back home from trying to repair the damage done at Geneva's Asiatic conference. He had been to Manila, where on September 8, 1954, seven other nations had joined the United States in signing the Southeast Asia security pact which became known as SEATO. Dulles made an effort to have it nicknamed MANPAC, for Manila Pact, by way of emphasizing that it differed from NATO, but SEATO stuck. SEATO did not rely, as did NATO, on contributions by each of the nations to a common armed force; its problem of defense was different. Its reliance was on the mobile striking power of the United States Fleet and Air Force, armed with atomic weapons, and it looked to land forces supplied by the member nations of the area if the occasion arose. In addition, SEATO embodied a concept first introduced into the anti-Communist defensive strategy by Dulles at Caracas, Venezuela, the previous March. The importance of this concept can await discussion in a later chapter. It was the concept that defense plans had to take into account aggression by subversion as well as by military action. The SEATO nations pledged themselves to combat both types and to apply the protection to all of Southeast Asia, including the Indochina states barred by the armistice terms from entering into alliances themselves.

The big objective of Russian maneuvering in Europe was to break up NATO, and it was scarcely surprising that the Chinese Communists disliked the spectacle of a similar defensive alliance growing athwart their path of conquest in Asia. Their reaction was to open up a threat against the Chinese Nationalist position opposite the mainland. Quemoy was the island where, in 1949, they had lost a bloody battle with the Nationalists at a time when victory might have enabled them to carry on and invade Formosa. In

Nationalist hands it remained an outpost symbolizing their failure to complete the conquest of China, and also an interdiction to effective use of the port of Amoy for coastal shipping. While the eight free nations were conferring at Manila the Communists began shelling Quemoy from shore positions. The attack reached such heavy proportions by the time Dulles stopped in Taipeh on his way back that U.S. strategists became convinced the Reds intended invasion of Formosa. In addition to intense bombardment, the Peking radio was making most warlike threats, openly proclaiming intention of taking the island.

In his consultation with President Chiang Kai-shek, Dulles found the Free Chinese leader anxious for a mutual security pact with the United States. Dulles argued that he already had something more effective—the protection of the U.S. Seventh Fleet—but Chiang felt he was entitled to the same treaty protection as other free states in the area. Free China had not been invited to take part in the organization of SEATO chiefly because it would complicate the diplomatic posture of Great Britain, which had prematurely recognized Red China in 1950 as the lawful government and would thus be embarrassed by Chiang's presence. Without serious argument, Dulles agreed to open negotiations for a treaty, which were conducted by Assistant Secretary of State Walter Robertson and the Chinese Foreign Minister, George Yeh.

Real threat of war existed at Quemoy and Formosa when Dulles returned to the United States. President Eisenhower, vacationing in Colorado, held a session of the National Security Council in Denver, which Dulles attended, to discuss the threat.

The official American attitude had come a long way from July, 1949, when the State Department had issued a "White Paper" writing off the Chinese Nationalists and abandoning them to whatever fate they met. The influences at work on American policy makers to bring about the final downfall of Chiang, or at least U.S. recognition of the Peking government, form too complex a story for recounting here. While these influences did not succeed in prompting the U.S. government into action that might have given Free China its *coup de grâce*, they were reflected in an air of indifference to what happened. In 1950 the United States Information Service, anticipating that Formosa might soon fall to the Communists, sent out a directive to its Far Eastern field offices suggesting they pave the way for it by emphasizing that Formosa was not considered strategically important to the United States. In the face of public clamor after word of the directive leaked out in Tokyo, the State Department disavowed it as representing policy. Officially, however, the policy remained one of indifference until the Communists attacked in Korea in June of 1950.

Even at that time the turnabout in attitude toward Formosa was only 90 degrees. From indifference it switched to the realization that Formosa must at least be "neutralized." President Truman's order to the Seventh Fleet was to prevent Communist attacks on Formosa—but also to prevent Chiang from taking advantage of the Korean War, in case he could, by preventing him from attacking the Communists. Not until President Eisenhower removed the latter interdiction, as noted in a previous chapter, did our policy complete its 180-degree reversal.

The purely military value of Formosa can be argued both ways by military experts. It depends on what kind of war is going on. In an all-out, hydrogen bomb war it can be assumed that Formosa could be neutralized effectively by whichever side did not occupy it. In more limited action it is an important link in the island chain that runs from Japan to the Philippines. In two NSC meetings, one at Denver and the other in Washington, the evaluation was that Formosa in friendly hands *was* vital to the defense of the United States, though Quemoy and Matsu were not. The distinction here was between the military and political viewpoints. The political viewpoint, accepting the military judgment on Quemoy and Matsu, held that, nevertheless, the islands were important in relation to the defense of Formosa, for psychological reasons transcending the military difficulty, and therefore important to us if, as the military deemed, we needed to keep Formosa free.

Ever since the Korean fighting had ended, Dulles and the President had been guided by this underlying policy: to seek solutions of war situations and war threats by peaceful means, backed with a concrete display of force and a readiness to use force. The force to resist the Communists in the Formosa straits was already there, represented by the U.S. Fleet and Air Force installations in Japan, Okinawa, and other spots in the area, as well as the Chinese Nationalist Army, which was the next biggest free world land force in the Far East after Syngman Rhee's. But, pursuing his first move of seeking peaceful solutions, Dulles decided to carry the case to the United Nations. He had already resolved on this course when he emplaned at Taipeh to return to the United States.

As a result, New Zealand introduced a resolution inviting the Communists to come before the UN for a discussion of their claims to Formosa. The invitation was turned down by Chinese Communist Premier Chou En-lai in language both insolent and arrogant. At the same time the Communists stepped up their attack on Nationalist positions on Quemoy and other small offshore islands.

They captured the small island of Ichiang and threatened the Tachens, another group off the coast north of Formosa. The Tachens were of lesser strategic importance to Chiang than Quemoy and Matsu, but to yield them meant enhancing the psychology of retreat and defeat at a time when the Peking radio was dinning into Asian ears its boasts about conquest.

It was at this point that the President asked Congress for authority to use U.S. forces in defense of Formosa and the Pescadores. The response, as noted, was overwhelming. Chiang, knowing privately that the United States would not help him defend the Tachens, voluntarily evacuated those islands rather than waste manpower in a hopeless defense, and the Communist aggression advanced another step.

Now was the moment when it seemed important to have the American government say whether it would help defend Quemoy and Matsu. The question had come up in negotiating the mutual defense treaty, in conversations between Dulles and Foreign Minister George Yeh. One of the problems had been defining the scope of the U.S. guarantee in terms of territory: the State Department was not willing to make a commitment covering the mainland under which Chiang could automatically invoke our aid in a campaign aimed at reconquest, but at the same time it did not intend to sanctify the Communist aggression by denying his claim on the mainland. This was settled by avoiding mention of the scope of the Republic of China's sovereignty and agreeing that neither side would take action except by mutual consultation—a formula which permitted joint action in situations which called inherently for self-defense. The treaty mentioned certain Chinese territories by name and at one point in the Dulles-Yeh talks Dulles agreed to include Quemoy and Matsu by name.

President Eisenhower struck the two place names out when he saw the minutes of the talks. He felt the United States needed a certain flexibility in its defensive plans. At the same time he sent Chiang his personal assurance.

Nevertheless, pressure continued to have Chiang give up the islands to the Communists, on the theory that this would reduce the danger of war. The British were the chief advocates of this course. When the SEATO Council held its first meeting in Bangkok in February, Eden proposed having Chiang cede Quemoy and Matsu in return for a Communist cease-fire agreement and a pledge to settle the Formosa question peacefully. Dulles rejected the idea. It smacked of the same kind of appeasement employed at Munich when the Sudetenland was awarded to Hitler; it would, he was convinced, be equally unsuccessful. It would only whet the Communist appetite for more and, being open to interpretation as free world weakness, lead to assault on Formosa. Furthermore, he did not share Eden's idea that outside nations were entitled to tell Free China how to dispose of her own territory. "You can look on a map at the Scandinavian peninsula and say it would be better to have the North Sea between you and the enemy," he argued in one debate with European allies, "but you cannot overlook the human beings just to put water between you. If a hundred miles of water is better than five, why shouldn't five thousand miles be better than a hundred?"

Munich and Quemoy, in fact, present a picture of two ways to react to the brink of war. At Munich the Western statesmen were afraid to look war in the face, but war resulted, one that engulfed the world. At Quemoy the American government was prepared to fight. The Chinese Communists knew it. The result was a rather abrupt falling off of the Communist attack.

In April, 1955, Chou En-lai attended an Arab-Asian conference at Bandung, Indonesia. Force had got him nothing on the Formosa issue except the promise of heavy U.S. retaliation. He elected to change his tune. No longer did he talk of military conquest of Formosa, but of peaceful settlement of Peking's claim. It was the third notable victory for the Dulles policy of deterrence as tested at the brink of war.

21

. . . .

The Problem of Subversion

THE year 1954 was for Dulles a year of boiling activity on
diplomatic fronts around the globe. The Berlin conference set
in motion processes of diplomatic change which brought Western
Europe's indecision over the European Defense Community concept to a head. This required four subsequent trips to Europe. The
Geneva Asiatic conference, ending the warring phase of the struggle against Communism in Indochina, produced reaction in the
free world which resulted in creation of the Southeast Asia Treaty
Organization. This required one trip to Asia and another to Europe.
And the same year marked the emergence of a new principle in
the cold warfare against Communism: the concept of collective
defense against political subversion. An antisubversion clause went
into the SEATO charter as a companion to its military antiaggression provisions, but the principle took tangible shape earlier in the
year at the Tenth Inter-American Conference at Caracas, Venezuela.

Dulles had scarcely got back from Berlin when he emplaned again for the South American capital to fight for adoption of a doctrine designed to fend off foreign political penetration. Early in the previous century the United States, in the Monroe Doctrine, had served notice that it would fight to prevent military encroachment into the hemisphere. Originally a unilateral declaration, in 1945 the Monroe Doctrine's principle was accepted and endorsed by the twenty-one American nations in the Chapultepec conference, and it was incorporated in 1947 into the inter-American treaty written at Rio de Janeiro. But unity to resist military penetration was no defense against 1954-style Communist political penetration. What the United States proposed at the Caracas conference, which opened March 1, was a declaration of solidarity by the states of the hemisphere expressing their determination to preserve their political integrity by joint action against Communist subversion.

It was more than a theoretical exercise. Communists had achieved a practical stranglehold on the government of a Central American state, the Republic of Guatemala, by steady infiltration of labor unions and political groups through party members who at first concealed their allegiance and their disciplined connection with each other. In the familiar pattern of subversion, they acquired effective control of various public groups and organized a "popular front" to support Jacobo Arbenz for president when the time came to choose a successor to Dr. Juan José Arevalo, who was not entitled to succeed himself under the terms of the Guatemalan constitution. Arbenz' main rival was the man serving Arevalo as chief of the armed forces, Francisco Javier Arana; he was assassinated on July 18, 1949, by Arbenz sympathizers.

After Arbenz' election in January, 1953, the Communists openly proclaimed their Communism. The secretary-general of the Guatemalan party, José Manuel Fortuny, was a leading spirit in a "kitchen cabinet" of Communists and fellow travelers which had Arbenz under its thumb. Fortuny's party was recognized by the Cominform newspaper in Bucharest as the Guatemalan agent of international Communism. Article 32 of the Guatemalan constitution forbade foreign-directed political parties, but in his message to Congress on March 1, 1953, Arbenz answered clamor for a ban on its activities by stating that the government would permit "all, absolutely all" political beliefs.

During the year immediately preceding the Caracas conference the orientation of Guatemala's rulers had been expressed too clearly to leave any doubt as to where they looked for political coaching. They followed the Moscow line at every turn. Influential members of the government had joined in condemning "imperialist aggression" against North Korea and charging the UN forces with using bacteriological warfare there. Guatemala refused to join the other isthmus states, grouped in an organization known as ODECA, in condemning foreign ideologies in the hemisphere. The government voted against putting "intervention of international communism" on the agenda for the Caracas meeting. Fortuny took a two-month trip to Moscow and came back in time to direct strategy to be followed by Foreign Minister Guillermo Toriello.

Toriello's line at Caracas was that by seeking to ban Communism in any American state, the U.S. proposal was in effect an attempt to interfere in the internal affairs of American states. It was an argument that carried a certain amount of plausibility. The Bolivian representative, for example, argued (before voting *for* the resolution) that Guatemala should be permitted to choose any form of government, and if the country wanted anarchy it was entitled to have it. Toriello also sought ingenuously to disclaim Moscow's influence, asking rhetorically, "What is international communism?"

Dulles answered in terms sharper than diplomats normally use. "It is disturbing," he said, "if the foreign affairs of one of our American republics are conducted by one so innocent that he has to ask that question. But since the question has been asked, it shall be answered. International communism is that far-flung clandestine political organization which is operated by the leaders of the Communist party of the Soviet Union. Since 1939 it has brought fifteen once-independent nations into a state of abject servitude. It has a hard core of agents in practically every country of the world. The total constitutes not a theory, not a doctrine, but an aggressive, tough political force, backed by great resources, and serving the most ruthless empire of modern times. . . .

"The disciplinary requirements include a firm insistence that loyalty to the movement, which means in effect loyalty to the leaders of the Communist party of the Soviet Union, shall take precedence over every other obligation including love of country, obligation to family, and the honor of one's own personal conduct. These conclusions are not speculation; they are established facts, well known to all who have seriously studied the Communist apparatus. . . .

"Within all the vast area, now embracing one-third of the world's people, where the military power of the Soviet Union is dominant, no official can be found who would dare to stand up and openly attack the Government of the Soviet Union. But in this hemisphere, it takes no courage for the representative of one of the smallest

The Problem of Subversion

American countries openly to attack the government of the most powerful. I rejoice that that kind of freedom exists in the Americas, even if it may be at times abused. But the essential is that there be a relationship of sovereign equality. We of the United States want to keep it that way. We seek no satellites, but only friendly equals. We never want to see at the pan-American table those who speak as the tools of non-American powers. We want to preserve and defend an American society in which even the weak may speak boldly, because they represent national personalities which, as long as they are free, are equal."

Debate lasted for two weeks, during which Dulles' newly appointed Assistant Secretary of State for American Regional Affairs, Henry Holland, and John C. Dreier, ambassador to the Organization of American States, had to do some diplomatic arm-twisting among some of the Latin states. The final vote was 17 to 1— Guatemala being the sole negative—with two abstentions.

"Words alone will not suffice," Dulles had said during the debate. "What we need to do is to identify the peril; to develop the will to meet it unitedly, if ever united action should be required; and meanwhile to give strong moral support to those governments which have the responsibility of exposing and eradicating within their borders the danger which is represented by alien intrigue and treachery."

The resolution adopted at Caracas, after condemning the activities of international Communism in American states and expressing determination to combat it, recommended two lines of action: (1) "Measures to require disclosure of the identity, activities, and sources of funds of those who are spreading propaganda of the international Communist movement or who travel in the interests of that movement, and of those who act as its agents or in its behalf"; and (2) exchange of information on these points between governments.

The words of the resolution did not, in fact, suffice, though the peril had indeed been identified. During March and April, Guatemala appointed a number of special consuls to posts in northwest Honduras. In May strikes broke out in the territory to which they had been assigned. The Honduran government called for expulsion of three of the consuls, accusing Guatemalan Communist labor organizations of having fomented the strikes. Meanwhile a Communist freighter, the *Alfhem*, loaded 2,000 tons of arms in the Polish Communist port of Stettin, with a falsified manifest describing the cargo as machinery, hardware, chemicals, and optical glass. The ship set out for Dakar, but its orders were changed several times en route to conceal its destination, and it finally arrived in mid-May at Puerto Barrios, Guatemala, to be unloaded under guard, in the personal presence of the minister of defense. It carried 15,424 cases containing rifles, machine guns, artillery, and miscellaneous military equipment.

"By this arms shipment," Dulles announced at a news conference May 25, "a government in which Communist influence is very strong has come into a position to dominate militarily the Central American area. Already the Guatemalan government has made gestures against its neighbors which they deem to be threatening and which have led them to appeal for aid. The Guatemalan government boasts that Guatemala is not a colony of the United States. We are proud that Guatemala can honestly say that. The United States is not in the business of collecting colonies. The important question is whether Guatemala is subject to Communist colonialism. The extension of Communist colonialism to this hemisphere would, in the words of the Caracas resolution, endanger the peace of this hemisphere."

On June 8 Arbenz, with approval by the Congress which he summoned in the night, suspended constitutional guarantees, imposed censorship, and instituted a Communist-type reign of terror in which hundreds of persons were arrested on suspicion of opposing the government, some being beaten and otherwise tortured and some being killed. In the face of this development, capping the possibilities of Communist-armed military domination of an isthmus which contains the Panama Canal, a revolution against the Arbenz government broke out in mid-June, headed by Colonel Carlos Enrique Castillo Armas, who invaded from Honduras with a few hundred armed men. Proof of the popularity of Castillo Armas' cause came when the rebel ranks were quickly swelled by some two thousand sympathizers inside the country, and within two weeks the Arbenz regime was overthrown.

Communists accused Dulles and his brother Allen, head of Central Intelligence, of having instigated the revolt and supplying the rebels with U.S. arms. Whatever connection Allen had with it, if any, is something that must await recital in Allen's own story; as for Foster, the charge was on a par with the Communist claim that when he visited the 38th parallel in Korea in June, 1950, he gave the signal for the South Koreans to attack. Nevertheless, the Mexican Communist, Diego Rivera, painted a symbolic mural in which the faces of both Allen and Foster appeared among those involved in the revolution. Both brothers, perversely flattered by the imputation that they had the power to overturn a government and amused by the evil looks which Rivera had given their faces, obtained colored reproductions of the mural to keep as souvenirs.

Collective defense against subversion was also made a part of the alliance built up in Asia against Communist encroachment. The story of Indochina has been written about mainly as a military problem—as we examined it in Chapter 18—but the military side is only half the story. The ending of hostilities opened a new phase of history for the area; it ushered in the inevitable processes of change in human and national relationships. The SEATO mechanism that was put together after the Geneva Asiatic conference was first of all a defensive military alliance, differing in pattern from NATO though built on the same basic collective defense principle, but it was also a defensive antisubversive alliance. Since the settlement at Geneva was based on obvious Communist belief that the field was wide open to conquest by subversion, the non-military aspect of SEATO may prove in the long run to be the more important.

At the moment of truce, Vietnam became a divided state. The northern half was held in the disciplined grip of Communist troops under a Moscow puppet, Ho Chi Minh. The truncated free Republic of Vietnam was left drifting and leaderless, shattered in morale, preyed on by pirates masquerading as religious sects, with its head of state, the Emperor Bao Dai, enjoying a sybaritic absentee existence on the French Riviera. In the almost total disintegration of political authority in the wake of the military debacle, Bao Dai appointed a comparative unknown, Ngo Dinh Diem, as premier to rally the anti-Communist forces if he could. Only a miracle, it seemed, would make it possible.

Yet the miracle took place. It came about through the dedication and stubborn integrity of Ngo Dinh Diem; through steadfast moral and economic support by the United States; through the creation of a military deterrent to further conquest in SEATO; and lastly but importantly through the identification in connection with SEATO that subversion was the weapon which needed to be countered. The SEATO charter said in Article II that the member states, separately and jointly, would by means of continuous and effective self-help and mutual aid, maintain and develop their individual and collective capacity to resist armed attack "and to prevent and counter subversive activities directed from without against their territorial integrity and political stability."

Part of the bargain for Beedle Smith's return to the Geneva conference was agreement by France and Britain to join in the "united action" project which had fallen through prior to the conference. SEATO, between the "united action" concept following Berlin and the signatures of eight nations on a treaty at Manila on September 8, 1954, had more ups and downs than a movie serial. Even with the British agreement to take part, there was a dispute at Manila over identifying the aggression referred to in the treaty as Communist aggression. Britain was unwilling to use the word "Communist" in view of its relationship with Communist China, and Dulles insisted that the United States meant Communist aggression. The dispute was compromised by leaving out the adjective in the treaty text, and adding an "understanding of the United States of America" which said that this country in executing the treaty "does so with the understanding that its recognition of the effect of aggression and armed attack and its agreement with reference thereto in Article IV, paragraph 1, apply only to Communist aggression but affirms that in the event of other aggression or armed attack it will consult under the provisions of Article IV, paragraph

2." The intent was to make a distinction between attempts at conquest by Red armies, and area fighting, such as that which had occurred in northern Burma after Chinese Nationalist troops under General Li Mi, cut off from Formosa when the Communists overran the mainland, crossed the border and caused trouble for the Burmese government for several years.

With all controversies over the treaty resolved, and with the date for signing publicly announced, a final hitch arose exactly one hour before the ceremony. Dulles was at the U.S. Embassy, drafting a statement to read at the signing, when he got a telephone call from a foreign minister saying that his government agreed with the U.S. position that aggression must be defined as Communist aggression. The minister had just been instructed that, unless the treaty was changed accordingly, he was not to sign.

Dulles left his press officer, Carl McCardle, to complete drafting the statement, and he drove over to see his friend. What transpired remains their secret, but when the time came for the signing, the two of them walked in together and nobody ever learned that there had been an eleventh-hour byplay which put the treaty in its final jeopardy.

South Vietnam was not a member of the organization, nor was Laos or Cambodia. The Geneva settlement had prohibited any of the three French Indochina states from joining such alliances. SEATO, however, extended its protection to them with a protocol designating all three as "states and territories as to which provisions of Article IV and Article III are to be applicable." Under SEATO's two-sided shield, South Vietnam was given a chance to recover a place among the free nations, but it was still touch and go whether

Diem was a leader possessing the necessary character and stamina to pull the country together.

The British had written him off completely. The French were openly sabotaging his attempt to establish native central authority. Dulles had not met him personally, but on the basis of the U.S. Embassy's reports from Saigon, he concluded that no other figure promised greater hope for the country and the only choice for the United States was to back him. On a Far Eastern trip in February and March, 1955, Dulles got his first chance to meet Diem and was impressed by his qualifications as the kind of patriot needed by the times.

Diem's problems were herculean. First of all he had to absorb in the south the flood of refugees from the Communist north, which eventually totaled 800,000. With economic and personnel help from the United States, the Philippines, and other nations, he handled that problem and got the refugees settled. His personal popularity with the masses, on which the democratic future of Vietnam depended, grew with each trip he made through the country. But the real challenge to his authority, which continued to cast doubt on the country's future, came from two religious sects known as the Cao Dai and the Hoa Hao, and from a gang of river pirates known as the Binh Xuyen. Under the venal French colonial administration the Binh Xuyen paid Bao Dai for their operating concessions, providing money on which he lived in style abroad. It was as fantastic as if President Eisenhower decided to live in Scotland so that he could play golf at St. Andrew's, and "sold" the New York police to a gangster mob in return for a cut on the take.

Diem's ability to deal with the Binh Xuyen was hampered by the questionable loyalty of the native Vietnam army's French-trained chief of staff. Even after Diem achieved sufficient popular backing to sack the officer, General Ely, as commander of the French forces, restrained him from moving against them with plausible arguments that it would lead to disastrous civil warfare at a time when the Communists menaced from the north.

Because Diem's survival as premier under such conditions was problematical, President Eisenhower decided to appoint a personal representative to study the situation and report to him. He selected General J. Lawton ("Lightning Joe") Collins, one of his wartime subordinates in the European theater. After several months Collins, under the persuasion of General Ely, became convinced that Diem could not master the situation. Collins' estimate, at variance with that of the Embassy, caused vacillation in Washington for a period of four weeks during the late spring of 1955, though not at the State Department. Dulles, Deputy Undersecretary Robert Murphy, and Assistant Secretary Walter Robertson all stoutly maintained, with logic, that there was no point in abandoning Diem unless a better, or at least equally good, leader could be found.

During this period there was a NATO Council meeting in Paris, and the three major Western powers made use of the occasion to hold their own separate discussions of the Indochina situation. Three sessions were held on the future of Vietnam.

At the first, Premier Edgar Faure announced that France was through backing Diem. France, he said, had come to the conclusion that Diem was incapable of pulling the country together. He was anti-French, stubborn, strong-willed, and refused to take outside counsel. Dulles replied that the United States knew of no figure in the country capable of replacing Diem, certainly none who had any more chance of success regardless of Diem's supposed handicaps.

Then Faure took a surprising tack. He said that since Vietnam was a source of friction between France and the United States, France was unwilling to have it remain a source of trouble and would offer to withdraw from Vietnam.

What effect Faure intended by this proposal could only be guessed by the Americans. They guessed that Faure expected Dulles to say: "Oh, no, please don't do that!" and perhaps to add that the U.S. would give up its support of Diem for the sake of friendlier relations with France. Dulles, at least, sensed that Faure was engaging in a psychological rather than serious maneuver for he made no attempt to question Faure on what he meant by French withdrawal. Instead he said, "No, if this is such a serious point between us, we'll withdraw." But he added that in any event the United States would support an independent government.

This response was obviously a surprise to Faure. He, likewise, made no attempt to plumb the meaning of American withdrawal to find out whether it meant economic withdrawal, cutting off military aid to the French, or what. The session amounted to a diplomatic Alphonse and Gaston act and ended inconclusively.

The effect of it, however, was to bring Faure back the next evening in a frame of mind to talk things out. "This question is not important enough to bring serious disorder between us," he suggested. "We both offered to give up our interests in Vietnam. But we know that if one gives up it would be an abandonment by both of this country, and that would be bad."

"I said we would support an independent government even if you do withdraw," Dulles reminded him.

Faure went on to say that when he mentioned French withdrawal he didn't regard it as a clash with the United States. It would, he said, be a "gradual procedure," and he thought the two countries should attempt a common approach. With that, the meeting got down to a discussion of Diem's shortcomings and what could be done about them. Sir Harold Caccia, one of the British delegation, said British information was that Diem, whether the West liked him or not, had achieved a strong political position.

Dulles said that, speaking with the kind of frankness the gravity of the situation called for, he could agree with Faure that Diem might not have all the qualities which the three countries would like to see in the head of the Vietnam government.

"But we should not look on him as a calamity we have to bear," said Dulles. "He is a nationalist; he is anti-Communist; he is a force needed if the country is to be saved from Communist control. We must accept the fact of his willfulness, that he is anti-French and probably anti-American. President Rhee of Korea, for example, occasionally attacks me personally. I don't like it, but I realize that these qualities are required by the situation. Diem and Rhee are not amenable to the kind of guidance we might want to give, but they have the qualities the situation needs."

Faure said he would think it over and write a memorandum about it. He did, sending it to Dulles at the Embassy residence next evening shortly before the official dinner for visiting ministers which was to wind up the NATO meetings.

The third and final session on Vietnam was held at Faure's official residence, the Hôtel Matignon, after the NATO dinner. Faure, Macmillan, and Dulles came in their dinner jackets. Dulles acknowledged receipt of Faure's memorandum, which suggested a six-point program for the three governments to follow. It called for a political enlargement of the Diem government; "peaceful solution" of the problem of the sects; cessation by Diem of anti-French propaganda; retention of Bao Dai in his existing role; removal of any French and U.S. functionaries who disturbed Franco-American "harmony"; assurance that French economic, cultural, and financial relations with Vietnam would be maintained.

Dulles rarely pounded the table—his usual anger reaction was to turn beet red—but he did that night. He did it not to express anger but to emphasize the conviction behind his words, expressed with the impressive eloquence of which he was capable when he was fighting to get across the concept of international relations in which he believed.

"Some of these things," he told Faure, "are based on the assumption that Diem will take orders from us." He said the United States could accept the objectives of the French proposals, but that it could not accomplish them by dictating to Diem. "I don't see anyone who can take Diem's place," he went on, "and therefore the situation requires that we gamble on Diem. Any other course is disaster. But we cannot undertake to get a dependable answer from Diem on these proposals. We can only seek to win his trust and confidence. We cannot go to Diem and dictate to him that he should take Mr. A, Mr. B, Mr. C, or Mr. D into his government, and I am thankful this is so with the spirit that prevails in Vietnam today. The fact that the Diem government is supported largely by our money does not give us the right to dictate to it." He cited the U.S.-Philippine relationship for Faure's benefit, pointing out that friendship exists between the former ruler and former colony because of mutual confidence and trust. The best course of action, he argued, was to convince Diem that the French were backing him and not trying to overthrow him.

The result of the meeting was grudging agreement by the French to support Diem, but it failed to be reflected in any change of attitude by the Binh Xuyen back in Saigon. President Eisenhower, troubled by the situation, summoned Collins home for a personal report. "I sent Collins out to give me his personal estimate," he said. "Why should I disregard it?"

Perhaps in the knowledge that Collins was advocating withdrawal of U.S. support from Diem, the Binh Xuyen chose the moment of Collins' report in Washington to launch an attack on Diem's palace. Diem responded firmly. He ordered the army to move against the sects and in a short time they were subdued.

It was a turning point, from which the country moved steadily ahead. Elections were held which dismissed Bao Dai as the head of state, confirmed Diem's authority, and created a constituent assembly which drafted a constitution. Under the Geneva agreement Diem's government was supposed to start conversations with the Vietminh in July, 1955, to set up regulations for a national north-south election the following year which was to determine the political future of the country. Diem refused. His government had refused to sign the Geneva agreement, but a more important reason was that conditions of repression in the north made "free and democratic" elections impossible, as the Geneva agreement required. Despite Diem's defiance, the Communists made no trouble about it. Kremlin boss Nikita S. Khrushchev gave an explanation of it in a speech in Moscow on July 17, 1956. Primarily Khrushchev was complaining of the failure to hold the election, citing it as an example of bourgeois disregard of "electoral laws."

Backhandedly he paid tribute to the strength that had grown in South Vietnam behind SEATO's antiaggression and antisubversion shields. Why, asked Khrushchev, had the scheduled elections not been held? "Because," he answered himself, "a so-called democratic state has firmly entrenched itself in South Vietnam and now holds that part of Vietnam in its hands."

22

. . . .

Nasser and the Dam

THERE was a weekend in mid-July, 1956, when yachting of one sort or another occupied the attention of four prominent world figures.

Egypt's Gamal Abdel Nasser was visiting Yugoslavia's Marshal Tito on his Istrian island retreat of Brioni, a modern pleasure dome of the kind which only successful dictators can afford in these days of high taxes. Brioni is a neat island whose green lawns and white-stone walks and buildings look as well manicured as the poshest parts of Palm Beach or Miami. On a bluff overlooking the sea Tito has a large stone palace, modern in style without being severe, pleasing in effect but lacking any individuality of character such as that of Newport mansions built by capitalist tycoons of another era. There is a wide stone terrace on the seaward side, and steps leading down to a small mole where the Yugoslav president keeps powerful speedboats in which he likes to roar about in the Adriatic waters where Roman galleys once plied. Within a short run by speedboat of this palace is the tiny island of Vanga on which Tito has a small imitation Burmese Buddhist temple. To this island Tito took Nasser, personally piloting the boat across; they were awaiting the arrival the following Wednesday of a third neutralist figure, India's Jawaharlal Nehru, who also got a speedboat ride as part of his visit.

In the Western Hemisphere, on the same weekend, John Foster Dulles was at Sodus Point, New York, east of Rochester, to attend a regatta of Dragon sailboats, a one-design class originating in Scandinavia, for which he had put up the John Foster Dulles trophy. He had donated the cup in 1955, intending to present it then, but the "summit" conference at Geneva had prevented. In 1956 there was no business to interfere.

Both Dulles and Nasser had more on their mind that weekend than yachting. Nasser had business with Tito, and later on with Nehru; but also in his thoughts was the fact that his ambassador to Washington, Ahmed Hussein, was en route back to his post with instructions to accept a U.S.-British offer to help Egypt finance a high dam at Aswan on the Nile—a $1,300,000,000 undertaking which would take twelve to fifteen years to complete and would rank with the greatest engineering projects of all time in size. Dulles knew that it was no longer the simple matter of receiving the Egyptian acceptance, for events had taken place since the offer was made which altered the factors then existing. Indeed the dam project's overtones in world politics called for reassessment of the offer against the developments of three turbulent years since Dulles, making his first fact-finding and impression-gathering trip to the Middle East as Secretary of State, had stopped first in Cairo to see Mohammed Naguib and had met Nasser, the man who really led the ruling military junta which Naguib ostensibly headed.

Dulles had taken off on his Middle East trip on May 9, 1953, seeking the answer to four major problems which the area presented. What could be done to protect the security of the Middle East? How could the United States help the former colonial states, whose protectors had been Britain and France, to preserve the independence they had acquired since the war? What could be done to promote their economic development? Was settlement possible in the dispute between the Arabs and Israel, which had smoldered menacingly ever since the UN-arranged truce of 1949? There were individual problems galore: for example, Prime Minister Mohammed Mossadegh's irresponsible handling of the nationalization of oil in Iran; but the other problems were region-wide.

In accordance with his established custom, after he returned Dulles made a speech reporting on the trip. In it he enunciated a policy of impartiality on behalf of the United States in the Arab-Israeli dispute. Impartiality on the part of the United States was something the Arabs found it hard to believe in; they were convinced from the circumstances under which the State of Israel had been set up by the UN with U.S. backing, and by the immediate U.S. support for it, that America was really the friend of their enemy.

The main impression Dulles had brought back was that in all the crosscurrents of motive and interest in the area there was one thing which some of the states—the "northern tier," which bordered on Russia—had in common. This was a fear of Russian aggression which was more than ideological, being rooted in generations of experience with Russian expansionist practice. These states, he suggested, might find it advantageous to enter a military alliance for their common protection. Any such development, he said, would have to be indigenous, with the countries involved deciding whether they wanted Western powers in it as partners. Two previous attempts to create Middle East defense organizations in partnership with member states of the area had come to nothing because Egypt objected violently. Egypt, which was attempting to oust the British from their base on the Suez Canal, did not want them to remain even as partners.

As a result of the Dulles suggestion, Turkey and Pakistan formed a mutual defense alliance on April 2, 1954. A year later Iraq joined, making it the "Baghdad Pact." Great Britain, whose military treaty with Iraq was running out, knew that the Iraqis were doubtful about renewal and, to avoid another such "colonial" conflict as that with Egypt over the Suez base, joined the pact as a means of putting its military arrangements in that area in line with the nationalistic trend of the times. Iran joined before the year was out.

One feature about the development of the Baghdad Pact not generally known is that it was 100 per cent indigenous in its growth. After Dulles threw out the original suggestion, Turkey took the ball and put it in play. When the two-nation alliance was enlarged at Baghdad it was a surprise to the State Department as well as to Nasser, who by then had replaced Naguib. Literally the United States had taken no step to urge the pact between Dulles' speech in June, 1953, and early 1956, when he sent Deputy Undersecretary Loy Henderson to a pact meeting under instructions to promise U.S. support to its economic committee but not to join, despite British and members' pressure for U.S. adherence. The State Department heartily approved each development, giving encouragement to Iran, for example, when Russia threatened that state diplomatically for announcing intention to adhere. But despite the assumption by foreign policy observers that behind the scenes the United States had been actively promoting it, the action actually came from the states themselves.

One element of motivation in the original Dulles suggestion—now forgotten in assessing the results—is that it was made at a time when the Korean War was still in progress. Negotiations toward truce were taking an encouraging course, but bitter experience had shown that the West could not safely bank on a few encouraging signs of reasonableness on the part of the Communists. The thought behind the "northern tier" concept was that as long as Communism showed any reliance at all on military aggression it behooved nations on its borders to insure themselves against it by collective defense.

The effect of the pact on regional politics was to draw sharp reaction from Nasser in Egypt. Primarily he saw Iraq emerging as Egypt's rival for leadership of the Arab states, though his public objection was that Iraq was endangering her sovereignty and Arab independence by establishing ties with the West.

It made no difference to Nasser that the United States, operating through Ambassador Henry A. Byroade in Cairo, was holding aloof from the pact and at the same time using its influence with Britain toward helping Egypt accomplish her objectives in the Suez Canal dispute. One of the U.S. reasons for not joining the Baghdad nations was the desire to maintain its neutrality in the Arab-Israeli conflict, and Israel also was objecting to the pact. Israel regarded any Arab strengthening as a threat to her security. Nasser insisted on regarding it as a blow to his interests.

While the pact was developing, however, other events were

taking place in the Middle East. Iran's Premier Mossadegh, all but openly threatening the United States to turn his country Communist if his oil demands were not met, posed a blackmail threat which Dulles and President Eisenhower met by flatly refusing to pay. This stand involved a calculated diplomatic risk. Mossadegh's subsequent overthrow at the hands of Iranian mobs came more by "act of God" than by diplomatic pressure; but his removal did open the way for slow, plodding recovery of Iran from the brink of Communism. For this job Dulles adopted the technique he had urged on Dean Acheson in connection with the Japanese peace treaty: give one man the job to do and make him responsible. He picked Herbert Hoover, Jr., an engineer thoroughly familiar with the oil business. Hoover brought it off successfully, and his success prompted Dulles to pick him for undersecretary when Beedle Smith took a job in private business.

The area's main problem, however, remained the Arab-Israeli dispute. To deal with that, Dulles picked a foreign service officer, Francis H. Russell, to act as his special assistant. Russell's assignment was not the same type as Hoover's; Dulles did not consider the problem one that could be turned over to one man; but he did instruct Russell to spend full time on it and keep him constantly advised on all departmental actions, and foreign developments, bearing on it.

As part of the problem—potentially separate from it, but contributing to its possible solution—Dulles appointed movie czar Eric Johnston to see what he could do to get Arab states together with Israel in joint use of the waters of the Jordan River in a development similar to the Tennessee Valley Authority. Better utilization of the Jordan had been a dream in the area for years, and since it was wholly an economic scheme it was thought that agreement on peaceful division of the waters, if it proved possible, would help at least in some degree to foster a climate promoting political settlement. But the Arabs maintained enormous suspicion that anything connected with Israel was booby-trapped, and after Johnston's first trip around the circuit the universal outside judgment was that he had flopped and the project was dead. A Washington correspondent, seeking at the time to badger a State Department official into admitting this as the basis for a story, got a reply which he still cherishes as a reminder that some of the men who patiently try to cope with foreign problems are capable of humorous perspective on themselves. The official replied: "Oh, I wouldn't say that Johnston flopped completely. I think he did some good. He turned the situation from hopeless to bad."

From the time of Russell's appointment in October, 1954, to August, 1955, the Arab-Israeli problem got the most exhaustive examination from all agencies of the U.S. government involved in foreign policy, including the National Security Council, that it was possible to give. The study started with the most basic of questions: Is the Arab-Israeli dispute a problem soluble through diplomacy, or something that could only await the passage of time to rearrange the power factors? If it can be solved, what are the main factors? What can and should be done to rearrange the factors in favor of settlement? How should it be done? The answer to these questions reached early in 1955 was that they were capable of solution; and that solving them would require outside help, but that active great-power mediation would be resented. How to do it was the next question.

The public result of this study was another speech by Dulles on

August 26, 1955, delivered to the Council on Foreign Relations. Although it was cautious and generalized in committing U.S. policy to a new course, this speech made two offers toward ending the conflict. It offered U.S. guarantee of Arab-Israeli frontiers—provided the states involved could agree on them. It offered monetary contribution toward compensation of the Arab refugees who had lost their homes in the creation of Israel.

The United States had already begun to hear rumors that Egypt was shopping for arms in Communist markets. Within weeks after the speech was made the rumors became official. Egypt had made a deal with Czechoslovakia of cotton for arms—just how big remained obscure. It introduced an entirely new element into the picture, upsetting the balance of military power in the area which the United States, Britain, and France had been trying to maintain since 1950, and threatening an arms race.

Late in September, when many of the world's foreign ministers were in New York for the annual meeting of the UN General Assembly, Dulles gave a dinner in his suite at the Waldorf-Astoria for Britain's Harold Macmillan, France's Antoine Pinay, and Russia's V. M. Molotov. All four had been at the "summit" conference where the "spirit of Geneva" was created. The meeting was billed as a discussion of "procedural" questions connected with the impending foreign ministers' meeting at Geneva, and it was, to the extent that the four agreed they would limit the conference to about three weeks; but mainly the three Westerners took occasion to protest to Molotov about the Egyptian arms deal.

Pinay, Macmillan, and Dulles in turn pointed out to him that the three nations had been trying to prevent outbreak of hostilities between Egypt and Israel by preserving an arms balance in the

Middle East. Molotov blandly maintained the arrangement with Czechoslovakia was nothing more than a "commercial transaction." Macmillan replied that none of the three Western governments could regard it as such, and Pinay added that creation of an imbalance in the area increased the threat of war and ran counter to the "spirit of Geneva" which the Russians were seeking so hard to keep alive. The participants in the meeting got the feeling that Molotov was impressed by their argument, but they never broke down his claim that it was all "commercial," though he did promise to pass their views along to his government.

Israel's reaction to the deal was to apply to the United States for arms to offset the Egyptian buildup. Domestic pressure was heavy on the U.S. government to grant Israel's request, amounting to about $65,000,000. The State Department, however, saw danger in that kind of response: it would lead to an arms race which Israel could not hope to win. The Communist bloc had enormous surplus stocks left over from the war, obsolete for its own purposes but valuable in an area which had no experience with advanced weapons. If it came to an arms race, Israel's 1,800,000 population could not hope to absorb as much as the surrounding 40,000,000 Arabs. In addition, the State Department reasoned that it would be fatal to American interests to be jockeyed out of its chosen policy of neutrality in the dispute and forced to take one side—Israel's—against the other.

While tension built up as Communist ships delivered tanks and airplanes to Egypt, two other developments injected new complexities into the cold-war maneuvering over the area. Russia began making offers of economic aid as well as arms to the Arab countries, and Nasser put urgency into an old economic dream of Egypt's:

building a high dam at Aswan that would impound Nile waters so as to add, by irrigation, some 25 per cent to Egypt's arable land.

The Aswan dam, as something designed to improve the miserable economic conditions under which the average Egyptian lived, appealed to the State Department as a worthy project for aid. Ever since King Farouk's overthrow, U.S. interest in Egypt had been based on the tentative judgment that the military junta was motivated more by genuine desire to improve the people's lot than by desire for personal power. Nasser put his request on a crash basis: he wanted to start work during the Nile's low-water period in June, 1956. The difficulty was that it was an enormous engineering and financing job. Nevertheless, the United States and Britain, making a crash response by the standards of democratic procedure, scraped together $70,000,000 between them in an attempt to allow Nasser to undertake preliminary work immediately, building cofferdams and diversion canals that would prepare the way for raising the dam but which would not be wasted effort if the rest of the project was delayed. They did this despite Nasser's increased showing of friendship with the Communists and despite the fact that Britain was considerably more disenchanted with his performance than was the United States. The offer was followed by arrangements with the World Bank for a $200,000,000 loan, and plans for the United States to contribute another $200,000,000 over a period of years to take care of the foreign exchange requirements.

But after the offer was firm, Nasser changed his mind about speed. He notified the United States he did not feel it necessary to begin work in 1956, and that when it started he wanted to do it in one piece. He raised objections to requirements of the World Bank designed to protect Egyptian resources and ensure the stability of the loan. As part of his pressure he hinted that Russia had made him an offer. His minister for national production announced in January—without Soviet contradiction—that Russia had offered a loan of $300,000,000 repayable over fifty years.

This offer, if genuine, dramatized the campaign of economic competition with which the Communists had quietly been penetrating the free world. Aid offers from Russia had first turned up in Afghanistan, then in India. It consisted chiefly of offers to sell equipment on easy terms and supply technicians to assemble it and teach its use. In India, which the United States was patiently cultivating, it provided competition which was not too serious as long as Nehru clung to his announced policy of neutrality and nonalignment with either power bloc, but in the Middle East, where Nasser gave signs of actively playing off both sides against each other for his own benefit, it posed a more dangerous threat.

American reaction was of two types. One was the impulse to outbid Russia. The other, expressed in Congress, was to cut off all aid to countries which tried to deal with both sides. Dulles rejected both approaches. Trying to outbid Russia, he said, would permit the Russians, simply by making offers around the world, to achieve cheap propaganda victory and drain the United States of its resources. Cutting off aid likewise was shortsighted because it might force needy countries to rely on Russia and implied that the U.S. motive for granting aid was to "buy" friendship.

Attempts to steer a course between the two opposite reactions to economic competition led to considerable national debate about U.S. policy toward neutrals. President Eisenhower, Dulles, and Vice-President Nixon made separate attempts to articulate what it was. Their statements were so contradictory in phraseology that they defied reconciliation. Each attempt to rationalize policy only made the contradictions more pronounced. But, regardless of what the leaders said policy was, action taken by the United States made it plain that each country was being considered on its merits against the background of American resources and American interests. The United States continued to honor aid requests from neutrals but still continued to give the lion's share to its friends. In the fiscal year 1956 America's economic aid was divided 58 per cent to nine friendly countries of the Far East, 8 per cent to friendly European nations, and the rest to neutrals, including India and Yugoslavia.

But the spectacle of Nasser, seemingly more and more pro-Communist, apparently about to win U.S. help on one project almost as costly by itself as America's entire world economic expenditures for 1956, began to have an effect on friends as well as neutrals. Stout allies like the Philippines and Pakistan began to ask themselves whether it was worth-while to take sides in the world struggle if by holding aloof the reward was help from both camps. Nasser was making it look as though the United States could be played for a sucker. When the State Department, growing more and more suspicious of his intentions, authorized France to divert some Mystère jet fighters from NATO production for delivery to Israel, Nasser responded by withdrawing Egypt's diplomatic recognition of Formosa and recognizing Communist China. It was a move without any economic or other substantive motive for Egypt, and Dulles interpreted it as a petulant one revealing how far Nasser had departed from his original objective of rebuilding his country for his people's benefit.

The Middle East's hot war flared periodically and subsided as

UN truce machinery tried to keep border incidents under control, but its cold-war tension mounted steadily toward a grand climax. Nasser was a problem child, not only because we wanted his friendship but because national independence was in the U.S. tradition, a bond of sympathy which caused us to strain our basic ties with such colonial powers as England and France when emerging independence clashed with their colonial interests. America was pulled in both directions. It was the basic dilemma of the Middle East: how to reconcile our tradition of kinship with the longing for national independence with the hard fact that we had to retain our special relationships with our proved friends, who mean more to us than neutrals.

On the Aswan dam issue Britain, despite her annoyance with Nasser, was still willing to take part in the project. The assumption had grown that Egypt did not want Western help on the dam and would turn to Russia. The new Soviet foreign minister, Dmitri Shepilov, had visited Cairo. United States intelligence reports conflicted on what offers he had made, but Russia had never denied the Egyptian announcement of a loan offer. Furthermore, Nasser's change of mind about speed on the project, and his raising of objections about the conditions, all pointed in the same direction.

For Dulles, a moment of cold-war climax had come.

It was necessary to call Russia's hand in the game of economic competition. Dulles firmly believed the Soviet Union was not in a position to deliver effectively on all her economic propaganda offers, for reasons which we shall examine in the next chapter.

It was necessary to demonstrate to friendly nations, by act rather than by oral explanation, that U.S. tolerance of nations which felt it necessary to stay out of Western defensive alliances could not brook the kind of insult Nasser presented in his repeated and accumulated unfriendly gestures.

It was necessary to make the demonstration on a grand scale. In Ceylon, the new neutralist premier, Bandaranaike, was talking about selling the Russians radio time on a station which the United States had built. It would mean nothing to react by dismantling and removing the station—the gesture would be too petty.

Nasser combined the right timing, the right geography, and the right order of magnitude for a truly major gambit in the cold war.

The drama was heightened when Ambassador Hussein announced that he had returned to accept the American offer, and to drop all previous objections about the details. Despite some small clues of American attitude dropped by State Department officials in testimony on appropriations bills, the general public assumption was that the United States had won out in the competition with Russia to build the Aswan dam, for reasons Nasser did not explain.

Consequently, when it was announced, following a fifty-minute talk between Dulles and Hussein after they both reached Washington, that the United States was withdrawing its offer to help finance the dam, the effect was electric. The drama had come to a climax with a highly unexpected twist.

Why had Dulles waited so long? Why did he turn down Nasser so brutally, without a chance to save face? Why did he let it go at that, without making propaganda designed to point out the moral to neutrals? In effect, it was Nasser who created the dramatic spectacle. Until he sent Hussein back to announce that Egypt wanted the money for the dam, after all, the United States had gradually reached the conclusion from Nasser's disinterest that he did not intend to pick up the offer. Since it appeared he did not want the money, it seemed unnecessary to announce he would not get it. Only after he raised the issue publicly did it seem appropriate to answer.

The choice was between letting him down easily, through protracted renegotiation that came to nothing, or letting him have it straight. Since the issue involved more than simply denying Nasser money for a dam, a polite and concealed rebuff would fail to make the really important point. It had to be forthright, carrying its own built-in moral for neutrals in a way that the ormolu of applied propaganda would not cheapen.

As a calculated risk the decision was on a grand scale, comparable in the sphere of diplomacy to the calculated risks of war taken in Korea and Formosa.

It risked opening a key Middle East country, one whose territory bracketed the strategic Suez Canal, to Communist economic and political penetration. It risked alienating other Arab nations, controlling an oil supply without which Western Europe's mechanized industry and military defenses would be defenseless.

Dulles' bet was placed on his belief that it would expose the shallow character of Russia's foreign economic pretensions and that most nations would accept the thought that there comes a time when tolerance must give way to firmness. He risked the prestige of the United States on those beliefs, knowing it would bring reaction on a commensurate scale, and counting on U.S. power and resourcefulness to cope with the change and movement in Middle East and cold-war politics which it would bring about. His experience at sailing in diplomatic waters convinced him the breeze would be better if he took a new and independent tack. Nasser reacted one week later, almost to the hour, by seizing the

Suez Canal—but not, surprisingly, by turning immediately to Russia for aid on the dam. The future of that project remained for the moment obscure, an unknown quantity in the maneuvering that was to follow.

23

· · · · · · · ·

Nasser and the Canal

Nasser's seizure of the Suez Canal Company precipitated the sharpest crisis the Western powers had faced in the Middle East, and before it was over produced a tremendously shocking split among the Western powers themselves. It brought a crisis within a crisis, the second being of such historic scope as to create a completely new understanding of motives in "neutral" parts of the world which added immensely to the stature of the United States as moral leader in the fight for peace.

Simultaneously with this development there occurred an equally fundamental crisis within the Communist world's satellite empire, one which interacted with events of the Middle East to the benefit of the United States, but not to the good of the Western world as a whole.

In the course of the canal crisis—during which Dulles was suddenly stricken with an abdominal attack which required an operation for cancer of the intestine—Dulles' intervention with Britain and France on behalf of the United States twice fended off the outbreak of fighting. A third time the fighting did begin, sparked by an Israeli attack on Egypt which prompted Britain and France, deliberately ignoring the advice of the United States and acting on their own, to launch an offensive aimed at seizing the canal. In close consultation with President Eisenhower, Dulles wielded the influence of the United States for peace so vigorously that fighting was stopped within a week.

This was "waging peace" with genuine skill. There was still a fourth war-threat incident when the Russians prepared to capitalize on trouble by sending "volunteers" to Egypt. The consequences of such action, in the light of Chinese "volunteers" in Korea, could have been disastrous. Eisenhower's reaction to it—for by this time Dulles was in the hospital—was to follow the Dulles doctrine that stopping an enemy at "the brink" was the best way of avoiding war. Through public warning the President served notice on Russia that the United States would use force to prevent any such move.

Facing a powerful enemy bent on aggression, Dulles believed that willingness to face "the brink" was the best policy. Facing a weak and misguided neutral, Dulles believed that the best course was to swing moral opinion to bear on him and show him, if possible, in what way he was misguided. Despite the rejection of this theory by the British and French, the Dulles method prevailed in the end.

Dulles was in Lima, Peru, attending the inauguration of a new president, when Nasser announced the canal seizure in an impassioned nationalistic speech saying that Egypt intended to use the shipping revenues to pay for building the Aswan high dam.

British authorities sent Dulles a request to fly immediately to London to confer with them and the French on a course of action, but he declined. He did, however, assign Deputy Undersecretary Robert Murphy, one of the solidest and most experienced career diplomats in the business, to leave immediately for London to represent the United States. Dulles returned to Washington from South America on Sunday, July 29, the same day Murphy arrived in London.

One day's conferences in London impressed Murphy with the immense danger to world peace which Nasser had caused.

Murphy found the French quite ready to go to war with Egypt on the canal issue. The international waterway was of course vital to the economic well-being not only of France and the United Kingdom but of all Western Europe. Through it went the oil of the Arabian peninsula and the Persian Gulf on which the industrial machine of Europe operated and on which depended the ability of NATO's military units to meet attack.

The French were already neck deep in trouble in North Africa. Independence movements had forced them to relinquish control in Tunis and Morocco and threatened the allegiance of Algeria, a vast area of important mineral potential which the French felt was vital to their position as a major world power. They knew Nasser was encouraging the Moslem insurgents and that his Cairo radio was inciting rebellion against French rule. Some of the French officials had become obsessed with the belief that if Nasser could be removed their troubles would be over—an irrational belief, but one that became, with some, an *idée fixe*. Nasser must go; if the British would join in the undertaking, the task would be so much the easier.

Britain's motives did not entirely overlap those of France, though the British had no reason to love Nasser, who had ejected them from the Suez Canal in 1954. The canal's accessibility was more vital to Britain than to France. In addition to threatening a situation in which Britain might be forced to adopt a more expensive transportation route for oil around the Cape of Good Hope, the seizure flouted British prestige in a way that was bound to have repercussions adversely affecting British oil positions on the Persian Gulf, from which she derived approximately enough profit to pay for the oil she needed. Beyond that practical consideration was the psychological: once the proud and undisputed ruler of the seas, Britain had been receding, step by step, from world dominance since the time when Winston Churchill had doughtily declared that he had not become the King's first minister to preside over the liquidation of the British Empire. If Britain could not cope with a ha'penny dictator like Nasser, she was through as a world power.

Under the spur of these motives, the impulse of the British and French was to go to war. The French had no reservations about it; for them the decision was simple. For the British it was more difficult. There were elements in the government which had scruples about reverting to force as a solution.

Murphy, listening to their talk, drafted a cable to Washington on Monday night, July 30, which rated the chances of war very high. After reading it on Tuesday morning Dulles went over to the White House to discuss it with the President. It was on this occasion that Mr. Eisenhower asked him to go to London himself, immediately, a request that resulted, as we noted earlier, in his departure with scarcely two hours' notice.

As he headed east, Dulles knew that if war was to be averted it was up to the United States to prevent it. He had noted that Nasser, somewhat taken aback by the violent reaction which his nationalizing of the canal had created, had quickly moved to assure the world that traffic would go on as usual albeit under Egyptian control. Dulles reasoned that the most logical way to handle the situation would be to convene all the nations affected by possible closing of the canal and talk collectively to Nasser about it.

Between Washington and his first stop at the U.S. base at Argentia, Newfoundland, Dulles spent his time drafting a paper representing the U.S. idea of what action should be taken. With astonishingly little editing, it subsequently became the Tripartite Statement of August 2, issued as a communiqué after his consultations in London. It called for a conference of the eight countries remaining of the signers of the original 1888 Suez Canal convention together with sixteen others who represented the greatest tonnage using the canal or whose trade pattern depended on it. This was the origin of the first Suez conference, held in London on August 16 to 23 inclusive. Dulles was away from Washington exactly seventy hours on that trip, and when he got back he knew the risk of war was still great but that he had bought time for cooling of tempers and calmer discussion.

Russia, India, and Egypt herself were among the nations invited to the first conference. Nasser rejected the bid. Dulles had proposed Geneva as a meeting place in the hope that on neutral ground Nasser would be willing to talk, but the British insisted on London, and thus it was no surprise to Washington that Nasser refused to journey to his enemy's capital. Greece also refused, on account of her strained relations with Britain over Cyprus, but twenty-two nations did convene, including Russia and India. The result was creation of a five-man committee under Australian Prime Minister Robert Gordon Menzies which subsequently went to Cairo and sought to persuade Nasser in five days of meetings to accept the eighteen nations' proposal as a basis of negotiating the dispute. Nasser rejected the overtures.

Dulles made one of his periodic vacation trips to Duck Island while the Menzies committee was in Cairo. The Suez problem was of course uppermost in his mind. Thinking it over in the light of his legal training, it seemed to him that the users of the canal had the equivalent of an "easement" on the waterway, a legal right that they could band together to protect and exercise against the man who threatened to deprive them of its use. On his return from Duck Island he discovered that the British and French were again planning to resort to war, and were making no effort to find some peaceful alternative to the direct negotiation which they had sought and which Nasser had rejected.

For a second time Dulles supplied the original thinking that the situation required of a man determined to make peaceful methods prevail. He cabled Eden outlining a proposal for organization of a Suez Canal Users Association which would hire its own pilots, look after maintenance of the canal, and pay Egypt a fair proportion of the tolls as a sort of rental.

This plan was first announced by Eden himself in the House of Commons. The State Department's motive was to work at the job of keeping the peace, not to claim credit for its ideas; it was only too glad to have Eden adopt the idea. Dulles happened to have a news conference scheduled for the following day; he endorsed the Eden plan and said the United States had been consulting about it.

There was enough difference between Eden and Dulles' explanations of the strategy involved in the plan, however, to raise some questions. Eden had said: "But I must make it clear that if the Egyptian government should seek to interfere . . . Her Majesty's Government and others concerned will be free to take such further steps . . . as seem to be required . . . either through the United Nations or by other means, for the assertion of their rights." His words seemed to threaten Nasser with force if Egypt failed to co-operate with SCUA. Dulles had said: "It is not our purpose to try to bring about a concerted boycotting of the canal. I think under those conditions [blocking of the waterway by Egypt] each country would have to decide for itself what it wanted its vessels to do."

Eden was sorely beset from the outset of the crisis by his own political situation. Although the powerful Labour opposition whole-heartedly backed his initial strong protests to Nasser, when Britain's course seemed to be heading for war the opposition swung against him. Within his own party, however, were diehard Tories who clamored for display of British force in the old Britannia-rules-the-waves pattern. British public opinion grew more and more antiwar as time went on—in fact, some long-standing editorial critics of Dulles hailed him at one stage as a hero for counseling peace—but Eden had his party leadership to consider, too.

The effect of this British internal tug of war about policy showed up in two ways: it caused Eden to make his speeches sound as war-like as possible in an effort to keep his Tory diehards quiet in Commons, and it caused him to waver between the forthright French advice to fight and be done with it and the steady American advice not to fight but to negotiate.

The seeming difference over SCUA's role in strategy between the United States and Britain, arising out of the remarks quoted above, later led to charges from across the Atlantic that Dulles had first agreed to an organization with "teeth," capable of sanctions against Egypt such as boycotting the canal, only to back down later. Lack of time for complete understanding of purpose on both sides of the Atlantic may have entered into this erroneous impression, but in fact and on the record U.S. policy did not go through the ups and downs it was credited with. It was consistent and purposeful.

The basic purpose, whether Eden understood it privately or not, was to assert for the canal users the enjoyment of the international waterway's facilities as a matter of right, not of Egyptian sufferance; and to create a situation in which, if traffic was stopped, Nasser would be responsible and could be brought to answer before the world. Nasser understood the purpose if Eden did not, for he made the most meticulous effort not to interfere with transit of the canal. Up to the end he maintained the position of a man who could say: "What's all the shouting about? Your ships are going through, aren't they?"

Despite the British wavering, however, a second Suez conference was held in London from September 19 to 21 inclusive, and SCUA was organized on paper by fifteen of the original twenty-two nations, with arrangements made for bringing it actively into being. Before emplaning for home Dulles had a final talk with Eden, urging him again to play it so that Nasser would be the one to take hostile or obstructive acts against the users before attempting to carry the Suez dispute to the United Nations. Only in such event, Dulles argued, would the British and French have a case which the UN would support.

Then, on landing at Washington, Dulles was greeted by the news that Britain and France had independently lodged a complaint before the UN's Security Council. Somewhat annoyed, the U.S. could do nothing more than back up its allies.

The Security Council consideration of the dispute took from October 5 to 13 inclusive. Egypt, so far unwilling to negotiate, was invited to attend the discussions and sent its foreign minister, Dr. Mahmoud Fawzi, to New York, backed by Nasser's trusted lieutenant, Wing Commander Ali Sabry, who exercised the back-of-the-scenes authority. Progress toward settling the dispute came, however, not from Security Council efforts but from the personal diplomacy of the UN's Secretary General, Dag Hammarskjold.

Hammarskjold proposed that he get together the foreign ministers of the three countries chiefly concerned—Britain, France, and Egypt—and see what compromise could be made. His plan had the virtue, by excluding participation of the United States, of also excluding Soviet Russia, which of course was present at the Security Council ready to use her veto to keep trouble alive if possible. "I will be acting merely as a chaperon," Hammarskjold told Dulles. The usually sober-faced American grinned. "My understanding of a chaperon," said Dulles, "is a person whose job is to keep two people apart. Your job is to get the parties together."

Accordingly, on Wednesday, October 10, the four men—Hammarskjold, Selwyn Lloyd, Christian Pineau, and Fawzi—met without aides around a low coffee table in Hammarskjold's 38th-floor office with its view over the East River and the flat roofs and factory chimneys of Brooklyn. The talk was mostly in English; Fawzi and Hammarskjold were completely at home in that language as well as French; Pineau understood English well though he preferred to speak in French; Lloyd could understand most of Pineau's French. Only occasionally did they call in an interpreter.

In a series of intense discussions in this setting during the rest of the week, the three foreign ministers under Hammarskjold's patient and sleepless chaperonage agreed on a set of six principles that were to guide future negotiations of the canal dispute. They were: (1) no discrimination against transit through the canal; (2) respect for Egypt's sovereignty; (3) insulation of canal operations from the politics of any country (a principle which the U.S. considered highly important); (4) fixing of canal tolls by agreement between Egypt and the users; (5) allocation of a "fair proportion" of revenues for canal developments; and (6) arbitration of compensation to be paid to the old Suez Canal Company which Nasser had expropriated.

These principles were approved unanimously by the Security Council at a night session, October 13-14. Dulles left New York believing the parties would carry out a plan for beginning actual negotiations under the guidance of the six principles at Geneva on Monday, October 29. The dispute still was not settled, but it seemed that time and patience would do it, and peaceably.

24

· · · · · · · ·

The Alliance Splits over Egypt

No sooner had the Security Council set the disputing nations on the path of settlement when sensational news began to come out of the capitals of satellite Europe: first from Warsaw, then from Budapest. They distracted public attention from the Suez crisis but did not obscure the latter completely. In the press there was a news leak from Cairo that there was to be a negotiators' meeting at Geneva on October 29, but there was denial from London that Egypt had presented new proposals. Monday, October 29, arrived without any forgathering of plenipotentiaries and, with the headlines black with news of the Communist revolt, most newspaper readers had forgotten the date at Geneva.

In Washington, at 2:15 P.M. that day, Israel's ambassador, Abba Eban, called at the State Department to keep an appointment with Assistant Secretary William Rountree. Eban had just returned from Tel Aviv, having been called home for consultation, and his arrival in Washington coincided with disquieting reports of military mobilization in Israel. These reports, which threatened to give an entirely new and menacing tone to the Middle East crisis, already had caused President Eisenhower to send Israel's premier, David Ben-Gurion, two personal messages taking note of the mobilization and urging him not to initiate any step that would disturb world peace.

One other official was present at the Eban-Rountree interview. He was Fraser Wilkins, officer in charge of Arab-Israeli affairs. Eban told Rountree that Israel's mobilization was defensive in motive, not aggressive. It was prompted, he said, solely by fear of attack from neighboring Arab states which had been conducting provocative raids across Israel's borders. Israel felt obliged to take all precautions.

Eban was a very able ambassador but was also fairly loquacious. He had spent about half an hour developing this theme when Wilkins was urgently called from the room by Rountree's secretary. She showed Wilkins a dispatch that had just come over the news ticker: an announcement that Israel had launched an invasion of Egypt's Sinai Peninsula.

Wilkins took the yellow ticker copy back into Rountree's office. He waited until Rountree finished his sentence, then broke the news. Eban brought the interview to an end immediately, saying he would have to return to the embassy to read his reports.

Thus did the United States learn that plans made behind its back by three of its allies and carried out in secret had taken effect. The full scope of the plan was still not apparent, but already U.S. intelligence had collected a long series of out-of-pattern bits of information, pieced them together, and predicted what was about to happen. Next day, when the British and French issued their ultimatum to Egypt and Israel, the whole tragic maneuver was out in the open.

Only a day-by-day account of what had gone before, and what immediately followed, can give an adequate picture of the jarring crisis it produced, one so tremendous that for some time it crowded even the incredibly gallant Hungarian revolt out of first position for attention.

October 16 was the critical date, but the collusion went back further than that. It was on October 16, in Paris, that Sir Anthony Eden and Selwyn Lloyd were persuaded by Guy Mollet and Christian Pineau to go along on a plot which the French had already cooked up with the Israelis. This was only three days after the two foreign ministers had participated with Hammarskjold in drawing up the six principles to guide settlement.

The plan was primarily Israeli in origin, though the French joined in willingly enough. The two nations were, after all, natural allies in the situation. Egypt was their common enemy.

Signs of growing affinity between France and Israel began to be noticed soon after the canal take-over by Nasser, though their significance was lost at the time. Menahem Beigin, one-time terrorist and leader of Israel's Herut party, which advocated expansion to Israel's "historic borders," visited Paris and was given the unprecedented honor of being asked to address the Chamber of Deputies. The head of Israeli intelligence, Colonel Yehashafat Harkabi, made a trip to France. The French ambassador to Israel became "the most popular man in the country" because, Israeli diplomats explained, he had become proficient in Hebrew; but another reason for their enthusiasm about him may have been that France very quietly supplied Israel with more than thirty of its latest jet fighter planes.

During this period Dulles and other officers of the State Department were repeatedly telling both France and Britain that any attack on the canal would bring disaster to the Allied cause. The American judgment was that it would have practical political effect only if it succeeded in toppling Nasser from power. The United States had no doubt that the British and French could mount the military power to seize the canal but did not believe this would automatically overthrow Nasser. On the contrary, the U.S. estimate of the Arab temper was that a touch of martyrdom as the victim of attack would only enhance Nasser's hold on the mob.

The big, underlying reason why the United States differed from its partners on the approach to Nasser was that the "colonial" attitude, making exception to the UN Charter's renunciation of force when dealing with weak or "backward" nations, threatened the loss of all Asia in the cold war with Russia for men's minds. Peoples who had undergone "colonial" treatment and recently won their independence by one means or another would look to Russia as their proclaimed champion, comparing Soviet propaganda with Western performance in a specific and dramatic instance against the background of past colonial history. But there were practical reasons, too, for U.S. opposition.

The U.S. warning was that, even if successful in taking the canal, Britain and France would get bogged down in the same kind of frustrating guerrilla warfare that was already plaguing France in North Africa; that attack would immediately invite blocking of the canal by Egypt and sabotage of the pipelines carrying oil from the Persian Gulf; that Europe would undergo a sharp oil shortage while painful adjustments were made in traffic patterns; that supply of oil from the Western Hemisphere would require dollars which the two countries did not have—and, finally, that they could not expect the United States to support them in any such venture.

But no American was on hand to repeat these warnings on October 16, when Eden and Lloyd conferred in Paris with Mollet and Pineau, and the wavering British allowed themselves to be persuaded. Since the active planning up to then had been conducted between the Israelis and the French, Eden and Lloyd were technically truthful later on when in speeches before the House of Commons they insisted that there had been no plotting with the Israelis. American officials who knew the inside story noted, however, that they always were careful to put it in terms of Israel, not France. Their dealings had been with France.

After October 16 a curtain came down over Middle East planning of Britain and France. No longer was there daily consultation across the Atlantic on plans for peaceful action. Dulles, even as he turned his attention to the new developments in Poland, sensed that something was wrong and cabled both Paris and London to see if Ambassadors Douglas Dillon and Winthrop Aldrich could find out what was going on.

Lloyd was vague in talking to Aldrich and stalled him in discussing what Britain intended. He misled Aldrich into believing that Britain still hoped to have talks with Egypt. American intelligence learned that France had given Israel many more Mystère fighters than Paris admitted officially. The United States noted an abnormal step-up in volume of communications between France and Israel. Then, toward the end of October, more ominous signs made themselves felt in Washington despite preoccupied fascination with satellite developments.

On Thursday, October 25, reports reached the State Department from Israel that the country apparently was beginning a military mobilization. The following day another cable reported these suspicious elements: the French and British seemed to know more about what was going on than did the Americans, but were evasive in talking; the Israelis brushed it off as being only partial mobilization, but the U.S. military attaché added that, judging by what he could see from personal observation, it was total.

Saturday morning, October 27, Dulles took these disquieting reports to the White House for consultation with the President. Dulles was scheduled to leave that day for Dallas, Texas, to make a speech, and Ike was due at Walter Reed Hospital for a medical checkup. Before the President left the White House he sent Ben-Gurion a personal message saying he hoped that Israel would take no steps endangering peace.

Sunday, October 28, Mr. Eisenhower was still at the hospital when a sizzling cable came in from Ambassador Edward B. Lawson at Tel Aviv reporting that Israel's mobilization was indeed total. Despite the government's protests that it was merely defensive, he was convinced that Israel intended military action. Herbert Hoover, Jr., acting secretary while Dulles was out of town, sped out to the hospital with it and came back with a second personal message from the President to Ben-Gurion. He also returned with instructions to arrange evacuation of Americans from the potential war area—Israel and her neighboring states—indicating not only the extreme gravity with which the United States viewed the developments but also the extent to which American intelligence had been able to piece together the nature of the secret plan and warn the President what was about to happen.

After his return from Texas on Sunday afternoon, Dulles issued instructions that the Arab countries be notified, through our ambassadors, of the appeals to Ben-Gurion and likewise warned against taking military action. He summoned Eban to discover whether he could explain Israel's mobilization, in view of his recent return from his capital, and got the same "defensive mobilization" story which Eban was recounting next day to Rountree when the news of the invasion broke.

The British were temporarily without an ambassador in Washington, Sir Roger Makins having been called home, and his successor, Sir Harold Caccia, not having arrived; the new French ambassador, Hervé Alphand, was absent from town. Dulles summoned the British and French chargés d'affaires, J. E. Coulson and Charles Lucet, informed them that if fighting broke out the United States probably would ask the United Nations to try to stop it, and asked support of the British and French governments. Coulson and Lucet promised to query their foreign offices and give him a reply.

Monday, October 29—the day Egypt had been willing to meet in Geneva to talk canal settlement—the British Mediterranean Fleet set out from Malta for Cyprus. This fact, when it became known, was the clinching proof of collusion in the three-nation attack on Egypt, if any were needed. This was the beginning of massive military movement on the part of Britain and France, and it occurred simultaneously with the Israeli invasion.

In Washington, immediately after his session with Eban, Rountree hurried to Dulles' office and informed him of the news. Senior departmental officers were summoned to the Secretary's office for conference, after which Dulles sent again for the British and French chargés, who arrived at 4:50 P.M. Dulles suggested an immediate appeal to the UN Security Council. The two men were still unable to reply on behalf of their governments and promised again to inquire. They left at 5:10. From their air of innocence, State Department officials concluded later that for security or other reasons their foreign offices had deliberately kept them in ignorance of attack plans.

The Israeli invasion, of course, represented a most serious crisis, and the President summoned an emergency meeting at the White House at 7:00 P.M. In addition to Dulles, those attending included Admiral Arthur Radford, chairman of the Joint Chiefs of Staff, Secretary of Defense Charles E. Wilson, CIA Director Allen W. Dulles, and Sherman Adams. At this meeting UN action was decided on, and Presidential Press Secretary James Hagerty was instructed to issue a statement reaffirming U.S. intention to adhere to the 1950 tripartite declaration by which the United States, Britain, and France agreed to maintain existing boundaries, control the flow of arms in the Middle East, and to take action within or without the UN to stop aggression.

One other event occurred that night, never revealed until now. The President took the highly unusual step of summoning the British chargé to the White House. The tall, lantern-jawed, blond J. E. Coulson arrived unnoticed at 8:15 and was taken to the President's study in the mansion; there, in the presence of Secretary Dulles and Colonel Andrew J. Goodpaster, Eisenhower ignored protocol to tell him personally how gravely concerned he was about the threat to peace. The President, angry clear through at what by this time he knew from intelligence sources was an Israeli-French-British plot to seize the canal, couched his language diplomatically but forcefully conveyed to the Britisher the depth of his feeling. Coulson, still in the dark, had no choice but to listen.

Tuesday, October 30, took the President to Florida on a quick campaign trip. In New York Ambassador Henry Cabot Lodge announced that he would ask the Security Council to deal with the Israeli attack on Egypt. En route back from Florida, Eisenhower got word during a stop at Richmond, Virginia, that Britain and France had sent an ultimatum to Egypt and Israel. It demanded immediate cessation of all fighting and withdrawal of military forces at least ten miles from the Suez Canal. With it went a demand that, in order to ensure the safety of the canal and its commerce, Egypt accept temporary occupation of key canal zone defenses and Port Said, Ismailia, and Suez by British and French forces.

The combined irony and ingenuousness of this demand quickly became apparent when Egypt scuttled ships all along the canal and the British-French military action turned into an ignoble fiasco, but its brutality was the point immediately apparent to U.S. officials. In effect the two nations informed Egypt that unless fighting stopped they would occupy Egyptian territory; and that even if it stopped they would occupy anyway.

As soon as he got back to Washington, Ike sent personal messages to Eden and Mollet urging them not to use force until the UN had a chance to act on the crisis. In New York, Lodge introduced a resolution calling on Israel and Egypt to stop fighting, on Israel to withdraw behind its armistice line, and for members to refrain from interfering. For the first time in Security Council history Britain and France exercised their right of veto against a U.S. resolution. The veto was repeated when Russia offered a similar resolution, stripped of the injunction against interference by other UN members.

Wednesday, October 31, saw the beginning of the British-French air attack on Egypt. Eisenhower announced that he would make an address by radio and TV to the nation that night, canceling a brief political campaign trip he had planned for that day. Dulles worked most of the day helping him prepare it. In New York the Security Council adopted a Yugoslav resolution calling an emergency session next day of the UN's General Assembly, where the veto could not be exercised. World capitals reacted strongly against the British-French stand, and Canada announced that it was halting delivery of jet planes ordered by Israel.

In his speech that night Eisenhower reviewed the crowded series of developments in Poland and Hungary, as well as in the Middle East. "In the circumstances I have described," he said, "there will be no United States involvement in these present hostilities." They were words chosen with care, limited to the situation as it existed when he spoke. Then in five terse and eloquent paragraphs, which Dulles had written for him, he summed up the American viewpoint:

"In all the recent troubles in the Middle East there have, indeed, been injustices suffered by all nations involved. But I do not believe that another instrument of injustice—war—is a remedy for these wrongs.

"There can be no peace without law. And there can be no law if we work to invoke one code of international conduct for those we oppose, and another for our friends.

"The society of nations has been slow in developing means to apply this truth. But the passionate longing for peace on the part of all peoples of the earth compels us to speed our search for new and more effective instruments of justice.

"The peace we need and seek means much more than mere

absence of war. It means the acceptance of law and the fostering of justice in all the world.

"To our principles guiding us in this quest we must stand fast. In so doing, we can honor the hopes of all men for a world in which peace will truly and justly reign."

On Thursday, November 1, Israeli forces cut off the Gaza Strip and penetrated deeply into the Sinai Peninsula. Egypt collapsed a bridge across the canal and scuttled ships along its length. British-French air attack on Egypt continued. In Washington, with the General Assembly scheduled to convene in New York, Eisenhower asked his Secretary of State to go there personally to handle the U.S. case. Dulles took off by air on forty-five minutes' notice.

It was a misty, rainy day. While in the air, Dulles' pilot received word that bad weather had socked in all three of New York's airfields—LaGuardia, Idlewild, and Newark. While he circled above Philadelphia, Dulles worked on preparation of the U.S. resolution, weighing various considerations in discussions with his aides. About the time he finished, the pilot got word that minimum landing conditions existed at Newark, so he slid down through the overcast and Dulles rushed by automobile to the UN meeting, arriving late, while Sir Pierson Dixon of Britain was speaking. He got inscribed as speaker after T. F. Tsiang, the Chinese representative.

When he finally got the floor, late in the evening, Dulles spoke extemporaneously under strong emotion. "I doubt," he began, "that any delegate ever spoke from this forum with as heavy a heart as I have brought here tonight . . . the United States finds itself unable to agree with three nations with whom it has ties, deep friendship, admiration, and respect, and two of whom constitute our oldest, most trusted and reliable allies.

"The fact that we differ with such friends has led us to reconsider and re-evaluate our position with the utmost care, and that has been done at the highest levels of our government. Even after that re-evaluation, we still find ourselves in disagreement. Because it seems to us that that disagreement involves principles which far transcend the immediate issue, we feel impelled to make our point of view known."

Reviewing the facts that had brought about the meeting, Dulles agreed that recent moves had grown out of "a long and sad history of irritations and of provocations."

"But," he argued, "if we were to agree that the existence of injustices in the world, which this organization so far has been unable to cure, means that the principle of renunciation of force is no longer respected, and that there still exists the right wherever a nation feels itself subject to injustice to resort to force to try to correct that injustice, then we would have, I fear, torn the [UN] Charter into shreds and the world would again be a world of anarchy.

"All the great hopes that are placed in this organization and in our Charter would have vanished and we would be as we were when World War II began, with only another tragic failure in place of what we hoped would be—and still can hope will be—a barrier against the recurrence of a world war. . . .

"It is still possible for the united will of this organization to have an impact on the situation and perhaps to make it apparent to the world, not only for the benefit of ourselves, but of all posterity, that there is here the beginning of a world of order.

"We do not, any of us, live in societies in which acts of disorder do not occur. But we all of us live in societies where, if those acts occur, something is done by constituted authority to deal with them. At the moment we are the constituted authority. While we do not have under the Charter the power of action, we do have a power of recommendation, a power which, if it reflects the moral judgment of the world community, of world opinion, will, I think, be influential on the present situation."

Just twenty-four hours after he made this speech Dulles was stricken with cramp symptoms which led to his sudden operation. Had that dangerous operation proved fatal, he could not have asked for a more appropriate epitaph expressing the goal of his life's work than the speech he had just made before the nations of the world.

Dulles concluded the speech by introducing a resolution urging (1) that all parties involved in hostilities agree to an immediate cease-fire and halt movement of military forces and arms into the area; (2) that the parties to the Arab-Israeli armistice of 1949 withdraw all forces behind armistice lines and desist from raids; (3) that all UN members refrain from introducing military goods into the war area; (4) that, after cease-fire, steps be taken to reopen the canal; (5) that the Secretary General report on compliance; and (6) that the General Assembly remain in emergency session pending compliance.

When this resolution was brought to a vote after midnight it was approved 64 to 5. The only opposition came from Britain, France, Israel, and two British Commonwealth members, Australia and New Zealand.

Dulles remained at the session, though he had been working unceasingly with little sleep for five days, until the Assembly acted also on a resolution dealing with the Hungarian situation. Reaching his suite at the Waldorf after 4:00 A.M., he poured himself a slug of rye on the rocks, stirred it with his forefinger, and inquired cheerfully of aides: "When shall we go back to Washington? How about a takeoff at eight o'clock?" The younger men groaned involuntarily. The Secretary's sober face broke into a wide grin. "All right," he said. "I'll settle for leaving the hotel at eleven-thirty." But he himself was up and talking by telephone with the President at 9:30.

That same day—Friday, November 2—Canada's Minister for External Affairs Lester B. Pearson suggested organization of a UN police force, a suggestion subsequently adopted. There were anti-British disorders at Bahrein, one of the Persian Gulf oil centers. The British and French claimed destruction of the Egyptian air force.

And in Washington, retiring around 10:00 P.M., Dulles was awakened, after an hour's sleep, by stomach cramps. He went back to a fitful sleep but was roused again by a recurrence of pain at 2:00 A.M. Doctors were called. By five o'clock it was decided to take him to Walter Reed Hospital for tests; his symptoms indicated appendicitis. Top officials of the department were notified. Dulles talked to some of them personally, including Undersecretary Hoover, giving various instructions before departing at seven for the hospital.

After tests, the doctors decided on an exploratory operation, which was undertaken that afternoon and revealed a malignant lesion in the lower intestine. Dulles was under the knife for more than two hours, but after it was over the surgeons felt they had accomplished what they described as "complete removal of the diseased tissue." With Dulles out of action, Herbert Hoover, Jr., took charge of U.S. moves in the Middle East crisis, and Eisenhower assumed personal command of top-level strategy.

On Saturday, November 3, Britain and France rejected the UN's cease-fire resolution unless various conditions were met, one of them being acceptance by Egypt and Israel of the UN police force which Pearson had suggested. Egypt went on scuttling ships in the canal and four pumping stations on the Iraq Petroleum Company's pipeline across northern Syria were sabotaged, apparently with Syrian government acquiescence if not participation. This abruptly stopped the flow of oil from Iraq.

At the United Nations one day merged into the next as the Assembly sat through the night seeking to deal with the crisis. On the night of November 3-4 the Assembly adopted, 59 to 5, a resolution calling on the Middle East belligerents to comply with the previous cease-fire recommendation. It also approved a Canadian resolution requesting Hammarskjold to submit a plan within forty-eight hours for a UN police force. Hammarskjold was back the next night with a proposal that small nations make up the force, and it was adopted 57 to 0. At dawn on November 5—just about the time the Assembly was voting—British and French paratroops were landing at the north end of the Suez Canal. That same day fighting ceased between Egypt and Israel.

At this point a new danger arose from an outside source. It was November 5—election eve in the United States.

Soviet Premier Nikolai Bulganin sent strong messages to Eden, Mollet, and Ben-Gurion saying that Russia "is fully determined to apply force in order to crush the aggressors and restore peace in the East." He also sent Eisenhower a message proposing the U.S. and Russia join in forcibly putting down the Egyptian fighting.

The latter proposal Eisenhower promptly rejected as "unthinkable." He wasted no time replying to Bulganin: "The introduction of new forces under these circumstances would violate the United Nations Charter, and it would be the duty of all United Nations members, including the United States, to oppose any such effort."

This prompt and resolute action prevented what threatened to develop into a repetition of the Chinese "volunteer" episode in Korea, with consequences which undoubtedly would have been far more disastrous. At noon, Washington time, on November 6, while Americans were voting, Egypt appealed for arms and volunteers, but in London Eden announced acceptance of the UN's cease-fire demand to take effect at 7:00 P.M., and Egypt subsequently withdrew her request. In any event, the "volunteers" never materialized.

The turning point had been reached. Hostilities had been ended and the belligerents persuaded to pick up the broken pieces and try to live together once again.

Some six weeks later, after he had recovered with an amazing display of physical stamina and had plunged again into the thick of work by attending a NATO meeting in Paris, Dulles was questioned at a press conference about the practice of consultation among the Western allies, which the British and French had breached in their invasion. Dulles said it was a mistake for anyone to think that America's opposition to its allies was caused by their failure to consult us on the move.

"It is quite true," he said, "that the actual attack occurred without our knowledge, and came as a complete surprise to us. But there had been prior consultation about this matter for nearly three months . . . they knew our views; they knew why we were opposed to any such action. Our complaint is not that there was not a discussion of these matters; the point was that we considered that such an attack under the circumstances would violate the Charter of the

United Nations and would violate Article 1 of the North Atlantic Treaty itself, which renounces the use of force."

In his own mind Dulles regarded the decision to oppose Britain and France as quite the most significant policy decision taken by the United States since the war. The decision to enter Korea was simple by comparison, based on the knowledge that ultimate self-protection required fighting an enemy bent on aggression. This one required taking the painful course of breaking with close friends for the sake of UN principles.

It was made with full realization that such a break could not occur without strong repercussions—but the repercussions remained infinitely preferable to the alternative. The alternative was a disastrous breakdown in world order and almost certainly a new world war waged with nuclear weapons. In meeting the test successfully, the UN produced its greatest demonstration that even without armies of its own it was capable of effectively swaying world opinion on behalf of the principles of justice.

25

• • • • • • •

Unity in Western Europe

THE agony involved for the United States in deciding it had to break with its main European partners on the issue of force in the Middle East can be appreciated if it is set against the fact that European unity was what the United States wanted most to accomplish in foreign policy. From time to time other objectives forced themselves momentarily to the forefront; at times Middle East or Far East problems became more immediately important.

But the unity of Western Europe remained the solid core. Even at the moment of schism with Britain and France, even at the height of his personal anger, President Eisenhower made a point of reaffirming the basic nature of the ties. In his television speech following the start of the British-French attack on Egypt he said:

"We believe these actions to have been taken in error, for we do not accept the use of force as a wise or proper instrument for the settlement of international disputes. To say this, in this particular instance, is in no way to minimize our friendship with these nations, nor our determination to maintain those friendships. And we are fully aware of the grave anxieties of Israel, of Britain and France. We know they have been subjected to grave and repeated provocations."

Ike's profession of continued friendship was more than lip service to tradition. Blockage of Middle East oil quickly produced shortage in England and the Continent. The United States, which had set up a government-sponsored industry committee during the summer to study methods of making up shortage, did not believe it wise to throw the switch to put its plan into operation. The plan had been intended for use in case Nasser blocked the canal; to use it after the British and French had provoked blockage by their own action might disabuse the Arab nations of their new understanding that the United States was serious about refusing to make exception to its principles for the sake of its friends. It might, the government judged, nullify the dramatic effect of the demonstration which the United States had just made.

But the Arab world had to learn, too, that America was not casting its friends aside. That word was conveyed after the government became convinced in its own mind that Britain and France would withdraw their invasion troops and thus abandon the method of force. Director Arthur Flemming of the Office of Defense Mobilization announced that the Middle East Emergency Committee, which had been held in suspension, would resume its work, which involved such steps as rerouting oil from the Western Hemisphere to Europe and taking tankers out of mothballs to provide more carrying capacity.

The United States had no desire to deal out punishment to its partners—they had brought down enough on themselves. Prior to Dr. Flemming's announcement the government moved to make oil available to Europe without publicity. This was done in two ways: private companies, inquiring whether the government would object if they filled British orders, were told to go ahead. With the President's knowledge, Dr. Flemming made a trip to New York to meet with oil executives and to underline the government's desire that any European orders for oil be filled. Official government planning for such aid, he explained, had to await assurance that the British and French would withdraw from Egypt; otherwise, for the United States to appear to be siding with them might provoke Arab sabotage of the one oil pipeline still operating and cut off all Middle East supplies completely.

The story of the American oil industry's immediate response is told in the jump in oil shipments from U.S. Gulf Coast ports during November. Suez Canal traffic was cut off just prior to the first week of November; that week 287,000 barrels of oil were shipped to Western Europe from Gulf Coast ports. The next week shipments jumped to 1,484,00 barrels; the third week, to 2,247,000; the fourth week, to 6,608,000.

Official government sanction for a program of aid to Europe was announced on December 8. Before it came, the United States had shipped 16,282,000 barrels of oil to Western Europe since November 1.

And Dulles, making his remarkable recovery from a very serious operation, plunged immediately into the task of restoring the ties by leaving for Paris at the end of his first week back at work. He went to attend a NATO meeting at which Western Europe, having gone through a strongly emotional experience in its own affairs and having seen Soviet brutality break through the post-Stalin camouflage in Hungary, remembered anew the reasons that had brought it into existence and achieved a renewed realization of the need for perfecting the union. "I would not go so far as to say," said Dulles on his return, "that there are no scars that remain—no differences of opinion about past performance. But the best way to forget the past is to be planning for the future. That is a rule that I think applies to life in all its aspects, including international life. As we think about the future, and plan for the future together, there tends to be a healing of the old wounds, and I think that process is under way."

European unity was the first task Dulles tackled as the new administration took up the responsibilities of foreign policy; but any breakdown by geography of the major separate problems which confronted the United States fails to convey a sense of the furious pace forced on him. Particularly was this true during the year 1954. Nor does such a breakdown highlight the peaks of achievement and valleys of frustration recorded within a specific time span.

From an intense negotiation with the Russians at Berlin he went to Caracas to write the Dulles Doctrine of defense against subversion into the Pan-American community's world outlook. Scarcely back from there, he shuttled the Atlantic like a commuter, seeking to build Western unity before the Indochina conference, only to see it shatter. Resuming the attempt to rally the Allies after the Asian conference, he was in the midst of preparations for Manila's repair job when word came from Europe that the worst had happened and the French had capped their disgraceful shilly-shallying on the European Defense Community issue by defeating the treaty. While he was still in the Far East he got a cable from Anthony Eden suggesting that he continue on around the world to begin the EDC repair job on his way back. But the Formosa crisis had risen phoenix-like out of the ashes of Indochina and President Eisenhower had scheduled a National Security Council meeting in Denver to consider action. Dulles returned via the Pacific and stopped in Denver for the meeting. He remained in Washington only one weekend—thirty-six hours—before taking wing again for Europe to see what could be done about splicing the raveled threads of Western unity. It was this brief grounding which gave the Gridiron Club inspiration for its skit lampooning his travels. He seemed to live in an airplane; indeed, the small son of one of his security officers, who was taken periodically to the airport to bid his father good-by or welcome him home, identified the picture of a Constellation in a magazine advertisement by saying, "That's where Mr. Dulles lives."

At Bermuda Ike and Dulles had resisted French attempts to wriggle off the spot on which governmental espousal of EDC had put them in domestic politics. The EDC principle had been originated by the French in 1949 in an attempt to enlist West Germany for European defense in the face of Russia's postwar belligerence, and at the same time overcome the Frenchman's scruples about permitting the enemy which had invaded his homeland thrice within living memory to rebuild an army. EDC was to be a supranational army, mixing in one command soldiers of France, Germany, Belgium, the Netherlands, Luxembourg, and Italy to comprise the Continental component of NATO. Its virtue was that it carried built-in safeguards against the uncontrolled rebirth of German militarism. Also it opened promise that, once military fraternization was achieved under controlled conditions, the centuries-old rivalries which had made warfare a recurring cycle in Western Christendom would wither, and a friendship would be possible on which to build one foundation pillar toward durable peace.

France's governments, despite their frequent overturns, all clung to the EDC principle but none dared face the National Assembly for a showdown. Always it meant, to those in power, the risk of their jobs. Premier Laniel and Foreign Minister Bidault, with the issue looming once again at the time of Bermuda, sought to find whether the United States had an alternative which might be more acceptable to their domestic politicians.

Ike and Dulles firmly said no. The fact was they did have an alternative—German membership in NATO as a full-fledged partner—but to loosen pressure in any degree from the drive for EDC would, they knew, be tactically fatal. In any case EDC was preferable because of its embryonic element of European nationality-mingling and because uncontrolled partnership with Germany would be an even more bitter pill in French politics.

The Administration had been dubious of EDC's success, and even before taking office had considered whether to follow through or try a new approach. Dulles told Ike the EDC treaty was prostrate and it would take his full force and backing to revive it. Ike, who had played so big a part in turning NATO from an idea to a defense force, decided to nail the U.S. flag to the EDC mast and scud for a showdown. He sealed the decision by sending NATO's commander, Albert Gruenther, a confidential message, promising support, and a New Year's greeting to Konrad Adenauer, putting his position on record. Thus even before taking office Ike made the unification of Western Europe the dominant theme of U.S. foreign policy. Dulles' first speech in office and his first trip abroad were devoted to it.

Unity in Western Europe

The EDC showdown finally came a year and a half later, and it came as defeat. Dulles, scheduled to meet Eden and the others in Manila for the SEATO conference, discussed with Ike the advisability of abandoning that journey and returning to Europe.

"Let the French stew awhile," Ike suggested. "They've got to realize that NATO is not the exclusive responsibility of the U.S." It was decided the best course was to let Eden, who planned to skip Manila, explore the possibilities of an EDC substitute in Europe. As a reminder to France that America had heavy obligations on the other side of the world, Dulles enlarged his travel schedule to make stops in Formosa and Japan.

When Dulles returned, Eden had come up with a substitute idea. In 1948 Britain had signed a treaty at Brussels with France and the "Benelux" countries—Belgium, the Netherlands, Luxembourg—creating economic and social ties and containing some defense provisions. It had never amounted to much. Eden proposed to enlarge its membership and its defense features. Dulles decided to fly over to talk to him about it, and to visit Germany at the same time. Konrad Adenauer had staked his prestige on a pan-European policy and had sought to lead his nation, for its own good, into the new relationship with its western neighbors. He was left in an awkward position by EDC's defeat. He needed reassurance that the United States would continue to plug for the goal he was seeking.

In France Premier Pierre Mendès-France was feeling the effects of "stewing." In a cocky mood stemming from the domestic popularity he had acquired for ending the Indochina War, he had tackled the EDC issue. At a meeting of EDC nations at Brussels he trotted out some ideas for revising the treaty already negotiated among the six countries and merely awaiting ratification. Since adopting his revisions meant renegotiating the treaty, the partners refused. Mendès dwelt on the need for satisfying his countrymen for the brutalities of German occupation; in the private session Netherlands Foreign Minister J. W. Beyen reminded him scornfully but politely that others besides France had suffered German occupation and accepted the EDC treaty without the caterwauling of the French. Mendès returned to Paris in a defiant mood and posed the vote by which EDC was defeated. The United States felt that, had he wanted, he could have won adoption of the original treaty, his popularity representing the difference between victory and defeat.

The calculated show of disinterest by the United States had brought home to France the consequences of its action, in sober afterthought. The idea penetrated the French that perhaps they had, after all, brought on the "agonizing reappraisal" of which Dulles had warned—and they had. When Washington press dispatches reflected official discussion of taking Germany directly into NATO and leaving an "empty chair" for France, the prospects of isolation began to be felt. Mendès invited Dulles to stop by Paris, too, but Dulles declined. Mendès renewed the plea, asking him if his time did not permit a full visit, at least to stop at Orly airfield long enough to exchange a few words. Again Dulles refused.

The result was that when nine nations met in London late in September to consider Eden's plan, Mendès was a chastened man. It was not France which caused trouble over the substitute. In fact without much difficulty the substitute was agreed on in one week's meetings. In place of a commingling of troops, the enlarged pact adopted the principle of setting weapons limitations on the members. It was the first effective disarmament system ever adopted, and remains the only one. NATO set goals toward which members built their military strength; Brussels set ceilings on the buildup, with French fears about Germany in mind. One of EDC's weaknesses had been the hold-off position of Britain, which felt its world position dictated some aloofness toward the Continent. At London, as contribution toward the elusive goal of unity including Germany, Eden pledged four British divisions to the Continent, Dulles followed by reiterating a pledge of American troops which President Eisenhower already had given EDC, and the effect was electric.

Thus was Europe's will to unite for defense brought to fruition with Germany included. Under the Brussels formula Germany became NATO's fifteenth member on May 5, 1955, in Paris.

For five years this had been the major goal of Western policy, its origins antedating the Eisenhower administration. For the same five years the major goal of Soviet foreign policy had been to prevent it. Even after the London agreement Molotov was uttering threats of the dire consequences. On November 21, 1954, he warned that ratification of London's work would "jeopardize the existing possibilities of settling outstanding problems." On January 15, 1955, he said it would make "meaningless and impossible" any negotiation over Germany. The Soviets even canceled treaties of friendship and alliance with Great Britain and France to emphasize their threats.

But once the treaty had been ratified, the Russians changed their tune. Once they knew for certain they had lost the five-year fight, signs appeared that Russian policy was undergoing change. The first omen was notification by the Russians that they were ready to sign that Austrian treaty which had been lying around since

Berlin. It was a sensational turn in Russian policy. On December 17, 1954, Molotov had handed Austria a note saying the Brussels treaty would "create new obstacles to settlement of the Austrian question." On February 8, 1955, he said Austria's future could not be examined "independently of the German question." Now, ignoring both these warnings, he was ready to conclude a treaty more favorable to Austria and the West than what he had been offered at Berlin.

Even more startling was a reversal of attitude toward Yugoslavia. Ever since Tito had been expelled from the Cominform, Russian leaders, and Communists everywhere, had been heaping vituperation on him. With their usual shameless disregard for consistency, suddenly the leaders decided on a pilgrimage to Tito. Khrushchev and Bulganin swallowed four years of Russian billingsgate about Tito's "Fascist hireling" tendencies, while *Pravda* blandly discovered the new truth that independent national Communism as practiced by Yugoslavia was entirely compatible with Moscow Communism.

These were not the only signs. In UN disarmament discussions, Russia budged for the first time off its long-standing, rigid propaganda positions on military manpower strength with some proposals for limitation. The new proposals actually were plagiarized from the French and British and were by no means acceptable, but for the first time there were signs of Russian movement. Though the Russians had warned no negotiations would be possible if Germany joined the West, now they indicated a desire to negotiate some more.

Such moves, though significant, were in the realm of tactics and were reversible. The concessions in Austria and Yugoslavia were of first magnitude. Austria's independence was quickly sealed in a treaty signing at Vienna in return for a pledge of neutrality—a pledge which the little nation had made readily at Berlin without effect. It was on the trip to Vienna for the treaty signing that the idea for the "summit" conference at Geneva originated.

Russian hints about willingness to negotiate drew greatest attention from Britain and France. Their publics were closer to the threat of war and yearned for any action giving hope of release from the tension under which they lived. Their governments were no less sophisticated about the possibilities of negotiation but had a political sentiment to contend with that did not exist in the United States. Hints from London and Paris appeared to the effect that now might be the time to have the summit meeting about which Churchill had been talking so long. Churchill had meanwhile retired, but his idea lingered on in Eden, now prime minister.

Dulles had the feeling that, with a tremendous five-year corner turned in Europe, it might indeed be profitable to make another probe of Russian intentions. He was, however, opposed to the idea of a summit meeting, for dealing with the Russians required detailed legal commitments, carrying their own instruments of enforcement, to be any good. This was a problem for technicians, not heads of government. How could the heads of government, whose time was necessarily limited, make any lasting agreements in a few days? His formula was to have the technicians reach agreement first, then assemble the heads of government to ratify. He left for Europe skeptical of the summit suggestion, but he did not close his mind to it.

The trip involved a stop in Paris for the ceremony in which Germany formally joined NATO. Three days later, on a winy

Paris afternoon, at 3:35, Dulles met with his partners, Harold Macmillan and Antoine Pinay, at the Quai d'Orsay for a talk about meeting again with the Russians. Pinay, presiding as host, invited Macmillan to lead off, and he broached the British ideas.

It would be good, Macmillan said, if the West took the initiative in asking the Russians to negotiate again. The real question was what kind of agenda to adopt and whether the meeting should be at the summit or a conference of foreign ministers. He proposed there be a summit meeting—not one designed to discuss substance, but one which would explore negotiable possibilities and in effect lay out an agenda for a foreign ministers' meeting. In other words, he said, he was proposing reversal of the usual procedure.

Pinay commented that he agreed with Macmillan. He said French public opinion required another meeting, and he thought there should be nothing specific or limited about the agenda in advance.

It was Dulles' turn. He said he found Macmillan's suggestion "interesting and ingenious." Meetings held without adequate preparation, he went on, were not likely to succeed. They tended to lead to substantive agreements of seeming validity which lacked the precise detail necessary in dealing with the Soviets and, therefore, sometimes gave the impression that agreement had been reached when there was no agreement, and raised false hopes among peoples longing for peace. Furthermore, he pointed out, the President of the United States was head of state as well as head of government, and took his responsibility with him when he traveled. His attendance at a foreign conference for more than a few days was out of the question. Macmillan's idea of an exploratory conference, limited in duration, limited in effect to finding an agenda on which the foreign ministers could negotiate, appealed to him as an acceptable compromise with his viewpoint. But, he said, he could not answer that day. His colleagues understood why; it was something on which he wanted to consult Ike.

This he did, and within twenty-four hours it was agreed among the three governments that an invitation would go forth to the Russians, one that resulted in the convening at Geneva, July 18, 1955.

The summit conference, one of the best publicized high-level international gatherings in history, produced three things: an intangible something called the "spirit of Geneva"; a proposal by President Eisenhower for reciprocal "open sky" inspection by the United States and Russia of each other's territory; and an agenda for a foreign ministers' meeting to convene at Geneva in October.

Of these results, the effects of the spirit of Geneva proved the most important. It meant different things to the two sides. To the Russians it had a propaganda meaning: it was a phrase intended to foster the idea that the new Kremlin leaders were reasonable men, abjuring war as an instrument of Communist policy in favor of "peaceful coexistence." Peaceful coexistence had a reassuring sound in Europe among democratic peoples who were only too anxious to be told the Russians did not really want to attack them and would live in peace with them. The message which Russia sought to convey to Western Europe was: "Relax. We aren't going to hurt you."

On the other side of the Iron Curtain it had a different meaning. It was meant to convey the idea to satellites ruled by a thin crust of Communists with guns, and populated by peoples who wanted freedom but had no means to achieve it, that the West—particularly the United States—was trying to reach a live-and-let-live arrangement with Russia: in short, to suggest subtly that the two opposing big powers were seeking a "deal" confirming each other's status, thus sanctifying the Communist enslavement of the satellites. The Russians gave token of this in the use they made of news photographs taken of the Big Four heads of government.

Responding to the usual demand for pictures, the four gathered one day in the courtyard of Geneva's Palais des Nations for still and newsreel cameramen. The left-to-right in the picture they presented was Premier Bulganin, President Eisenhower, Premier Faure, Sir Anthony Eden. Men sitting alone for a portrait tend to look solemn and have to be cajoled to "smile, please." Men being pictured in a group, by photographers shoving each other so as not to be crowded out of a good angle, tend to find the performance amusing. The shots showed all four of these world statesmen in jovial spirits, smiling and laughing at each other.

After the conference the Russians took this picture, cropped Faure and Eden completely out of it, and blew up to barn-door size the portion showing a smiling Bulganin and a smiling Eisenhower exchanging good feelings. This subtle promotion of U.S.-Russian amity, suggesting a "deal," was exhibited in pictures all over the satellite countries. When the foreign ministers assembled in October, photographers could not understand why Dulles refused the usually routine requests for a Big Four picture or why he always sought to duck behind someone when the four were together for other than picture-taking reasons. They did not know that it was the propaganda use of summit pictures, undercutting the U.S. campaign for satellite "liberation," which made Dulles camera shy. Eventually, by prearrangement with Molotov, they got the Russian to confront Dulles unexpectedly at one meeting and thrust out his hand. When Dulles saw the resulting picture next morning on page one of the Paris edition of the New York *Herald Tribune,* he let out a hearty laugh, heaving his shoulders with mirth. "They can't make much propaganda out of that," he said. "I look as if I had just swallowed a dose of castor oil."

The spirit of Geneva had a third meaning to the West itself. It represented the private conclusion by the three governments that Russia did not want war. There was a difference between this conclusion and the idea Russia was assiduously cultivating in Western Europe. In the latter case the motive attributed to Russia was a change of heart: the new leaders were not like Stalin; they believed in being peaceful. In the case of the statesmen the interpretation of motive was that, having mastered the hydrogen bomb and done their own experimentation, the Russians had learned what a transcendentally destructive weapon it was and for the first time knew the truth that, regardless of what blow they might strike, they themselves stood to be wiped out in the second blow.

This was not, however, the whole of the informed Western interpretation of what the Soviets wanted. As far as Dulles was concerned, he read in the Russian attitude a desire for easing of Western pressure based on serious internal and external difficulties for the Kremlin.

In some of his public allusions to this belief, Dulles used the word "overextended" to describe the Soviet position. The idea that the Soviet Union was "weak" or "losing the cold war" caused editorial horse laughs among many critics far less able to judge than he. Dulles did not, of course, mean the Soviet Union was weak. It was, he knew, the second most powerful nation on the globe's face. But he did believe it was feeling the strain of overcommitment, and that it was overhauling its policies because of this strain.

We noted in the preceding chapter that this belief played a part in the mammoth calculated risk of the Aswan dam decision. Those who looked on the Soviet Union as "taking the initiative" in this period displayed an enormous insensitivity to assessment of the major international development of 1955: the loss by Russia of a five-year battle to prevent Western Germany's alignment with the West. Was it taking the initiative for Khrushchev and Bulganin figuratively to crawl over broken glass to do penance before Tito? Was it the generosity of success that caused Russia to expend its control in Austria in the abortive hope that by the example of "neutrality" West Germany could be denied the West?

Dulles thought not. He was convinced the Soviet Union was groping for new policies because it knew—even better than Western intelligence—that its old policies were not succeeding. He believed loss of West Germany was the most decisive diplomatic defeat Russia had suffered since the collapse of its ill-fated pact with Hitler prior to war. Thoroughly familiar with his own problems, which were being pointed out to him daily, he also had a keen eye for Russia's problems.

He knew the technical progress that had taken place in weapons since the end of war, and how expensive the new ones were. He remembered the contest in Russia between those who believed in more consumers' goods and those who wanted to maintain priority for war industry. Though the latter, in Khrushchev's person, had won out, he could grasp the tremendous economic drain involved in trying to catch up with American weapons development in an economy one-third the size, and one which had never licked its agricultural problem.

The economic problem was not confined to Russia itself. Immediately after the war Russia had squeezed the economy of its new satellites for its own benefit, and reduced standards of living. The squeezing process was at or near its limit. It might not be easy for Russia to maintain its rule without easing up. Communist China, a notch above satellite class, was seeking to industrialize and build up a large military establishment. This put Russia under additional drain. Finally, Russia was making economic promises to neutral countries, apparently feeling under necessity to match the foreign-aid program of the United States at least to some degree. It would not be easy for Russia, in the long run, to live up to the hopes this campaign had aroused.

The Russian propaganda motive for seeking to create a spirit of Geneva in Western Europe was transparent. As such, Dulles knew it would cause short-range trouble. The West could not defend itself against the immediate repercussions by combating a pious slogan like "peaceful coexistence"—it could gain no mileage with democratic peoples by acting more bellicose than the Russians.

About the only course open to the West was to accept the immediate setbacks sure to result from the new peaceful line and patiently continue the effort to educate the public in ways that would be convincing that Russia's reasonableness did not stem from a change of heart. The Geneva foreign ministers' conference was devoted to giving Russia a chance to demonstrate before the world that there was something more than propaganda in the spirit of Geneva. Ike warned the American people on his return from the summit that the next meeting would be the "acid test." The President said:

"Then is when real conciliation and some giving on each side will be definitely necessary."

Geneva in October, 1955, rounded out the technical side of the diplomatic maneuver that had begun twenty-one months before in Berlin. For half the conference Molotov tried to keep alive the spirit of Geneva generated at the summit without really altering any Russian position. The heads of government, Bulganin included, had agreed in the agenda directive that "settlement of the German question and the reunification of Germany by means of free elections shall be carried out in conformity with the national interests of the German people and the interests of European security." The acid cut through the layers of "spirit" on the words "free elections." In mid-conference Molotov took a trip home and when he returned it was plain that Moscow had ordered him to fall back on the old Stalin-type line: concede nothing.

Dulles, who had attended the summit meeting as the senior member of Ike's supporting delegation, had made a hard effort to determine whether there was anything at all which the West could do to persuade Russia to permit German reunification. He refused to believe that a reunited but neutral Germany—if that was what Russia was indicating in its Austrian maneuver—was the answer. From long association with Germany he believed neutrality simply was not in the nature of the German people; left to a temporary artificial neutrality, they would be a prey to the old urges of national expansionism. "What is it you want?" he asked Molotov at one point, in candid puzzlement. "Tell us what will satisfy you and we'll see what we can do about it." Molotov replied with the usual propaganda clichés about preventing the rebirth of German militarism.

Trying to cut through the propaganda, Dulles reasoned that, if there was anything at all underneath, perhaps a European security treaty would allay Russian fears. He got together with Macmillan and Pinay in advance of the October meeting in drafting an "outline of terms of treaty of assurance on the reunification of Germany." It provided for renunciation of the use of force, withholding support from aggressors, limiting forces and armaments, and provided for inspection and control, including a special warning system to guard against surprise attack. The three unveiled it first to NATO members at Paris and got some unexpected reactions. Luxembourg's urbane and witty Joseph Bech commented with profound satire: "Luxembourg is not disposed to guarantee the security of the Soviet Union. The disparity is too great." Nevertheless, it was an offer the West could live with, if all that Russia wanted was genuine protection against Germany, and Pinay presented it at Geneva on behalf of the West.

Since Molotov had built so much propaganda on the "security" line, it was hard for him to reject the outline out of hand. The more he sought to evade it the deeper in trouble he got. His weekend in Moscow straightened him out, and his reply on return demonstrated what the West had suspected but hoped was not true: Russia's only terms for reunification of Germany were a Germany completely within Soviet control.

There were those on the American side who thought the West was being equally rigid. Why not, they asked, give Germany a chance to achieve reunification by agreeing to the Austrian condition of neutrality? Austria had not agreed to remain defenseless; she was entitled to an army. She had only agreed not to join military alliances. But it was not the United States or Britain which was preventing West Germany from undertaking to offer Russia a promise of neutrality; it was the West German government under Konrad Adenauer. Like Dulles, Adenauer did not believe neutrality was either possible for the German people over any length of time or wise in any case. Indeed, the Western powers in essence recognized the right of Germany to be neutral if she wished, for under their formula of free elections to unite the country they implicitly conceded that a new independent government could choose any course it wished—alliance with Russia, neutrality, or alliance with the West. Nor had any postwar American State Department been any less willing to concede that eventually the Germans were free to choose their own destiny.

Had there been no progress, then, between Berlin and Geneva? Not on German unification. But there had been changes in favor of the West. The Federal Republic had been accepted as an equal partner; Austria had its independence; the Soviet satellite system's frontiers were shortened and left more exposed to the magnetism of freedom which everywhere drew individuals across the line in desperate life-gambles to win it. Pressure had been constant and alertly applied. As a study in "initiative" the three conferences were much more deeply significant than the standards applied by those who could see initiative only in such superficialities as which side issued the invitation to a conference or which side offered loans to a neutral.

26

. . . .

"Liberation"

Two events which occurred soon after the Eisenhower administration took office had a more profound effect on American
foreign policy than the fact that governmental authority had just
changed hands from Democratic to Republican. One was the death
of Josef Stalin on March 5, 1953. After a quarter century's one-man
rule it left his successors in a state of demoralization from which
it took them three years to emerge. The other was Soviet explosion
of a hydrogen bomb in August of the same year. Russian mastery
of thermonuclear fusion as well as atomic fission brought an end
to American monopoly of the ultimate in power weapons.

If it seems that these two events have intruded only casually in
the recital of the official part of the Dulles career, it is because
tacitly they provided a background against which everything else
occurred. As a connoisseur of the importance of change in human
affairs, Dulles calculated his moves, from the moment these factors
injected themselves into the world situation, toward exploiting
them for the benefit of the United States.

309

For Dulles, the absorption he shared with the American public in seeking to learn what changes were taking place in the nature of the Communist high command was not an end in itself. It was the beginning of plans for using the influence of the United States, in so far as it could be brought to bear, toward seizing the opportunity for loosening the Kremlin's grip on its satellites.

"Liberation" was the underlying motivation of Republican foreign policy as applied to Communism, as Dulles shaped it. To him it represented the difference between a dynamic and a static response to dynamic Communist expansion. He believed static response was doomed to eventual defeat. Liberation meant the kind of crusading belief in their own ideals which characterized the American people in the early stages of their growth. "What we need to do," he said, "is to recapture to some extent the kind of crusading spirit of the early days when we were darn sure that what we had was a lot better than what anybody else had. We knew the rest of the world wanted it, and needed it, and that we were going to carry it around the world. The missionaries, the doctors, the educators, and the merchants carried the knowledge of the great American experiment to all four corners of the globe." He looked on the Democratic policy of "containment" as static. While it resolutely opposed further expansion of Communism, by the definition of its author, George Kennan, it refrained from interference with Communism internally.

Dulles did propose to interfere, and the death of Stalin, by coincidence at the time he achieved a position making it possible for him to direct the interference, enlarged his opportunity. As a student of human nature he knew that rivalries between Stalin's heirs were as inevitable as death, and that they would take time to resolve. The effectiveness of interference could be enhanced during the confusion while the new lines of authority were being worked out. Dulles conceived it as peaceful interference—not necessarily polite by diplomatic standards, but peaceful.

Yet the impression that grew out of the 1952 presidential campaign was that Ike and Dulles were recklessly inciting captive peoples to rise and revolt only to face sure slaughter.

In the Republican platform of 1952 the references to liberation were these: "They [the Democrats] profess to be following a defensive policy of 'containment' of Russian Communism which has not contained it. . . . The supreme goal of our foreign policy will be an honorable and just peace. We dedicate ourselves to wage peace and to win it. . . . We shall encourage and aid the development of collective security forces there [Western Europe] as elsewhere, so as to end the Soviet power to intimidate directly or by satellites and so that free governments will be sturdy to resist Communist inroads. . . . It will be made clear, on the highest authority of the President and the Congress, that United States policy, as one of its peaceful purposes, looks happily forward to the genuine independence of those captive peoples. We shall again make liberty into a beacon light of hope that will penetrate the dark places. . . . It will mark the end of the negative, futile, and immoral policy of 'containment' which abandons countless human beings to a despotism and Godless terrorism which in turn enables the rulers to forge the captives into a weapon for our destruction. . . . The policies we espouse will revive the contagious, liberating influences which are inherent in freedom. They will inevitably set up strains and stresses within the captive world which will make the rulers impotent to continue in their monstrous ways and mark the beginning of their end. Our nation will become again the dynamic, moral, and spiritual force which was the despair of despots and the hope of the oppressed."

Even in the style of hyperbole common to campaign literature, this plank promised nothing more than (1) refusal to recognize the permanence of Russian domination of satellite nations; (2) peaceful opposition to such domination; and (3) limiting the counteraction to setting a shining example of liberty in the free world. Ike, speaking on August 20, said the United States should "tell the Kremlin that our government will never recognize the permanency of the Soviet Communist rule over these captive peoples of what were eighteen independent countries." Even without allowing for the flamboyance of "telling the Kremlin," what he said stayed within the formula. And in a speech on October 6 to the Council on Foreign Relations in Chicago Dulles was even more specific about the limitations of the "liberation" policy.

He said it was meant to "activate the strains and stresses within the Communist empire so as to disintegrate it." He added: "Activation does not mean armed revolt. The people have no arms and violent revolt would be futile; indeed it would be worse than futile, for it would precipitate massacre." He said that if the United States "got off the fence" of containment the captive peoples themselves would exploit the possibilities of "peaceful divorce" from Moscow, for "most of them have had long experience in winning freedom; losing freedom; and regaining freedom."

"They need no lessons from us, nor help from us," he said, "other than the kind of support which the American people have traditionally extended to other freedom-seeking peoples, and that means, most significantly, confidence that we shall not hereafter sell them out."

In short, what Dulles meant and what he specifically defined was an operation no more warlike than Joshua's march around the walls of Jericho. His concept was too simple for general acceptance; his slogan, "liberation," was gross oversimplification of what he had in mind. One of history's most monstrous oversimplifications is the equation $e = mc^2$. When Einstein produced the formula, it meant nothing by itself to those who had not gone through the enormous calculations behind it; and it took infinite labor thereafter to demonstrate that it actually was the key to releasing the energy of the atom. "Liberation" was the distillation of a similar amount of background thought by Dulles, and he knew it would take much time and zeal to translate it from theory into practice. His faith in the unquenchability, over the long run, of mankind's hunger for individual freedom was not generally shared. More than three years later, when publication of the secret Khrushchev speech to the Twentieth Party Congress had shaken international Communism to its roots, Dulles reiterated his belief that crumbling of such despotism was inevitable. The literal and still unbelieving correspondents at the press conference where he spoke wanted to know when the crumbling would take place. He replied he did not know whether it would take ten years or longer; headlines on the story—modest ones, being based more on the "names make news" formula than in belief in his theory—reported literally that Dulles predicted the breakup of Communism within ten years.

Signs of breakup came much sooner. Without help from the outside beyond the steadfast reiteration that the United States would never acquiesce in enslavement, cracks began to appear in the Iron

Curtain's wall of Jericho. They showed up first in Poland, in mid-October, 1956, followed almost immediately by revolt in Hungary. When they appeared, and when they developed fissures much greater than anyone had imagined, those who had accused the Eisenhower administration of rashness for "instigating revolt" by its talk of liberation were foremost in clamoring that the United States "do something."

The fact was that liberation policy was not predicated on violent, one-step revolt. The U.S. government felt that to interfere in Hungary with troops would risk world war, even apart from the fact that to do so would have required violating the neutrality of Austria. Nevertheless, there was no lack of admiration and respect for the cold courage displayed by the Hungarians. "It would have been wrong for us to urge violence," Dulles said at the time, "because we could not have helped them. But I don't say it was wrong for the Hungarians to use violence. It would be a sad day if people were not willing to shed their blood for freedom. Hungary's fight for freedom is an inspiring spectacle. It makes us feel a great respect for the people who engaged in it. The demonstration has to be made from time to time that people are willing to die for freedom."

After the Hungarian revolt burst on American consciousness and produced a sense of frustration because the liberation policy made no allowance for exploiting it with tangible American aid that could make the country free, U.S. officials checked broadcasts of the Voice of America and of Radio Free Europe, a privately financed organization, to see if indeed the government was guilty of inciting violence which it was not prepared to back up. They concluded that perhaps a few broadcasts of Radio Free Europe might have been interpreted as urging revolt, but not the official broadcasts. Nevertheless, government officials, Dulles included, tremendously regretted that a false impression had been built up as to what the United States intended.

For the sake of the human lives involved, however, the United States preferred the evolutionary method adopted by the Poles, based on restrained determination. In Poland it took the form of popular pressure to oust the Moscow-picked head of the Communist party, Edward Ochab, and reinstate a purged former Communist, Wladyslaw Gomulka, who, while reiterating his belief in the Communist form of society, put Poland's interests above Russia's interests for Poland. The restrained determination was expressed when Gomulka, facing an angry Khrushchev who had flown in from Moscow to demand a halt, quietly faced his own "brink of war" by threatening to fight. Khrushchev backed down.

In Hungary events went further and faster when the people demanded ouster of the Communist stooge, Ernest Geroe, and forced acceptance of Imre Nagy. Under Nagy's five-day government Hungary moved to cut its ties with Russia by abandoning membership in the military alliance known as the Warsaw Pact. Following this, on Sunday morning, November 4, 1956, Russian tanks ringed the city of Budapest and began a bloody job of crushing the revolt. Nagy was deposed and a Hungarian puppet, Janos Kadar, installed in his place.

But, despite the brutal, overwhelming force of the Russian action, the Hungarian people were not daunted. By passive and continued active resistance and strikes they made a shambles of Kadar's government.

All of Russia's might could not quench the will for freedom, for Hungary never again would become the complacent satellite she had been, whatever the final outcome. Revolt in Hungary had exploded several theories about the permanence of Communism. It had proved the falsity of the belief that "you can't fight tanks with stones and bare fists." It had shown that people indoctrinated from the beginning of their education with Communist dogma were still capable of finding in themselves the latent desire for freedom.

On a broader scale, at one stroke it ended Soviet reliance on satellite armies. In Hungary the local troops fought the Russian troops. In Poland they had threatened to fight. It could happen elsewhere. Henceforth no Russian war planner could safely count satellite divisions as part of the Soviet fighting power, for in the clinch they might start shooting the wrong way.

Russia's satellite empire was in deep ferment. Dulles had believed it when the dramatic signs were lacking, partly out of the multitude of small indications of which the government knew and kept to itself, but basically out of an intuitive feeling for the forces that motivate human beings.

The question was, why had Russia taken one course in Poland and another in Hungary?

This cannot be answered by the superficial explanation that Poland said it would stay in the Communist fold and Hungary insisted on independence. The answer cannot ignore what was going on in the rest of the world at the same time.

In the light of Poland, in the light of the first stages of the Hungarian revolt, and probably in the light of other satellite difficulties about which only the Kremlin knew, on October 30 the Soviet Central Committee issued an amazing document. It was the kind of document which is not drawn up in a day, but represents careful study and formulation. It contained an offer to all the satellites to negotiate withdrawal of Russian troops from their territories.

Since the Russians knew only too well that it was the presence of their troops which maintained Communist governments in power, this was nothing short of sensational. It did not, of course, amount to *withdrawal* of troops, but as an evidence of the extent to which the Kremlin estimated it needed to appease satellite opinion its implications were tremendous.

But October 30 was the same day on which the British and French delivered an ultimatum in the Suez crisis. There is no way of proving in court that the spectacle of Western forces committing aggression emboldened Russia to retract her proffered appeasement offer from Hungary, but from the chronology the conclusion is inescapable that the two crises interacted to Hungary's tragic disadvantage. No amount of Russian propaganda could conceal the damage to the Communist cause which the Russian move in Hungary effected in the rest of the world; yet had the West not given them an excuse, the probability is that Hungary would have come out with at least the degree of independence within Communism that Poland and Yugoslavia enjoyed.

The results were, for Dulles, confirmation of his previous conviction that the changes which Communist technique already had been undergoing were manifestations of defeat, not of success.

It was necessity, not a new outlook on life, which dictated Soviet moves; of this he was sure. He believed it to be a necessity produced by steady Western pressure. At the same time, since it was change, he recognized that it opened a new phase of danger to the West. Once free peoples truly became convinced that the danger of war had receded, it was inevitable they would relax the strong and determined defensive posture which had brought it about. Both sides now had the capacity for massive retaliation. Both sides knew hydrogen warfare would be fatal not only for the enemy but for themselves. In effect this canceled out—as long as both sides retained the power—and inaugurated a phase of political and economic competition in which the dynamic threatened the static as strongly as before.

In fact, Dulles noted, the new Soviet line posed a curious dilemma for the United States: the more that Russia moved toward conformance with the accepted democratic standards, toward what the United States wanted it to be, the more dangerous it became— up to the final point of actually changing character into a democratic state based on the sanctity of the individual.

It was this which led him to turn his thoughts to what course the free world needed to take to meet the new challenge. He knew relaxation was inevitable, though he could not predict in what form it would show up. By the time the problem-identifiers were picking up evidences of this relaxation in such events as Iceland's request for NATO's troops to leave, Dulles already regarded the emphasis on such military symbols as of diminishing importance in the new scheme of things. It was not that military defense was any less vital, but that more than military union was needed in future.

This thought caused him to propose, in a speech in April, 1956, to Associated Press editors in New York, that the time had come when NATO needed to grow into an expression of the political philosophy of its members, which embraced most of Western Christendom. The key passage of his speech was:

"None of our governments is predatory. We want military power to be used as a community force to prevent aggression and not as a national force for aggrandizement. But the unanimity of our thinking upon the great basic issues makes it apparent that the time has come to advance NATO from its initial phase into the totality of its meaning.

"Western civilization has made an immense contribution to the welfare of the whole world. It has been a dynamic force which, like everything human, has made its mistakes. But on the whole it has reflected an enlightened view of the nature of man and of his God-given right to enjoy life, liberty, and the pursuit of happiness. Furthermore, the Western view of the nature of man has made it inevitable that its influence should on the whole be a liberalizing influence. But the Western nations can feel that their greatest success was to have brought to much of the world a knowledge, a political freedom, and an economic opportunity which it had never enjoyed before.

"But the mission of the West is not completed . . ."

What did he mean by "totality of meaning" for NATO? The literal-minded, who could only see that "NATO is coming apart at the seams," tended to interpret it as embarking NATO on some new international Marshall Plan. The fact that he could not produce a blueprint plan to explain it made it baffling.

His concept was too immense for easy explanation, being no less than the political unity of Western civilization for the sake of durable world economic betterment and peace. It was idealistic beyond the normal grasp. When Cardinal Wolsey, in co-operation with Pope Leo X, devised the Treaty of London in 1515 as an inducement for all Christendom to unite, it was for a tangible purpose: to fall upon and destroy the infidel Turk. Though it was ratified by all the great powers before the end of 1518, it kept the peace of Europe a scant thirty months. Dulles was calling Christendom together for an intangible purpose: "The peoples who make up the Atlantic community ought, in increased unity, to resume their greatness; and true greatness is not to be measured by ability to impose on others what they do not want, but by ability to find new ways whereby all men can better realize their aspirations."

Dulles did have specific ideas, if not a blueprint. He had expounded them rather concretely as far back as 1942. But they needed re-examination in 1956. Characteristically, once NATO had accepted his idea of exploring the possibilities for enlarging its scope, he selected one man, Foreign Service Officer Julius C. Holmes, to head up State Department consideration of the problem and generate ideas for the three-man committee which NATO had appointed, and to act as staff officer for Senator Walter George.

Dulles knew the problem was not lack of ideas, nor lack of yearning on the part of peoples everywhere to find a formula for enduring peace; the problem was finding a formula moving gradually enough toward the goal of unity so as to win acceptance by the mass of people accustomed to the past standards of nationalism. Some contributions of national sovereignty would have to be made toward international peace and order. Unless they won wide acceptance, unless the people saw greater benefits to be derived from the resulting arrangement than from the national power they were giving up, proposals toward this end would defeat their own purpose. If there was to be change from the past, it would have to be slow and cautious. But the timing was right. NATO had indeed come to the end of a phase and it must either grow or die, in accordance with the laws of nature.

We have already seen how independent action by the British, French, and Israelis against Egypt, conceived and initiated in secrecy, shook NATO to its foundations only a few months after this drive to give NATO its "totality of meaning" got started. Before the reasoned effort to return to it could proceed it was necessary to reaffirm that the alliance did indeed have a permanent, indestructible base in the common outlook of the English-speaking peoples. Both President Eisenhower and Dulles, in their pronouncements of opposition to Britain's course in the Suez crisis, had made clear they believed it still existed.

One internal political result of Suez in Great Britain was the accession to power of Harold Macmillan, who replaced Eden as Prime Minister. Firmly committed to the belief that Anglo-American unity was the keystone without which the Western alliance could not survive, Macmillan made a trip to Washington in which he proclaimed the necessity for "interdependence" and arranged a second Bermuda conference, which was held at the end of 1957. As invariably happens when the West indulges in quarrels of its own, the Russians provided a powerful impulse to renewed Western unity, first by launching Sputnik, the first man-made earth satellite, on October 4, 1957, and then by exploiting to the utmost the threat it implied in Russian weapons technology. A natural law of compensation in international relations seems to have been operating automatically to regulate the cold war since 1945's fighting stopped: each time the West indulged the luxury of internal dispute, the Kremlin seized the moment of weakness as a propitious time to increase its threats; each time the West was thus reminded of the relentless hostility of its rival, it drew together for self-protection.

27

. . . .

Piecemeal Negotiation

WHILE he joined with others in the task of restoring and perfecting Western unity, Dulles kept sight of the other side of the problem, which was reaching peaceful accommodations with the Russians if it was possible. Always back of his firmness in dealing with the Communists and his refusal to be beguiled by their specious brand of "coexistence" was the knowledge that progress had to be made in reducing the threat of war, not only because that was his life's mission but because war now meant world-wide nuclear devastation.

Out of his continual search for areas in which it might be possible to reach agreement with the Russians, out of his failure to find response in the tackling of major problems in the various conferences of 1954 and 1955, he came to the conclusion that one of the areas in which the Russians might be open to negotiation was the field of arms control.

Dulles, the pragmatist, did not consider the Russians capable of entering agreements solely for the humanitarian objective of reducing cold-war tensions. They could be expected, however, to show interest in agreements which promoted their own national interests. Perhaps there could be found an area of negotiation which promised advantage to both sides, so that neither East nor West would feel it was endangering its national security by giving up something, where each would be contributing an equal amount to lowering the pressure in the power balance. If such an area could be found, the agreement would require the kind of mutual enforcement and control that would provide escape in the event one party subsequently decided the arrangement no longer protected national interests and began to violate it.

Arms control gave promise of being a field worth exploration because weapons technology had taken a great leap forward with the discovery of the mass destruction capabilities of the A and H bombs. Refinement of delivery systems by means of missiles, as well as attempts to devise protection against the diabolic devices, had led the two sides into a deadly armaments race that had become fantastically expensive.

It was on this theory that the attempt was made in 1957 to reach an arms control agreement with Russia through the five-member United Nations disarmament subcommission in London. The Soviet representative on the group was Valerian Zorin; the American, Harold Stassen, President Eisenhower's special adviser.

Stassen's instructions in the day-to-day course of the London meetings were issued by the State Department, but the basic policy was evolved by the National Security Council only after the most thorough consultation among all the affected government departments, resulting in what eventually was made public on August 29,

1957, as the Western "package plan" arms control proposal. Before the proposal was formally submitted at London, Stassen was superseded in fact, though not in name, as head of the American delegation. Contemporary accounts hinted that he had made a serious blunder, but its precise nature was never revealed.

What Stassen had done was to make the tactical mistake on June 11 of giving Zorin an informal preview, on paper, of the Western plan before it had been cleared by the Allies. Insiders to the negotiations say Stassen did not deviate more than a hair's breadth, if at all, from U.S. government-confirmed policy. But his act had two effects: it aroused the resentment of the Allies, who are always fearful of anything that smacks of an American attempt to negotiate over their heads with the Russians; and because of Stassen's known political ambitions it aroused the suspicion of government officials at home that in his eagerness to create a reputation as "the man who negotiated peace" he would commit the United States to some unsound position just for the sake of achieving an agreement with the Russians.

Dulles took immediate steps to repair the harm. He dispatched Julius C. Holmes, a top career officer, to London to keep Stassen in check. Stassen himself was called back to Washington and reprimanded. Dulles also placed the special staff working on problems of disarmament and atomic energy under his own direct supervision. From that time on he personally read all the cables and papers relating to the London negotiations and personally directed the formulation of instructions.

The American plan was still in the process of being described piecemeal before it was unveiled as a whole in textual form. One feature of it was a proposal to provide safeguards against surprise attack. This carried authorization for inspection flights over the territory not only of nations represented in the subcommission but of other countries of Northern Europe, whose consent, of course, was essential. In order to make sure there was no repetition of the previous incident on the score of Allied resentments, Dulles flew to London to present that feature of the plan to the Russians on August 2.

When finally submitted in text on August 29 the plan had a number of interrelated features—interrelated because the West was not willing to let the Soviets pick and choose, taking some features and rejecting others. It was willing to make certain concessions only if the Russians accepted others. But the conspiracy-minded Communists suspected the West's motive in seeking control posts on its territory was espionage rather than enforcement inspection. With one of their typical retreats behind a smoke screen of "spy" charges, they shifted the battle into the United Nations General Assembly, apparently hoping to stampede the organization into backing their simply articulated but dangerous campaign to "ban the bomb."

Such was the growing world sophistication about Communist motives and propaganda, however, and such was the reasonableness of the Western proposals, that the Russians got nowhere with their campaign. The end result was that the Assembly adopted a resolution supporting the principles of the Western plan by overwhelming votes. Only the Communist bloc nations opposed it.

In the midst of this failure to advance the cause of arms control the Russians launched their Sputnik. It created in the West a somewhat panic-stricken reaction to the implications of Soviet superiority in missiles, stirring up a debate over the adequacy of military power. In characteristic fashion Khrushchev made energetic propaganda use of the spectacular Russian achievement in the conquest of space, and proposed a summit conference.

For the leaders of Europe it was a shopworn maneuver of deception. By the fall of 1957 there were few, if any, statesmen of the West who believed there was any profit in negotiations with the Soviets. Experience had taught them the simple truth that the Kremlin's leaders had no sense of give-and-take, and looked on conferences only as a method of wringing concessions from the West under threat.

Yet such was the impact on the public mind of the expansion of the Russian threat in a novel and unknown dimension of experience that the summit appeal recreated an old illusion for many people in the democracies—the illusion that the world's great problems could surely be solved if the top men met around a table in a spirit of good will.

The summit appeal was timed to inject confusion into the December, 1957, meeting of NATO in Paris, which heads of government planned to attend in an attempt to restore confidence to the Alliance in the wake of the two shocks of Suez and Sputnik. In the countries where popular vote is the basis for power, statesmen often have to operate at two levels: on the facts as they know them to be, and on the facts as the public believes them to be because of what it reads and hears. In the long run facts have a way of asserting themselves, but in the midst of a propaganda campaign where one side enjoys the capacity for total secrecy while the other moves only under microscopic public examination, the half-truth and quarter-truth public impression is difficult to cope with.

Despite the pressure this put on some of NATO's heads of government, and despite initial private misgivings of some nations within the conference sessions, the organization agreed on a response to the summit appeal which was both firm and reasonable. It refused to be frightened into action, but it did show willingness to talk. The technique devised was to have the ambassadors of the United States, Great Britain, and France make a series of visits to the Foreign Office in Moscow to see if an acceptable agenda could be agreed on which would promise results from a summit conference. These private visits quickly petered out to nothing, providing another demonstration that there was no good will behind the Soviet mask of peaceful intention.

For his part in engineering NATO approval of this response to the Soviet maneuver, Dulles withstood a great deal of abuse. But at NATO's next ministerial council session in Copenhagen the following May he got something of an accolade from his peers as the man who had saved them from being too rash in December. For the first time his combination of patience and firmness gained him a measure of popular and editorial respect in quarters previously hostile to his methods.

Fighting off Khrushchev's summit maneuver did not divert Dulles from his effort to probe Soviet policy for signs of willingness to undertake some arms control and reduction. He regarded Sputnik as having provided an opportunity for starting the job in one field— that of outer space—with a clean slate. In speeches he pointed out that it would be far easier for the nations to get together on a set of rules for peaceful use of space when they were in the process of finding out about it than it would be after independent explorations of it led to clashes of interest.

Resumption of the effort involved a lengthy correspondence between President Eisenhower and Bulganin, and later Khrushchev after Bulganin had been demoted. Ike sent one letter to which Khrushchev responded favorably in part. It contained the suggestion that if Khrushchev did not want to discuss the political side of disarmament, there were still opportunities to study its technical aspects. A technical conference was convened at Geneva during July-August, 1958, and resulted in scientific agreement on the essentials of a world-wide inspection system comprising inspection posts at stated intervals, seaborne detection monitors, aerial patrols, and the like. A technical conference on surprise attack also was convened but came to nothing.

In its political aspects, Khrushchev's part of the correspondence was devoted to advocating a proposition just as superficially appealing, and as basically unsound, as his campaign to "ban the bomb." It was his proposal to "end nuclear tests," seeking to exploit public alarm all over the world about the increase in radioactive fallout resulting from continued testing.

At one point—in March, 1958—Khrushchev made the grandstand gesture of offering to end tests if the other nuclear nations would do the same. Accepting it would have meant relying on the Russian word that they had stopped, and could have led to charges and countercharges of violation as the nations monitored each other with their existing detection devices. The President and Dulles agreed that it had to be turned down, as it was, quite promptly.

Yet within a few months, on August 22, 1958, the United States made a somewhat similar proposal, offering to cease tests for a year provided Russia did the same and provided work started on setting up an inspection system that would permit the ban to be continued under safeguards against violation.

What had caused the change?

Piecemeal Negotiation

It was a decision by Dulles that his responsibility for the international relations of the United States required him to take into account certain "imponderables" which were not the concern of agencies like Defense and AEC. Each of the latter had definite missions: Defense was expected to make the military establishment as powerful and up to date as its appropriations permitted, not to worry about what foreign nations thought; AEC was expected to push atomic development and safeguard its secrets, not to brood about world tensions. The State Department, however, did have to weigh not only these considerations but the impression which the image of the Untied States created in the rest of the world.

It involved the basic question of what the great power of the United States stood for. Did it represent only a determination to keep ahead of Russia in arms competition, which in the past had always ended in war? Or did it stand for peace, for a policy of maintaining American power for self-defense and for the safety of its friends but not for destruction of a rival? The imponderables of this situation convinced Dulles that the U.S. must take the initiative in attempting to convince the world, and the Russians too, that the arms race need not go on. If total mistrust on both sides prevented a reversal of the trend, it was still possible to substitute something else—the capability for mutual enforcement.

It was not that the U.S. opposed the *idea* behind some of Khrushchev's slogans, like "ban the bomb." Complete elimination of A and H bombs would benefit the purely American strategic interest, since it would tend to restore the value of our ocean frontiers in guarding against attack. But at the same time it would harm our European allies, since it would upgrade the conventional-arms superiority of the Communist world which is so close to them.

However, if there was no possibility of eliminating nuclear weapons it made sense for each nation with the capability to adapt them to its own defense requirements through continued testing.

Balancing the ponderables and imponderables led the government to conclude that it would reach a certain plateau in weapons development if it completed some tests it had planned for October, which it did, and reduce the "loss" involved in cessation. Then it joined Great Britain and France in a second Geneva conference with Russia, tackling the political side of the problem, on October 31. During the early days of November the Russians engaged, without public announcement, in a concentrated series of tests of such high radioactive yield that it pushed the level of Russian-created fallout above the level of the U.S. and Great Britain combined. Russia was entitled, under the conditions of her offer, to hold the tests, but the world would not have known about them had they not been picked up by Western detection and publicly announced by the AEC—illustrating the danger of Khrushchev's simple formula of "end tests forever." Because of the Russian action the U.S. announced that it considered itself relieved of the voluntary obligation it had assumed, but it made no move to resume testing.

The political Geneva conference on cessation of nuclear weapons tests ground away for months in the characteristic style of East-West negotiations. Dulles held tenaciously to his interest in using the issue as the entering wedge of a demonstration that the wit of man was capable of finding a way out of continued inching toward self-destruction. As late as March, 1959, when he was in his fatal illness at Washington's Walter Reed Hospital, he was reading cables about the Geneva negotiations and dictating suggestions to those who were carrying on along the course he had set.

28

. . . . . .

Three Crises

IN THE final year of his life, Dulles had to face three major crises
in the foreign relations of the United States. The first stemmed
from revolt in Iraq, which posed a great challenge to the Western
position in the entire Middle East. Dulles helped retrieve the situation from total disaster, but in the net it was a setback for the
United States. The second crisis came in the renewal by the
Chinese Communists of their old threat against Formosa, which
forced the U.S. once again to look war in the face but in the end
proved the soundness of Dulles' policy of no retreat. The third involved Berlin, the enclave of freedom within the Iron Curtain
whose presence became too much for Nikita Khrushchev to bear.
The Berlin crisis was still unresolved when Dulles died.

The beginning of the events which thrust Iraq to the center of
the world stage occurred on Sunday night, July 13, 1958, when
elements of Iraq's 3rd Army Division moved from their base at
Baquba into Baghdad, 30 miles away. They surrounded the royal

palace, the residence of strong man Nuri as-Said, the radio station, the telegraph headquarters, the airport, and strategic bridges and roads. They cut the British and American embassies off from effective communication by stationing tanks and troops around them. With amazing stealth and efficiency they attacked all the key spots at the same time.

By 5:30 A.M. Monday the rebel radio announced to the world that the pro-Western royal government of Iraq had been overthrown and a new regime had been formed. The nature of the new government could not be judged immediately from the names of the new cabinet members, but the prominence of a couple of obscure military figures—Col. Abdul Salam Arif and Brigadier Karim Kassem—indicated the uprising might be a Nasser-type "officers' rebellion" rather than a Communist coup.

With such information as there was at hand on Monday morning, Dulles called at the White House to consult with President Eisenhower on what to do. The development was a tremendous jolt to American policy, for Iraq was the only Arab member of the Baghdad Pact, the alliance designed to defend the Middle East against Communism. If the new regime turned out to be Communist in disguise, it meant that Russia had leapfrogged the "Northern tier" of Middle East states and set up a headquarters capable of subversion throughout the entire area. If Nasser was back of the revolt, it meant he had all but surrounded Lebanon, Jordan, and Israel.

Some 18 months previously, in an attempt to cope with a situation in which Syria was steadily undergoing Communist infiltration, Dulles had evolved a program which became known as the "Eisenhower Doctrine," in which Congress approved the use

of American troops to help any country of the area defend itself—
but only if it requested help—against attack from a Communist
country or a country "under the domination of international Communism."

It did *not* guarantee against Communist takeover in a country
where the government acquiesced in the takeover. The doctrine,
therefore, had not applied when Syria seemed about to go Communist, for the leaders did not ask for help. There was no way,
either by Congressional resolution or by administrative fiat, that the
United States could forbid any country to go Communist.

Rumors of plots against the Iraqi government were heard by
American intelligence during the late spring and early summer,
but Middle East rumors are always hard to assess and it was the
situation in Lebanon, rather than in Iraq, which caused the U.S.
primary concern. Opposition to the re-election of pro-Western President Camille Chamoun had reached the stage of open rebellion.
But efforts of the U.S. and U.N. to end the fighting seemed to be
bearing fruit when the Iraqi revolt changed this outlook overnight.
Chamoun's government, fearful that the psychology of the moment
would encourage the Lebanese rebels to renew and step up their
attacks, appealed for help. Jordan, which had barely nipped a plot
apparently timed to coincide with Iraq's, felt similarly exposed.

In Washington, after consultation with London, Ike and Dulles
decided the only course was to send U.S. troops to Lebanon. The
British took the responsibility for Jordan. Dulles explained the
decision in these words:

"Our decision to move troops into Lebanon, which was made
within a few hours without enough time for adequate explanation,
was made for one reason, and one reason alone. We were convinced

that if we did not, there would not be a single one of the small and relatively weak governments all the way from Morocco to the Pacific which would feel safe from the potential threat of individual aggression and assassination such as took place in Iraq. We acted to give a feeling of stability to such governments so that they would not automatically collapse, or feel that to be a friend of the United States was a liability in terms of independence or of life itself. . . .

"We took action without any thought that our response would solve the problems of the Middle East. In fact we recognized that it would make them more difficult. The overriding consideration was wholly that if the small nations felt themselves the actual or potential targets of individual aggression or of civil strife fomented from without, the whole situation would collapse."

When the U.S. decision was taken the government did not know whether the troops would have to fight their way ashore against rebel opposition (the landings turned out to be peaceful) or whether developing events would take them on into Iraq. It was not until Thursday night of that week that the U.S. and Britain knew the limits of their actions. By then they were agreed there was nothing to be done about Iraq. There was no one left of the former legitimate government to appeal for outside help, nor any figure around whom Iraqis opposed to the new regime could rally.

A major significance of the action itself, however, was in the fact that the U.S. did not hesitate to take positive military action even though when it did so it ran the risk of a military clash with Russia. This significance was heightened by the fact that when the chips were down Russia shrank from direct reaction.

The flash danger point of the Iraqi revolt subsided in a relatively short space of time, but within about six weeks of the Baghdad eruption another crisis, one deliberately created by the Communists and therefore even more menacing as a possible cause of war, broke out on the other side of the world. On the night of August 22-23 Chinese Communist shore batteries began an intense shelling of Quemoy and a couple of smaller islands in Amoy harbor. It revived all the problems for U.S. policy that the earlier attack against the Quemoy and Matsu groups had called up in 1954-55, which we examined in Chapter 20.

In the previous Quemoy crisis, we noted that despite general acceptance of the proposition that Formosa and the Pescadores should be defended, there was a great preoccupation with the question whether "related positions" included the Quemoy and Matsu groups and whether, therefore, they were specifically included in the U.S. pledge of protection. This obsession cropped up again with greater intensity in the second crisis.

There were reasons why the government did not want to name the islands specifically, and they still applied: the islands were basically indefensible from the military standpoint, and it was unwise to risk prestige by saying we would not permit them to be taken; furthermore, if we started naming "related positions" specifically we would in effect be pledging American defense of every Nationalist-held pile of rocks off the China coast, or, by failing to name some, inferentially inviting the Chinese Communists to take them without opposition. At the same time, if the Communists intended to invade and conquer Formosa, the United States did not propose to let them start the process at Quemoy.

Precisely the same situation existed the second time. Within a week of the first outbursts of shelling, Peking radio was announcing China's intention to invade Formosa. Peking's refrain was so constant on this point that any informed observer should have been able to convince himself there was no question but that under the existing circumstances the U.S. had every intention of defending Quemoy. Yet such was the obsession with getting the government to say so publicly that Dulles was finally goaded into making a statement designed to make it even clearer. The President was vacationing in Newport, Rhode Island, and on September 4, after a trip to confer with him, Dulles made a statement in which he reviewed the facts and, recalling that the President was empowered by Congress to declare Quemoy a "related position," said: "Military dispositions have been made by the United States so that a Presidential determination, if made, would be followed by action both timely and effective." But, he said, there was no indication that the Chinese Nationalists could not handle the defense themselves with U.S. logistical support, and the U.S. hoped Peking would "stop short of defying the will of mankind for peace."

The obsession that the government must state positively, forthwith, that it would or would not defend Quemoy, period, still remained after Dulles' Newport statement. At his next press conference, in Washington, Dulles was asked why he had not explained U.S. policy, since his statement contained "no decision" and the American people were expecting enlightenment. He replied that it was "replete with decisions," clear enough, at any rate, to be read meaningfully by the Chinese Communists.

Despairing of adequately getting across his point that it was not real estate but principle the U.S. was defending, Dulles telephoned the President to say that a dramatization of the reasons for the policy was badly needed. Accordingly Ike made a radio-TV speech the same week in which he spelled out the reasons in clear fashion:

"If the Chinese Communists have decided to risk a war, it is not because Quemoy is so valuable to them. They have been getting along without Quemoy ever since they seized the China mainland nine years ago.

"If they have now decided to risk a war, it can only be because they, and their Soviet allies, have decided to find out whether threatening war is a policy from which they can make big gains.

"If that is their decision, then a Western Pacific Munich would not buy us peace or security. It would encourage the aggressors. It would dismay our friends and allies there. If history teaches anything, appeasement would make it more likely that we would have to fight a major war."

All the contemporary writing about what it all meant or was presumed to mean may have obscured a picture of the combined determination and restraint with which the U.S. acted. The Chinese Nationalist garrison on Quemoy returned the fire from the mainland, and the U.S. Seventh Fleet was authorized to convoy supply ships—up to the three-mile limit. This kept American ships out of shore battery range to avoid any "incidents" but bespoke the determination of the U.S., which also was displayed in the transfer of West Coast naval and air units to the western Pacific. The Chinese Communists transmitted false radio signals in an attempt to lure American planes over their coast, but did not succeed.

By refraining from any act that might be interpreted as "aggression"—even to the extent of getting an agreement from the Chinese Nationalists not to bomb the mainland gun positions—and by patiently helping supply the beleaguered island, the U.S. helped Formosa to nullify the Red threat, though at the cost of many hundreds killed, mostly Quemoy civilians.

In fact, what the U.S. did in the Formosa straits—as it had in Lebanon—was to *deter* a limited war instead of fighting it. At Quemoy our military attitude was quite correct: we made no bellicose move. Our political attitude was something else; it was the knowledge that we had the capability to act coupled with the willingness to act that deterred the Communists. There was a great deal of discussion in the United States at the time about the supposed lack of capacity to fight limited wars. In the modern world it is difficult to keep limited wars from becoming general wars. Those interested in the subject might find both Lebanon and Quemoy worth studying as examples of how to *avoid* limited war.

The determination behind the American restraint was what eventually got across to the Communists, for on October 6 they announced a seven-day truce, later extended.

The third crisis of 1958 was created by Nikita Khrushchev when in a speech in Moscow on November 10 he issued a call for the three Western nations which had occupation troops in Berlin to withdraw, and announced Russia's intention to sign a peace treaty with East Germany which would turn control of access to West Berlin over to the puppet East German government. West Berlin, said Khrushchev, had become a "cancerous tumor" inside the Soviet empire, and the West, by violating the Potsdam agreement of 1945, had forfeited its rights to remain there.

Khrushchev was quite right about West Berlin being a "cancer" from the standpoint of Communism. The attraction of freedom it represented had, over the course of ten years, drawn 1,400,000 East Germans to seek refuge there from the totalitarian repression under which they lived.

Three Crises

The three occupying powers, and indeed all West European nations, were outraged at Khrushchev's casual assumption that he could flout agreements that the Soviet Union had entered into in 1945 when the wartime allies dealt with the problems of defeated Germany, and the additional agreements signed in 1949 after the 1948 Berlin blockade failed. But at the same time they were alarmed because Berlin, situated 110 miles away by *Autobahn* from the nearest point in West Germany, was the West's most vulnerable position if it came down to a question of military force and not of law.

Khrushchev did not follow up his speech with a note until Thanksgiving Day, November 27, and it did not take the same line on the Potsdam agreements. During the intervening silence there had been a number of small signs indicating that in his original pronouncement Khrushchev had shot from the hip and his lawyers were finding it difficult to back up his references to Potsdam. There was one theory at the State Department that Krushchev, surprised by the vigorous Western reaction, came up with the six-months postponement in the hope that the Allies would make some counterproposal in the interim that would get him off the hook.

But the Russian threat could not be dismissed as a bluff. What it came down to was that Khrushchev was in earnest on a fundamental point: the West had to get out of Berlin. The reason concealed behind pious talk about the need for making peace with Germany, of guarding against the rebirth of German militarism, of giving West Berlin "freedom," was that Communism could not tolerate the example of democracy within its borders and intended to absorb the enclave into its own system.

339

Coming as it did just before an annual NATO meeting in Paris, the Berlin maneuver was accompanied by a renewal of demand for a summit meeting. Dulles' attitude was, as before, that such a meeting would be useless unless there were some promise it would produce accommodation of a sort.

With no difficulty he persuaded the Allies to insist on a foreign ministers' meeting and let it be the test whether a summit conference would be fruitful. He also saw an opportunity to take the diplomatic offensive by reopening the question of German reunification with the Russians. He set the department to work re-examining Western plans to this end, and his last foreign trip, in February, was devoted to forging Western unity on them. But in the midst of it he was stricken with cancer. He had been spared long enough to set the course of Western response to Khrushchev's challenge, but it was left to Christian Herter, his successor, to carry on from that point.

29

. . . .

The Peacemaker

URING the first few days of December, 1958, Dulles made a
trip to Mexico to attend the inauguration of the new president, Adolfo Lopez Mateos, as an official representative of President
Eisenhower. In the course of a reception at the American Embassy
Dulles stood shaking hands with guests for several hours while he
felt considerable abdominal pain. He was scheduled to go from
Mexico City to San Francisco to make a speech, and despite the
pain he decided to keep to his schedule because he had become a
public figure whose illnesses made headlines around the world.
With the Berlin crisis in a developing stage he did not want to
advertise the fact that he was not feeling up to par.

When he returned to Washington he went to Walter Reed
Hospital on December 5 for a check of his symptoms. In view of
his 1956 cancer they had a potentially ominous connotation. Examination proved, however, that what he was suffering from was
diverticulitis, an inflammation of the lower colon. It had no con-

nection with his previous cancer, and the only cure was complete rest and a soft diet.

As a good patient, he submitted to the requirements of treating the diverticulitis, but the mid-December meeting of NATO in Paris was imminent, and he felt it was enormously important to make sure the Allied response to Khrushchev's threat was firmly handled. He got his doctors' permission to make the trip, provided he skipped the usual official dinners and took as much rest as possible. After his return, Dulles went to Jamaica for further rest, where he stayed over Christmas and New Year's.

In January he was back at work. During the month he discovered he had an inguinal hernia on the left side, a common enough ailment which at some appropriate time could be corrected by minor surgery. On January 31 he kept an engagement to speak before the New York State Bar Association. His subject was "Peace Through Law." Neither he nor his hearers knew it would be the last public speech of his life. He had chosen a topic suitable for the occasion and the audience; but had he known he was uttering his valedictory it is doubtful if he could have summed up more lucidly or cogently his life's philosophy. Let us examine it in his own words:

> In the swift flow of daily events it is easy to lose track of the broad strategy of our foreign policy. We seek peace, of course. But we seek it in what seems to us the only dependable way—the substitution of justice and law for force. . . .
>
> Often peace is identified with the imposition by strong nations of their "benevolent" rule upon the weaker. Most of these efforts collapsed in war. . . .
>
> But the world of today is very different from the world of past centuries. It cannot be ruled.

Nevertheless, world peace through world rule is the creed of international Communism.

The reasoning is very simple. Physical matter, these Communists see, becomes more productive when it is ordered, [and] so, it is argued, people everywhere should be brought into world order and conformity of action, thought, and belief. This is the mission of the international Communist movement.

We and our allies reject this road to peace, no matter how trying and difficult may be the alternative. We know that human beings . . . are part of a spiritual world. . . .

Today, people everywhere, even within the Soviet Union, are becoming less servile. We welcome this. . . . Lasting peace will never be achieved in terms of a world-wide tyranny.

Another means of preserving the peace is the maintenance of a so-called "balance of power." Sometimes this works. But . . . whatever may be the desire to maintain a balance of power, the balance inevitably shifts—with results such as those experienced in 1914 and 1939.

We come then to the third method of preserving the peace. This is a system of order based upon the replacement of force by community justice, reflecting moral law. This has been the dependable basis for national order in many countries, but, until recently, there has not been any determined effort to apply it internationally. . . .

A most significant development of our time is the fact that, for the first time, under the charter of the United Nations, there has been a determined effort to establish law and justice as the decisive and essential substitutes for force.

What is vital here is to recognize that the renunciation of force under these conditions implies, not the maintenance of the status quo, but peaceful change. . . . This new and constructive approach was the distinctive contribution of the San Francisco conference in 1945. . . . The twin concepts of "international law" and "justice" were interwoven throughout the charter as the counterpart of the renunciation of force. . . .

The Communist bloc countries never honestly accepted the concepts of the United Nations charter, either as regards the renunciation of force or as regards the rule of justice and law. Indeed, these United

Nations concepts can no more be combined with Communist doctrine than oil with water.

International Communism believes that force is a legitimate means to advance its goals. . . . "Law" to Communists [is] the means whereby those in power suppress or destroy their enemies. . . .

Our attitude toward the use of armed force is a matter of principle and not merely an anti-Communist policy. This is shown by the fact that the United States has made clear, even to its good friends, that we are opposed to the use of force in the settlement of international problems. Upon its success may depend the very survival of the human race. . . .

It is easy to support a principle when those who violate it are those who proclaim themselves enemies. It is hard to do so when the issue is raised by friends. . . . While it is premature to say that the Suez affair marks a decisive historical turning point, it may so prove. . . .

Peaceful change and development are, therefore, significant among the nations of the free world. Perhaps, indeed, the pendulum is swinging too far in the direction of change. Law serves, not merely to settle specific disputes, but to provide a sense of security in daily living. A measure of stability is an essential ingredient of peace and order.

Change—even political and social change—should not be so impetuous as to paralyze forward planning or to wreak unnecessary injury upon established rights. While law is and should be subject to an orderly process of change, as required by justice, it should be a shield and a protector of those who rely in good faith on international engagements. . . .

To accomplish peace through law will take patience and perseverance. It will require us at times to provide an example by accepting for ourselves standards of conduct more advanced than those generally accepted. We shall be misunderstood and our motives misinterpreted by others who have had no such training as we in the doctrine of law. . . . There is no nobler mission that our nation could perform.

Soon after this speech Dulles took off, on February 2, for London, Paris, and Bonn—still in pursuit of allied unity and firmness in dealing with the Russians on Germany and Berlin—on what proved to be his last trip abroad. What he sought to learn was whether the principal allies, especially Great Britain, underneath all the brave words and surface unity, really had the stamina to risk war in the showdown rather than retreat at Berlin.

What personal impression he got of the European mood in the light of direct Soviet challenge he kept to himself, for immediately after his return he underwent an operation for his hernia. He had been wearing a truss, and he found it as uncomfortable as the hernia was painful. He was a tired man on February 9, the day of his return. Leaving the State Department by his private elevator for a White House call, he remarked to his personal security officer, Louis Jefferson, "When your batteries run down, you just have to stop and get them recharged."

On February 15, after a few days of rest in preparation, he underwent surgery at Walter Reed Hospital. The medical bulletin described the hernia operation as "successful," but added: "During the course of the operative procedure, tissue and fluid were removed for microscopical examination." The biopsy report next day carried the fateful news that free cancer cells had been found in his abdominal cavity.

President Eisenhower, totally reluctant to accept the abrupt loss of the man he considered the country's greatest Secretary of State, granted him an indefinite leave of absence, and Christian Herter stepped in as Acting Secretary to conduct the nation's foreign policy.

Dulles had left the department for what appeared to be a minor operation with an air of "don't touch things till I get back." He had been able in the past to make rapid recoveries and resume the direction of affairs with scarcely a break. When he learned he had a second cancer he knew it was different this time. He informed Herter he would not attempt to make decisions on anything except questions involving Germany, Berlin, and the Allied response to the Russian threats.

Treatment consisted of two types. As soon as Dulles had recovered sufficiently from the hernia operation he was subjected to massive radiation, daily receiving million-volt X-ray bombardment for periods lasting from one to five minutes. Later he was injected with radioactive gold. After a period, Dulles, though thin and gaunt, was able to leave the hospital for rides in Rock Creek Park with his wife, Janet, sometimes stopping off briefly at his home. After one such visit reporters waiting at the hospital found him quite concerned because his poodle, Pepi, seemed to have a cold.

Radiation treatments had done what they could. The doctors thought that rest in a warmer climate might promote his recovery, so Dulles accepted an offer of the use of Undersecretary Douglas Dillon's winter estate on Jupiter Island, Hobe Sound, near Palm Beach, Florida. Looking around the crowd of VIP's who had come to see him off, Dulles searched until he saw David Waters, who had been his speech and television adviser. "I've been looking for you, Dave," he said quietly, and, shaking hands, he turned and got into the plane. Waters, an amateur painter of merit, had done a portrait of Dulles, capturing with electric impact the stern qualities of a tough Secretary of State, and in the sittings the two had established a warm personal rapport. Mrs. Dulles gave the portrait to Princeton University.

On Jupiter Island, Dulles basked in the sun and floated in the pool. It discouraged him that he was not gaining back his strength as he had after previous illnesses. Then on Thursday of the second week he felt pains in his neck, and X rays taken the following day indicated a tumor. It was the final blow to his tenacious morale. He knew then he had not long to live.

On an unseasonably cold Sunday evening, April 12, Ike's airplane, the *Columbine III,* brought John Foster Dulles back to Washington for the last time. Before he alighted from the airplane he told Herter he had recommended his appointment to the President. Mr. Eisenhower called on Dulles at the hospital next day and it was arranged to withhold the announcement until around April 21, primarily to allow time for the President to get a medical report on Herter, who suffered from arthritis. The President, still unwilling to end their close association, asked Dulles to act as his personal consultant. Speculation on the imminence of the Herter appointment was so intense, however, that after going to Augusta, Georgia, the President on Wednesday morning, April 15, announced Dulles' resignation, to spare him from having to appear in the false light of one who was trying to cling to a job he could no longer fill. Herter's appointment followed before the week was out.

Tragic as it was, the circumstances of his resignation gave Dulles the opportunity, permitted few men, of learning what his contemporaries thought of him when they looked up from the judgments they made about specific problems in isolation and thought in perspective about his life's work. The outpouring of tribute was even greater after his death, but those after his resignation reflected how deeply the once unpopular man had made an imprint on his times. None was more eloquent than *The New Yorker*'s Washington correspondent, Richard H. Rovere, who wrote on April 16:

John Foster Dulles

For the former Secretary and for the President, these awful moments may be made slightly more endurable by the knowledge, which both must surely have, that there is today a far wider appreciation of Mr. Dulles' services than there has been at any other time, and that this appreciation is in no sense the product of sympathy or pity or piety. Many men, here and in other capitals, who a year or two ago would have welcomed his resignation now fervently wish it were possible for him to stay on; all the forthcoming negotiations over the future of Berlin and of the two Germanies could be faced with greater hope and confidence if he were directing American policy. . . . It is not only Mr. Dulles' power, skill, and experience that are missed today. It happens that his illness coincided with a new evaluation of his past policies and with a sudden awareness of his growth in office. The time may never come when it will be possible for anyone to say with assurance that his strategies over the years were more wisely conceived than those offered as alternatives, but it is possible to say now that certain of his strategies that his critics insisted would lead to disaster have worked out very well in the short run.

On the afternoon of his resignation Dulles received a call from the only visitor not a high official or a member of the family who was permitted to see him during his last illness. While he was Secretary, Dulles had to make appointments far ahead, and two years previously he had booked a full afternoon to talk to the Council of Methodist Bishops. The session was, of course, canceled when he became ill, but his friend Bishop G. Bromley Oxnam was permitted to spend a short time with him.

Dulles was alone. He looked up at Oxnam and said, "I sit here trying to decide what to do with my life in the days I have left. My first concern is my wife. Her life has been so intertwined with mine that I don't know what she will do alone." The bishop bowed his head in prayer, and tears came to Dulles' eyes. He apologized to Oxnam, saying the radiation treatment had upset him emotionally. They talked briefly about his affairs, about his plan to leave his papers to Princeton, about his work as Secretary. "It was so hard not to slip or surrender," he told Oxnam. "If you slipped there was war, and if you surrendered it was all over." Dulles said he had tried hard to do neither.

President Eisenhower made frequent visits to the hospital to see his old friend. He took Britain's Prime Minister Macmillan and Foreign Secretary Selwyn Lloyd when they came for a conference on Berlin problems, and Dulles, wearing a dressing gown over his clothes, took part in a discussion of plans for the Geneva meeting before they went on with Ike to Gettysburg. Early in May, 86-year-old Sir Winston Churchill paid a final call, accompanied by the President. By that time Dulles needed a wheel chair to get around.

As the days went on, public attention shifted to focus on the man now in charge of foreign affairs. Herter headed the U.S. delegation to the Western foreign ministers' meeting at Paris, at which the Dulles-generated plan for Germany and Berlin was approved by the Allies, and Herter led the delegation to Geneva when the East-West conference opened on May 11. It was while that conference was going on, at the end of its second week, that John Foster Dulles died, on Sunday morning, May 24.

President Eisenhower decreed an official funeral. At Geneva the foreign ministers recessed their deliberations to fly back for the funeral; Japan's foreign minister flew from Tokyo; and from Bonn flinty old Konrad Adenauer made the journey out of respect to the Western colleague whose equal flintiness he most admired. In Moscow Mikoyan said, "Dulles was a very great statesman. He was a strong partisan advocate. We like strong men. We do not like uncertain ones. I am very sorry that he is dead, and not only I, but the whole Soviet government." In one of Washington's most impressive ceremonies, the onetime U.S. Army major and late Secretary of State was laid to rest in Arlington National Cemetery with full military honors.

So ended the career of John Foster Dulles, his name permanently imbedded in the history of two decades tense with the greatest dangers under which mankind had lived since its beginning. In the solemn hush of Washington Cathedral, when the world's illustrious were paying him final tribute, there came a moment when the minister quoted, "Blessed are the peacemakers, for they shall be called the children of God." To one member of the congregation the word seemed to synthesize the entire effort of the Dulles career. "It seemed," wrote Arthur Krock in the *New York Times,* "that when it was uttered all around him stirred with the consciousness that 'peacemaker' was the perfect biography of the late Secretary of State."

Index

Acheson, Dean, 2, 5, 10-11, 111, 116, 117, 124, 126, 127, 139, 151, 161, 167, 169, 251
Adams, Sherman, 279
Adenauer, Konrad, 172, 294, 295, 308, 349
Aldrich, Winthrop, 85, 276
Alfhem, 234
Algeria, 264
Allen, George V., 173
Allison, John, 6, 123, 126, 179
Alsop, Joseph, 169-70
Alsop, Stewart, 10
American Radiator, 84
American Society of International Law, 137
Amoy, 335
Arab-Israeli problem, 252-54
Arana, Francisco Javier, 230
Arbenez, Jacobo, 230, 231, 235
Arevalo, Juan José, 230
Arif, Col. Abdul Salam, 332
Aswan Dam, 247-61, 263, 304
Atlantic Charter, 90-91, 96, 132
Auburn, N.Y., 30, 54
Auburn Theological Seminary, 30
Australia, 120
Austria, 298-99

"B₂H₂" resolution, 91
Bacon, Robert, 3
Baghdad, 331, 335
Baghdad Pact, 150, 249, 332
Ball, Senator, 91
Bandaranaike, 259

Bandung Conference, 174
Bank of France, 80-81
Bao Dai, Emperor, 236, 243, 244
Baquba, 331
Baruch, Bernard M., 61, 63-64, 101
Beigin, Menahem, 274
Ben-Gurion, David, 273, 277, 278, 286
Bergson, Henri, 51
Berlin, 103, 109, 185-86, 192-200, 331, 338-40, 341, 345, 346, 348, 349
Berlin blockade, 103, 109, 339
Berlin Conference, 193-203, 229
Bernau, Phyllis, xi, 161
Beyen, J. W., 296
Bidault, Georges, 196, 197, 205, 211, 294
Binh Xuyen, 239, 244
Blair House, 107
Bohlen, Charles E., 9, 142-143, 165, 263, 287
Bowers, Martha (Mrs. Robert Taft), 52
Bowie, Robert, 141
Boxer, U.S.S., 207
Bradley, Omar, 5, 6, 117
Bridges, Styles, 140
Brioni, 246
Britain, see Great Britain
British Guiana, 57
Brownell, Herbert, 130, 134, 136, 137
Bruce, David K. E., 6, 7
Brussels Pact, 109
Budapest, 272, 315
Bulganin, Nikolai, 286, 298, 302, 304, 306, 327, 328
Bureau of European Affairs, 173

351

Index

Bureau of Near East, South Asian, and African Affairs, 173
Burnside, General, 23
Burton, Senator, 91
Byrnes, James F., 8-9, 103
Byroade, Henry A., 6, 250

Caccia, Sir Harold, 242, 278
Cake, Ralph, 6
Cambodia, 208, 238
Cao Dai, 239
Caracas Tenth Inter-American Conference, 229-35, 292
Castillo Armas, Carlos Enrique, 235
Central Intelligence Agency, 162
Ceylon, 259
Chamoun, Camille, 333
Chapultepec Conference, 230
Charlemagne, 22
Chiang Kai-shek, 87, 88, 174, 178-179, 221, 223, 224, 226, 227
Chicago & Indiana Coal Railway, 77
China, *see* Free China; Red China
Chou En-lai, 174, 184, 212, 214, 225, 228
Churchill, Winston, 90, 91, 146, 187, 189-90, 209, 265, 299, 349
Clay, Lucius, 129, 133-34, 136, 137
Clemenceau, Georges, 65, 118
Clinton, Sir Henry, 23
Cold Spring Harbor, L. I., 40
Cole, "Old King," 37
Collins, Fred, 10, 15
Collins, J. Lawton, 6, 240, 244
Columbia University, 55
Columbine III, 156, 186, 192, 347
Commission on a Just and Durable Peace, 90, 165
Communism, 72-76, 88, 104, 109, 113, 119, 130, 141, 178-84, 191, 204-18, 219, 225-26, 230-36, 250, 310-14, 332, 339, 343-44
Conference on Church and State, 89
Conference on Intellectual Co-operation, 89
Confucius, 27
Congo Basin Treaty, 123
Constantinople Treaty of 1888, 262

Cooper, John Sherman, 116
Costa Rica, 60
Coudert, Frederick, 81
Coulson, J. E., 278, 279
Council of Foreign Ministers, 102, 106
Council of Methodist Bishops, 348
Council on Foreign Relations, 253
Cromwell, William Nelson, 55-57, 79
Cummings, Wilbur L., 79

Daily Worker, 141
Davies, John Paton, 143, 144, 146, 167
Davis, Norman H., 76
Dawes, Charles Gates, 78
Dean, Arthur H., xi, 82
de Gaulle, Charles, 201
de Lesseps, 57
Depressions, 77, 81
De Thou, Ambassador, 48
Dew Drop, 156
Dewey, Thomas E., xi, 95-101, 103-04, 106-07, 112, 113, 115, 129, 134, 156
Diem, Ngo Dinh, 236-44
Dienbienphu, 205, 206, 207, 211, 212
Dillon, Douglas, 159, 211, 276, 346
Diplomatic Memoirs, 44, 46
Dixon, Sir Pierson, 282
Donnell, Forrest, 110
Donovan, Robert J., 139
Dreier, John C., 233
Driscoll, Alfred E., 7
Duck, the, 36
Duck Island, 36-37, 42, 60, 106, 133, 146, 262, 263, 267
Dulles, Allen Macy, 22, 23, 29-30, 34, 36
Dulles, Allen W., xi, 30, 35, 36, 39, 104, 114, 162, 235, 279
Dulles, Avery, 39, 162-63
Dulles, Edith Foster, 22, 23
Dulles, Eleanor, xi, 161-62
Dulles, Janet Avery, xi, 30, 36, 39, 50, 54-55, 57-59, 71, 77, 84, 87, 106, 133, 155, 156, 157, 158-59, 161, 162, 210, 346
Dulles, John Foster, administrative troubles, 138-52; air travel, 77, 87-88, 92, 122, 153-63; ancestry, 22-30;

Index

appearance, 2, 10; arms control, 322-25, 328-30; Aswan Dam, 246-61; authorship, 17-21; Berlin conference, 193-203; Berlin crisis, 338-40; bipartisanship, 95-105, 113; birth, 22; boyhood, 27-30, 33-36; broadcasts, 154; death, 349; diplomatic training, 44-50; education, 29, 30-32, 50-53; European unity, 289-308; family relations, 158-63; foreign travel, 30, 50-51, 52, 57, 71-72, 78, 87, 92, 154-58, 341, 342, 344-45; Formosa, 219-28, 335-38; funeral, 349-50; illnesses, 97-98, 262, 284, 285, 341-42, 345-47, 349; Indochina crisis, 204-18; Iraq crisis, 331-34; Japanese peace treaty, 10, 13, 20-21, 116-118, 165; law practice, 54-60, 70-85; marriage, 57; parents, 22; peacemaker, 309-22; press conferences, 164-76; speeches, 18-20, 26-27, 92-93, 107-12, 113, 120, 133, 137, 187, 282-83, 312-13, 318-19, 333-34, 337, 342-44; sports, love of, 33-43; subversion, problem of, 229-45; Suez Canal, 262-71; unpopularity, 166-71; Versailles peace conference, 63-69
Dulles, John Watson Foster, 59
Dulles, Joseph, 23
Dulles, Lillias, 39
Dulles, William, 23
Dumbarton Oaks Conference, 92, 96-97, 101, 108

Eban, Abba, 272-73, 278
Eberstadt, Ferdinand, 39
Eden, Sir Anthony, 150-51, 196, 197, 210, 214, 215, 227, 263, 267-69, 274, 276, 280, 286, 287, 292, 295, 297, 299, 302
Edwards, General, 59-60
Egypt, 6, 246-61, 262-71, 272-88
Einstein, Albert, 313
Eisenhower, Dwight D., 4, 6, 7, 9, 11, 129, 137, 139, 140, 146, 149-151, 153, 154, 155, 172, 177, 178, 180, 186, 187, 189, 190, 191, 206, 207, 208, 215, 220, 221, 223, 224, 225,

226, 227, 240, 244, 251, 256, 263, 265, 273, 277, 280, 281-82, 286-87, 289-90, 293, 294, 295, 297, 301, 302, 305, 323, 327-28, 332, 336, 341, 345, 347, 348, 349
Eisenhower Doctrine, 332
Eisenhower: The Inside Story, 139
Eldridge, Art, 40
Ely, General Paul, 206, 240
European Defense Community, 15, 130, 190-91, 212, 229, 292, 293, 294, 295, 297
European Recovery Plan, 109
European unity, 289-308

Fairbanks, Charles W., 28
Farben, I. G., 84
Far Eastern Commission, 116
Farouk, King, 255
Faure, Edgar, 240-43, 302
Fawzi, Mahmoud, 270
Fechteler, William M., 6
Federal Council of Churches, 90, 96
Federal Power Commission, 112
Federal Reserve Bank, 80, 81
Fine, John, 133
Flemming, Arthur, 290-91
Foreign Affairs, 188
Foreign Operations Administration, 145
Foreign policy, 11-15, 16, 18-21, 131, 167, 177, 185, 188-203
Foreign Policy Association, 187
Foreign Service, 138
Formosa, 219-28, 292, 295, 331, 335-338
Forster, George, 24
Forster, James, 24
Forster, Jane Watson, 24
Forster, Matthew, 24-25
Forster, William, 24
Fortuny, José Manuel, 231
Fosdick, Harry Emerson, 30
Foster, John Watson, 3, 16, 22, 23-24, 25-26, 27-28, 33, 34, 44, 46, 47, 55, 58, 59, 162
"Fourteen Points," 64
France, 12-13, 14-15, 190, 204-18, 240-244, 263, 264, 267, 274, 276, 286,

Index

296, 327, 330
Franks, Sir Oliver, 119
Free China, 27, 111-12, 220-28
French National Political Science Institute, 129

Gallup Poll, 96
Gamarra, Don Esteban de, 48
Gaza Strip, 282
Geneva Asiatic Conference, 211-14, 229, 236, 237
Geneva Foreign Ministers' Meeting, 156, 160, 301-02, 330, 349
Geneva technical conference, 328
George, Walter F., 104, 176, 320
George Washington University, 51-53, 81
Germany, 12-13, 71-72, 77-78, 84, 152, 185-86, 192-200, 299, 306-08, 338-340, 345, 346, 348, 349
Geroe, Ernest, 315
Gieseking, Walter, 84
Goethals, George, 59
Gomulka, Wladyslaw, 315
Goodpaster, Andrew J., 279
Great Britain, 6, 122, 258, 263, 265, 267-69, 286, 295, 327, 330, 332, 333, 345
Green, Edward H., 79
Green Mental Science Fellowship, 32
Gridiron Club, 153, 293
Gruenther, Albert, 294
Guatemala, 230-35

Hagerty, Jim, 113, 279
Hague, The, 16, 44, 46
Hammarskjold, Dag, 270-71, 274, 286
Hangkow, China, 87, 111
Harding, Warren Gamaliel, 70
Harkabi, Yehashafat, 274
Harrison, Benjamin, 3, 22
Hart, Robert F., Jr., 39, 40-42
Harvard University, 55
Hatch, Senator, 91
Helena, 180, 181, 183
Henderson, Loy, 249
Henderson Harbor, 28, 34-35, 59

Herter, Christian, 340, 345-46, 347, 349
Hill, Senator, 91
Hiss, Alger, 175
Hitler, Adolf, 16, 17, 84, 89, 92
Hoa Hao, 239
Hobby, Oveta Culp, 164
Ho Chi Minh, 205, 211, 214, 236
Holland, 62
Holland, Henry, 233
Holmes, Julius C., 320, 324
Honduras, 234
Hong Kong, 87
Hoover, Herbert, Jr., 174, 251, 277
Horton, Mildred McAfee, 143
House Foreign Affairs Committee, 6
Hughes, W. M., 64, 65-68, 69
Hull, Cordell, 3, 9, 16, 92, 97, 98-101
Hungary, 281, 314, 315-16, 317
Hussein, Ahmed, 247, 259
Hydrogen bomb, 309

Ichiang Island, 226
Independence, 156
India, 256
Indiana State College, 24
Indochina, 129, 131, 154, 204-18, 229, 236, 292
Inter-American Conference, Tenth, 229-35
International Nickel, 84
Iran, 6, 248, 251
Iraq, 249-50, 331-35
Israel, 250-54, 263, 272-74, 276-78, 279, 282, 286, 332

Japan, 27, 121, 295, 349
Japanese peace treaty, 10, 13, 20-21, 116-28, 165
Jaretzki, Alfred, 78
Jefferson, Louis, 345
Jessup, Philip C., 193
Johnson, Robert, 147
Johnston, Eric, 251-52
Joint Chiefs of Staff, 5, 6, 117, 153
Jones, John Paul, 29
Jordan, 332, 333
Judd, Walter, 9

354

Index

Kadar, Janos, 315
Kapp, 72
Kassem, Karim, 332
Kennan, George, 9, 144-45, 310
Khrushchev, Nikita S., 244-45, 298, 304, 313, 315, 325, 327-28, 329, 330, 331, 338-40, 342
Knowland, William, 111, 221
Koo, Wellington, 119
Korean War, 14, 117-18, 119, 131, 177-84, 219
Kreuger, Ivar, 82
Kreuger & Toll, 82
Krock, Arthur, 350

Lamont, Thomas W., 71
Laniel, Joseph, 190, 294
Lansing, Robert ("Uncle Bert"), 3, 34, 59
Laos, 208, 238
Lawley, George, 38
Lawson, Edward B., 277
League of Nations, 18, 19, 69, 89, 91, 98
Lebanon, 332, 333, 338
Lehman, Herbert, 112, 113-14, 115
Leo X, Pope, 319
Life magazine, 20, 85, 187, 216
Li Hung-chang, 27
Lima, Peru, 154, 263
Li Mi, General, 238
Lincoln, Abraham, 25
Linder, Harold F., 6
Lloyd, Selwyn, 270, 274, 276, 349
Lloyd George, David, 63, 65
Lodge, Henry Cabot, 280
London, 210, 262, 264, 265-66, 296
London *Economist,* 123, 142, 217-18
Lourie, Don, 5, 140
Lovett, Robert, 107
Lucet, Charles, 278
Luciano, Lucky, 95
Luxembourg, 307

MacArthur, Douglas, 117, 125, 130
MacArthur II, Douglas, 7
Macmillan, Harold, 242, 253-54, 300, 307, 349

Mahan, Admiral, 109
Makins, Sir Roger, 210, 278
Malik, Jacob, 119
Manila Pact, 222
Mao Tse-tung, 123, 184
Marshall, George C., 104, 107, 108, 115, 165
Mateos, Adolfo Lopez, 341
Matsu Island, 220, 221, 225, 226, 227, 335
Matthews, H. Freeman ("Doc"), 6, 7
McCardle, Carl W., 5, 7, 155, 165-66, 172, 174, 176, 238
McCarran Act, 60
McCarthy, Joseph, 8, 139, 145, 147-149
McCormick, Vance C., 61, 63
McKay, Douglas, 137
McLeod, Robert Walter Scott, 140, 147
Medalie, George Z., 95, 96
Memoirs (Hull), 98
Mendès-France, Pierre, 212, 213, 214, 215, 295
Menemsha, 38-42
Menzies, Dame Pattie, 155
Menzies, Robert Gordon, 262, 267
Merchant, Livingston, 173
Mexico, 341
Mikoyan, Anastas, 349
Military Air Transport Service, 156
Military Defense Assistance Program, 111
Millikin, Eugene, 130
Mollet, Guy, 274, 276, 280, 286
Molotov, Vyacheslav, 160, 193, 194, 196-200, 215, 253-54, 297, 298, 302, 306, 307
Mond Nickel, 84
Monroe Doctrine, 230
Morgan & Company, J. P., 78
Morocco, 264
Morton, Thruston, 5
Moscow Four-Power Conference (1947), 108, 165, 201
Moscow *New Times,* 85
Mossadegh, Mohammed, 6, 248, 251
Munich Agreement, 227-28
Murphy, Robert, 155, 240, 264, 265

355

Index

Mussolini, Benito, 17
Mutual Security Administration, 145
"My Preparation for English," 31-32

Naguib, Mohammed, 247-48
Nagy, Imre, 315
Nash, Frank C., 6
Nasser, Gamal Abdel, 154, 274, 275, 332; dam and, 246-61; Suez Canal and, 262-71
National Conference of Christians and Jews, 96
National Security Council, 136, 146, 180, 223, 225, 252, 293, 323
National War Fund, 85
Nehru, Jawaharlal, 210, 247, 256
New Panama Canal Company, 57
New Yorker, The, 132, 190, 264, 347
New York Herald Tribune, 303
New York Life Insurance Company, 83
New York Post, 114
New York Produce Exchange, 57
New York Times, 14, 15, 167, 176, 350
New Zealand, 120
Nicaragua, 56, 60
Nicholas II, Czar, 45
Nicolson, Harold, 47, 321-22
Nitze, Paul, 6, 144, 145-46
Nixon, Richard, 256
North American Treaty Organization (NATO), 12, 104, 107, 108, 109, 110, 130, 191, 211, 222, 236, 240, 264, 287, 291, 293, 294, 297, 318, 319, 320, 326, 327, 340, 342
Nuri as-Said, 332

Ochab, Edward, 315
O'Connor, Roderic L., xi, 7
O'Day, Burnita, xi, 7
Ohio Westeyan University, 18, 92
Olds, Leland, 112
Oil, 290-91
Orlando, 65
Oxnam, Bishop G. Bromley, 348-49

Pakistan, 249, 257
Panama, 59-60
Panama Canal, 56-57
Panama Railroad Company, 56-57
Pan-American Exposition, 33
Panikkar, Ambassador, 182
Pearson, Drew, 98
Peking, 335-36
Pentagon, 5, 117
Pepin the Short, 22
Pescadores Islands, 220, 335
Phi Beta Kappa, 32
Philadelphia Bulletin, 165
Philippines, 120, 121, 257
Philippine Sea, U.S.S., 207
Phleger, Herman, 5, 155
Pierce, Henry Hill, 78
Pinay, Antoine, 253-54, 300, 307
Pineau, Christian, 270, 276
Poland, 79-80, 281, 314, 315, 316
Potsdam Agreement, 124, 338-40
Pravda, 298
Press conferences, 164-76
Price, William Jennings, 59
Princeton University, 30-32, 44, 55, 346, 349
Problems of Leninism, 141
Providence Journal, 10

Quartermaster Corps, 112
Quemoy Island, 220, 221, 222, 223, 225, 226, 227, 335-38

Radford, Arthur, 207, 208, 279
Radio Free Europe, 314
Red China, 204-18, 223, 305, 331, 335-38
Reed, Lansing, 78
Remington Typewriter Company, 77
Reparations Commission, 69
Reporter, 141
Reston, James B., 176
Revere, Paul, 29
Rhee, Syngman, 182, 183, 225, 242
Rivera, Diego, 235
Robertson, Walter S., 9, 161, 223, 240
Rockefeller, John D., Jr., 87

Index

Roosevelt, Franklin D., 82, 83, 90, 91, 96, 97, 101-02, 149
Roosevelt, Theodore, 3, 45
Roundtree, William, 272-73, 278
Rovere, Richard H., 132-33, 347-48
Rusk, Dean, 125, 126
Russell, Francis H., 251, 252
Russia, 11-12, 83, 102, 116, 124-25, 185, 186, 191-200, 201, 232, 244-245, 248, 254, 256, 258, 260, 263, 275, 286-87, 297-99, 301-05, 309, 315-18, 322-25, 327-28, 330, 334, 338-40

Sabry, Ali, 270
Salvation Army, 85
San Francisco, 126
San Francisco Conference (1945), 165, 343
Saudi Arabia, 174
SCAP, 117
Schacht, Hjalmar, 84, 192
Securities Exchange Act, 83
Seligman, Eustace, 79
Senate Foreign Relations Committee, 69, 110
Sevareid, Eric, 167
Shepilov, Dmitri, 258
Shimonoseki treaty, 27
Sinai Peninsula, 282
Six Pillars of Peace, 91
Smith, Alexander, 7
Smith, Walter Bedell, 141, 143, 215, 216, 237, 251
Sodus Point, N. Y., 247
Sorbonne, Paris, 32, 50-51
Southeast Asia Treaty Organization (SEATO), 213, 222, 223, 227, 229, 236, 237, 238, 295
"Soviet Foreign Policy and What to Do About It," 85
Soviet Union, see Russia
Sputnik, 325, 326, 327
Stalin, Josef, 309
Stassen, Harold, 145, 148, 323-24
Stephens, Tom, 113
Stettinius, Edward, 8-9, 101
Stevens, Will, 33-34

Stevenson, Adlai, 104, 216
Straus, Roger W., 96
Streibert, Theodore, 146, 148
Suez Canal, 6, 57, 154, 249, 262-71, 291, 326, 344
Suez Canal Users Association, 267-69
Sullivan, Algernon S., 55
Sullivan & Cromwell, 55-56, 57, 59, 71, 77, 78-79, 81, 82, 83, 84, 85, 86, 95, 107
Summerfield, Arthur, 133
Sumner, Lord, 69
Suydam, Henry, 174
Syria, 332, 333

Tachens, 226
Taft, Robert, 52, 107, 110, 129, 130
Taft, William Howard, 3, 52
TASS news agency, 164
Telecasts, 11-14
Temple, William, 92
"Theory of Judgment, The," 32
Tinoco, Juan, 60
Tito (Josip Broz), 88, 246-47, 298, 304
Tokyo, 120
Tomlinson, F. S., 179
Toriello, Guillermo, 231-32
Tourane, 215
Toynbee, Arnold, 92, 192
Treaty of London (1515), 319
Tripartite Statement, 266
Troyanovsky, Oleg, 160
Truman, Harry S., 10, 110, 115, 118, 120, 124, 128, 139, 156, 217, 219, 224
Tunis, 264
Turkey, 249

Union Theological Seminary, 30
United Nations, 92, 98-101, 108, 119, 181, 182, 183, 225, 263, 269-71, 286, 323, 325, 333, 343, 344
United Service Organization, 85
United States Iinformation Agency, 146, 147, 148, 224

Vandenberg, Arthur, 101, 107, 110, 111, 115-16

357

Index

Vandenberg, Hoyt, 6

Van Dusen, Henry P., 30

Van Kirk, Walter, xi, 92

Versailles Peace Conference, 16, 63-69, 118

Victor, Royall, 77, 78

Vietminh, 207, 213, 214

Vietnam, 208, 213, 214, 215, 236-245

Vincent, John Carter, 143, 144, 146,

Voice of America, 314

Von Luttwitz, General, 72

Wagner, Robert F., Sr., 107, 112

War, Peace and Change, 17-20, 88

War Industries Board, 61

War or Peace, 10, 15, 17, 20, 21, 102, 141

Warsaw, 272

Warsaw Pact, 315

War Trade Board, 61-62

Washington *Times Herald*, 143

Waters, David, 346

Watertown, N.Y., 22, 29, 30

Western Big Three Conference, 189, 191

Western Europe, 12-13, 15, 190

Western European Union, 15

White House, the, 6

Wilkins, Fraser, 273

Willkie, Wendell, 96

Wilson, Charles E., 137, 145, 155, 279

Wilson, Woodrow, 3, 16, 59, 62, 64, 65, 68-69, 70, 91, 118, 321-322

Wolsey, Cardinal, 319

World Bank, 255

World Court, 19

World War I, 61

World War II, 79

Yalta conference, 175-76

Yeh, George, 223, 226

Yugoslavia, 298-99

Zorin, Valerian, 323, 324